Maths
for Key Stage 2

It's a Maths extravaganza from CGP!

This brilliant CGP book is bursting with Maths questions for 9-10 year olds.
They're split into three difficulty levels to suit pupils of all abilities
— with plenty of fun challenge pages added in for variety.

Every topic from the Year 5 Programme of Study is covered,
and it's all perfectly matched to the latest National Curriculum!

What CGP is all about

Our sole aim here at CGP is to produce the highest quality books —
carefully written, immaculately presented and
jam-packed with helpful content.

Then we work our socks off to get them out to you
— at the cheapest possible prices.

Year 5

Contents

Section 4 — Fractions, Decimals and Percentages

Section 5 — Measurement

Section 6 — Geometry

Section 7 — Statistics

Published by CGP

ISBN: 978 1 78294 798 1

Editors: Chloe Anderson, Joanna Daniels, Liam Dyer, Zoe Fenwick, Shaun Harrogate, Hannah Roscoe, Ben Train, Ruth Wilbourne

With thanks to Emily Howe, Nicola Paddock, Ethan Starmer-Jones, Hayley Thompson and Jonathan Wray for the proofreading.
With thanks to Ana Pungartnik for the copyright research.

Printed by Elanders Ltd, Newcastle upon Tyne.
Clipart from Corel®

This book covers every topic that you need to learn in Year 5 Maths.
We've packed it full of questions and made sure there is the right practice for everyone.

You'll find examples at the start of each topic.
These are great reminders of how you might
answer some of the questions on the topic.

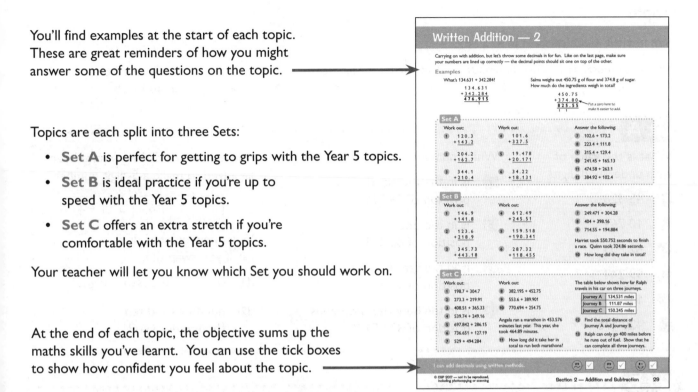

Written Addition — 2

Carrying on with addition, but let's throw some decimals in for fun. Like on the last page, make sure your numbers are lined up correctly — the decimal points should sit one on top of the other.

Examples

What's 134.631 + 342.284?

```
   1 3 4 . 6 3 1
 + 3 4 2 . 2 8 4
   4 7 6 . 9 1 5
```

Salma weighs out 450.75 g of flour and 374.8 g of sugar.
How much do the ingredients weigh in total?

```
   4 5 0 . 7 5
 + 3 7 4 . 8 0    ← Put a zero here to
   8 2 5 . 5 5       make it easier to add.
       1   1
```

Set A

Work out:
1) 120.3 + 143.2
2) 204.2 + 162.7
3) 344.1 + 210.4

Work out:
4) 101.6 + 327.5
5) 19.478 + 20.171
6) 34.22 + 18.131

Answer the following:
7) 102.6 + 173.2
8) 223.4 + 111.8
9) 315.4 + 129.4
10) 241.45 + 165.13
11) 474.58 + 263.1
12) 384.92 + 102.4

Set B

Work out:
1) 146.9 + 141.8
2) 123.6 + 218.9
3) 345.73 + 443.18

Work out:
4) 612.49 + 245.51
5) 159.518 + 190.341
6) 287.32 + 118.455

Answer the following:
7) 249.471 + 304.28
8) 404 + 398.16
9) 714.55 + 194.884
10) Harriet took 550.752 seconds to finish a race. Quinn took 324.86 seconds. How long did they take in total?

Set C

Work out:
1) 198.7 + 304.7
2) 273.3 + 219.91
3) 408.51 + 365.33
4) 539.74 + 249.16
5) 697.842 + 286.15
6) 736.651 + 127.19
7) 529 + 494.284

Work out:
8) 382.195 + 452.75
9) 553.6 + 389.901
10) 770.694 + 254.75
11) Angela ran a marathon in 453.576 minutes last year. This year, she took 464.89 minutes. How long did it take her in total to run both marathons?

The table below shows how far Ralph travels in his car on three journeys.

Journey A	134.531 miles
Journey B	111.87 miles
Journey C	150.245 miles

12) Find the total distance of Journey A and Journey B.
13) Ralph can only go 400 miles before he runs out of fuel. Show that he can complete all three journeys.

I can add decimals using written methods.

© CGP 2017 — not to be reproduced, including photocopying or scanning   Section 2 — Addition and Subtraction   29

Topics are each split into three Sets:

- **Set A** is perfect for getting to grips with the Year 5 topics.
- **Set B** is ideal practice if you're up to speed with the Year 5 topics.
- **Set C** offers an extra stretch if you're comfortable with the Year 5 topics.

Your teacher will let you know which Set you should work on.

At the end of each topic, the objective sums up the maths skills you've learnt. You can use the tick boxes to show how confident you feel about the topic.

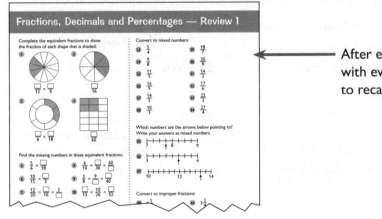

Fractions, Decimals and Percentages — Review 1

After every few topics there's a **Review** page
with even more practice questions — a perfect way
to recap all of the topics you've learnt leading up to it.

Each Section ends with some **Challenges**. These are a fun
and interesting way to practise lots of the skills and topics
you've covered in the Section.

They include loads of different questions and activities — you
might have to draw, make shapes, work with other classmates,
or create your own games!

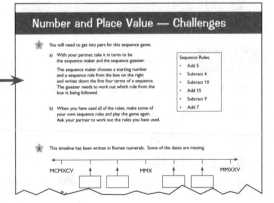

Number and Place Value — Challenges

1) You will need to get into pairs for this sequence game.
   a) With your partner, take it in turns to be the sequence maker and the sequence guesser.
   The sequence maker chooses a starting number and a sequence rule from the box on the right and writes down the first four terms of a sequence. The guesser needs to work out which rule from the box is being followed.
   b) When you have used all of the rules, make some of your own sequence rules and play the game again. Ask your partner to work out the rules you have used.

   Sequence Rules:
   - Add 5
   - Subtract 4
   - Subtract 10
   - Add 15
   - Subtract 9
   - Add 7

2) This timeline has been written in Roman numerals. Some of the dates are missing.

   MCMXCV   MMX   MMXXV

The **Answer Book** for this Year 5 Textbook has answers to all the questions. It also includes a mapping of the **Programme of Study**, and a suggested **Scheme of Work** that teachers can follow throughout the year.

Free printable resources including blank timetables and nets of 3D shapes can be found on our website:

www.cgpbooks.co.uk/KS2MathsResources

Place Value

Place value in five-digit and six-digit numbers might seem daunting, but you already know about four-digit numbers, so there's just a couple more things to learn.

Example

What is the value of the 4 in 473 189?

Hundred thousands	Ten thousands	Thousands	Hundreds	Tens	Ones	**4 hundred thousands**
4	7	3	1	8	9	or **400 000**

Set A

What is the value of each underlined digit?

1 4<u>5</u> 328

2 10 76<u>3</u>

3 <u>6</u>2 805

4 99 2<u>4</u>4

5 1<u>3</u>7 489

6 420 1<u>7</u>5

Which number:

7 is in the thousands position of 18 591?

8 is in the ones position of 63 409?

9 is in the ten thousands position of 91 354?

10 is in the hundred thousands position of 372 517?

The number cards below have been arranged to make a 5-digit number.

7	1	6	5	4

What new number do you get if you swap the:

11 ones and thousands digits?

12 hundreds and ten thousands digits?

Set B

What is the value of each underlined digit?

1 83 46<u>7</u>

2 51 <u>5</u>20

3 12<u>9</u> 386

4 <u>3</u>14 073

5 4<u>4</u>6 259

6 737 8<u>3</u>4

Write, in digits, the following numbers:

7 2 ten thousands and 2 tens.

8 1 ten thousand, 9 thousands, 4 hundreds and 3 ones.

9 4 hundred thousands, 4 tens and 8 ones.

10 What is the value of the odd digit in the number 76 484?

Look at the number 397 851.

11 What is the value of the even digit?

12 Which place is the 5 in?

13 819 044 people go to a concert. What is the value of the digit in the hundred thousands place?

Set C

What is the value of the:

1 5 in 65 021?

2 3 in 32 998?

3 2 in 146 724?

4 6 in 693 815?

5 2 in 428 973?

6 4 in 504 816?

7 7 in 730 591?

Look at these number cards.

9	2	3	8	5	1

Use all six cards to make:

8 a number with 5 hundred thousands.

9 a number with a 3 in the ten thousands place.

10 the biggest number you can.

Write, in digits, the numbers being described below:

11 6 hundred thousands, 3 ones, 9 thousands, 4 ten thousands, 1 ten and 8 hundreds

12 3 tens, 2 thousands, 5 ten thousands, 7 hundred thousands, 4 ones and 1 hundred

I know the place value of the digits in five- and six-digit numbers.

Writing Numbers

Now it's time to practise writing five- and six-digit numbers using digits and words.

Examples

Write sixty-two thousand, five hundred and thirteen using digits.

62 513

Write 916 728 in words.

Nine hundred and sixteen thousand, seven hundred and twenty-eight

Set A

Write these amounts using digits:

1. seventy-nine thousand, three hundred and forty-seven
2. twenty-four thousand, five hundred and sixty-four
3. eighty-three thousand, eight hundred and fifty-nine
4. sixteen thousand, seven hundred and five

Write these amounts in words:

5. 59 842
6. 12 296
7. 24 931
8. 68 074
9. 721 816
10. 955 302
11. 430 659

12. Write eight hundred and ninety thousand, four hundred and sixty-two using digits. Use the number cards below to help you.

| 0 | 8 | 4 | 2 | 9 | 6 |

13. Write five hundred and thirty-two thousand, one hundred and forty-four using digits.

Set B

Write these amounts using digits:

1. fifty-seven thousand, four hundred and eleven
2. twenty-nine thousand, nine hundred and seven
3. eight hundred and three thousand, eight hundred and seventy-six

Write these amounts in words:

4. 51 683
5. 490 274
6. 825 069

Write the odd number in words:

7. 37 124, 36 241, 37 426
8. 89 518, 98 150, 89 115

Cedric records the number of ants in his two ant farms. Rewrite his results in digits:

9. Two hundred and nine thousand, seven hundred and thirty-four
10. Four hundred and eighty thousand, and ninety-five

Set C

Write these amounts using digits:

1. four hundred and five thousand, six hundred and twelve
2. seven hundred and thirty thousand, five hundred and six
3. nine hundred and nineteen thousand, seven hundred and eighty

Write each even number in words:

4. 48 787, 48 877, 48 788
5. 553 626, 535 621, 555 265
6. 949 011, 949 014, 994 039

Write each odd number in words:

7. 63 104, 63 401, 63 506
8. 285 736, 258 672, 258 367
9. 704 147, 740 170, 704 414

10. Look at the incomplete number below:

Four hundred and [ ]-three thousand, [ ] hundred and [ ]-nine.

Which option below could be the completed number?

| 433 609 | 423 619 |
| 413 449 | 453 529 |

I can read and write large numbers using digits or words.

Counting in Powers of Ten — 1

Powers of 10 are numbers that are made up of 10 followed by zeros.
On this page, you'll be practising counting up and down in steps of 10, 100 and 1000.

Example

Start at 179 308 and count up 3 steps of 100.

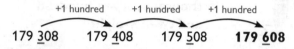

+1 hundred   +1 hundred   +1 hundred

179 <u>3</u>08   179 <u>4</u>08   179 <u>5</u>08   **179 <u>6</u>08**

When counting in steps of 100, the tens and the ones digits don't change.

Set A

Start at 45 666 and count:

1. up 2 steps of 10
2. up 3 steps of 100
3. up 1 step of 1000
4. down 5 steps of 10
5. down 2 steps of 100
6. down 3 steps of 1000
7. down 6 steps of 100

Count in steps of 100 to find the missing number in each sequence:

8. | 59 363 | 59 463 | |
9. | 27 801 | 27 701 | |

Count in steps of 1000 to find the missing number in each sequence:

10. | 32 887 | 33 887 | |
11. | 47 558 | 46 558 | |

Look at the numbers below:

| 525 427 | 521 127 | 521 477 |

Which number is:

12. 5 steps of 10 up from 521 427?
13. 3 steps of 100 down from 521 427?
14. 4 steps of 1000 up from 521 427?

Set B

Look at the numbers below:

| 45 539 | 48 519 | 48 939 |

Which number is:

1. 2 steps of 10 down from 48 539?
2. 4 steps of 100 up from 48 539?
3. 3 steps of 1000 down from 48 539?

Complete each sentence with the correct number (10, 100 or 1000):

4. 711 243 is 7 steps of ☐ from 711 943.
5. 64 481 is 10 steps of ☐ from 64 381.
6. 581 929 is 9 steps of ☐ from 572 929.

Write down the two numbers that are:

7. 3 steps of 10 from 290 567
8. 2 steps of 100 from 318 421
9. 4 steps of 1000 from 155 998
10. 7 steps of 10 from 467 323
11. 5 steps of 100 from 593 874
12. 6 steps of 1000 from 671 512

Set C

Start at 35 298 and count up:

1. 6 steps of 100
2. 2 steps of 1000
3. 4 steps of 10

Start at 816 934 and count down:

4. 9 steps of 100
5. 7 steps of 1000
6. 8 steps of 10

7. Start at 947 026 and follow the steps below:

   1. Count down 5 steps of 1000.
   2. Count up 3 steps of 10.
   3. Count down 7 steps of 100.

   What is the new number?

8. How many steps of 100 are there between 431 569 and 432 269?

9. Write down the two numbers that are 8 steps of 1000 from 723 418.

A company has £493 055 in a savings account. The money increases by £100 each month. How much money is there after:

10. 9 months?
11. 13 months?

I can count in steps of 10, 100 and 1000.

4 **Section 1 — Number and Place Value**

Counting in Powers of Ten — 2

There are two more powers of 10 that you need to know about — 10 000 and 100 000.

Example

Start at 273 692 and count down 5 steps of 10 000.

−1 ten thousand   −1 ten thousand   −1 ten thousand   −1 ten thousand   −1 ten thousand

273 692 → 263 692 → 253 692 → 243 692 → 233 692 → **223 692**

Set A

Look at the numbers below:

| 171 842 | 571 842 |
| 671 842 | 381 842 |

Which number is:

1. 1 step of 10 000 up from 371 842?

2. 2 steps of 100 000 down from 371 842?

Start at 465 160 and count:

3. up 1 step of 100 000

4. up 2 steps of 10 000

5. down 2 steps of 10 000

6. down 3 steps of 100 000

7. up 5 steps of 100 000

8. down 4 steps of 10 000

9. What number is 10 steps of 10 000 up from 600 000?

10. A termite mound has 697 319 termites. An anteater eats 10 000 termites every day. How many termites are left in the mound after 7 days?

Set B

Start at 662 451 and count:

1. up 3 steps of 10 000

2. down 2 steps of 10 000

3. up 2 steps of 100 000

4. down 4 steps of 10 000

5. up 3 steps of 100 000

6. down 3 steps of 100 000

7. down 5 steps of 100 000

Count in steps of 10 000 to find the missing numbers in each sequence:

8. 242 153 | ☐ | ☐ | 272 153

9. 388 578 | ☐ | ☐ | 418 578

Count in steps of 100 000 to find the missing numbers in each sequence:

10. 141 532 | ☐ | ☐ | 441 532

11. 970 113 | ☐ | ☐ | ☐ | 570 113

12. How many steps of 100 000 are there between 913 801 and 113 801?

13. Count up 4 steps of 10 000 from 286 420.

14. Count down 6 steps of 10 000 from 441 569.

15. Count down 7 steps of 100 000 from 708 088.

Set C

Start at 852 476 and count:

1. down 5 steps of 100 000

2. up 2 steps of 10 000

3. down 4 steps of 10 000

Start at 693 186 and count:

4. up 7 steps of 10 000

5. down 6 steps of 100 000

6. down 10 steps of 10 000

Count in steps of 10 000 to find the missing numbers in each sequence:

7. 618 694 | ☐ | ☐ | ☐ | 578 694

8. 71 532 | ☐ | ☐ | ☐ | 111 532

9. A sweet factory has 25 412 jelly beans. It makes 100 000 jelly beans an hour for the next 8 hours. How many jelly beans does it now have in total?

10. Start at 623 941 and follow the steps below:

   1. Count down 6 steps of 10 000.
   2. Count up 3 steps of 100 000.
   3. Count up 4 steps of 10 000.

   What is the new number?

11. Write down the two numbers that are 7 steps of 10 000 from 645 358.

I can count in steps of 10 000 and 100 000.

Number and Place Value — Review 1

What is the value of the:

1. 5 in 12 598?
2. 7 in 76 334?
3. 4 in 94 817?
4. 9 in 55 396?
5. 9 in 601 293?
6. 6 in 467 531?
7. 7 in 789 129?
8. 1 in 445 061?

Write, in digits, the numbers being described below:

9. 3 ten thousands, 1 thousand, 6 tens and 4 ones.
10. 4 hundred thousands, 9 ten thousands, 3 thousands, 5 hundreds and 6 ones.
11. 8 thousands, 5 hundred thousands, 2 tens, 6 hundreds, 4 ten thousands and 1 one.

Look at these number cards.

| 4 | 1 | 7 | 6 | 9 | 3 |

Use all six cards to make:

12. a number with a 6 in the ten thousands place.
13. a number with 7 hundreds.
14. the smallest number you can.

Write these amounts using digits:

15. eighty-four thousand, one hundred and twenty-five
16. twenty-seven thousand, five hundred and sixty-two
17. six hundred and ninety-six thousand, four hundred and three
18. nine hundred and three thousand, eight hundred and eight

Write these amounts in words:

19. 77 615
20. 13 243
21. 28 671
22. 40 522
23. 635 779
24. 981 232
25. 705 487
26. 430 063

Start at 382 524 and count:

27. up 5 steps of 10
28. up 3 steps of 100
29. down 2 steps of 1000
30. up 4 steps of 1000
31. down 3 steps of 10
32. down 7 steps of 100

How many steps of:

33. 10 are there between 513 968 and 513 908?
34. 100 are there between 514 268 and 514 968?
35. 1000 are there between 521 968 and 517 968?

Count in steps of 1000 to find the missing numbers in each sequence:

36. | 56 191 | | 58 191 |
37. | 187 423 | | | 184 423 |
38. | 96 815 | | | | 100 815 |

39. Count up 5 steps of 10 000 from 236 914.
40. Count down 8 steps of 10 000 from 119 998.
41. Count down 7 steps of 100 000 from 780 373.
42. Count up 9 steps of 100 000 from 96 542.

How many steps of:

43. 100 000 are there between 233 647 and 933 647?
44. 100 000 are there between 73 647 and 573 647?

Write down the two numbers that are:

45. 4 steps of 10 000 from 540 992.
46. 3 steps of 100 000 from 671 150.
47. 8 steps of 10 000 from 684 225.
48. 3 steps of 100 000 from 316 788.

Nice one! You finished all these questions!

Negative Numbers

You'll have first seen negative numbers in Year 4. Now you need to get to grips with using negative numbers in different situations — this could mean adding, subtracting or finding the difference between two numbers.

Examples

Start at 5 and count back 8.

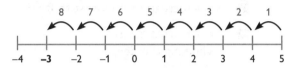

So 5 − 8 is **−3**.

Count forwards to work out −4 + 3.

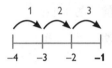

So −4 + 3 is **−1**.

A desert is −2 °C at night and 40 °C during the day. By how many degrees does the temperature rise?

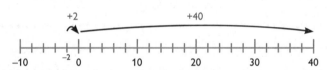

Start at −2 and count up to 0.
Then count from 0 to 40.
2 + 40 = 42

This means the temperature rises by **42 °C**.

Start at 5 and count back:

1) 6

2) 9

3) 11

Start at −11 and count forward:

4) 3

5) 7

Start at −2 and count back:

6) 5

7) 8

Count backwards:

8) 9 from 5

9) 5 from −6

Count forwards:

10) 3 from −7

11) 6 from −4

Count backwards to work out:

12) 2 − 9

13) 4 − 6

Count forwards to work out:

14) −3 + 7

15) −5 + 6

Count forwards or backwards to work out:

16) −5 − 3

17) −12 + 6

18) −7 − 4

Use the thermometer to answer the questions below.

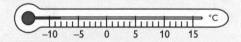

What temperature is:

19) 10 °C colder than 8 °C?

20) 5 °C warmer than −10 °C?

21) 12 °C warmer than the temperature shown?

This table shows the temperature on two different days.

	Morning	Evening
1	−8 °C	4 °C
2	7 °C	−3 °C

22) True or false? On day 1, it was warmer in the morning than the evening.

23) On day 2, was it colder in the morning or evening?

Set B

Start at −6 and count:

1. back 7
2. forward 3
3. forward 11

Count backwards:

4. 9 from 7
5. 12 from 4
6. 5 from −6
7. 8 from −10

Count forwards:

8. 3 from −7
9. 2 from −8
10. 6 from −4
11. 9 from −5

Count backwards to work out:

12. 2 − 7
13. 8 − 10
14. −4 − 6
15. −3 − 9

Count forwards to work out:

16. −4 + 2
17. −7 + 6
18. −5 + 13
19. −11 + 8

20. There is −£10 in a bank account. £12 is paid into the account. How much money is in the account now?

The table shows the depth compared to sea level of some creatures:

Whale	−27 m
Dolphin	−14 m
Shark	−19 m

21. Which creature is closest to 0 m?

22. Which creature is swimming the deepest?

Use the diagram to answer these questions:

23. Eric lives on floor 12 of a tower block. He gets the lift to floor −2. How many floors has he gone down?

24. Federica lives on floor 6. She takes the lift down 9 floors. What floor is she on now?

Set C

Start at −5 and count:

1. forward 3
2. back two 6s
3. back three 5s
4. forward six 4s

Count backwards to work out:

5. 4 − 9
6. 8 − 12
7. −7 − 6

Count forwards to work out:

8. −10 + 7
9. −4 + 8
10. −6 + 15

Count forwards or backwards to work out:

11. −9 + 4
12. −5 − 14
13. −8 + 18

What is:

14. 10 less than 3?
15. 15 less than 8?
16. 12 less than −6?
17. 10 more than −24?

18. A freezer is set at −18 °C. The door is left open and the temperature increases by 1 °C every hour.

How many hours will it take for the freezer to be at 3 °C?

Priya and Kevin play a video game twice. They write down their scores each time:

	Priya	Kevin
Game 1	−6	4
Game 2	2	−3

19. How many more points did Kevin get than Priya in game 1?

20. What was the difference between Priya's scores in game 1 and game 2?

21. They play a third game. Kevin gets 10 more points than he did in game 2. How many points does he get in game 3?

22. A colony of penguins is huddling together to keep warm. The temperature outside the huddle is −45 °C. Inside the huddle, it is 21 °C. How many degrees warmer is it inside the huddle?

I understand and can use negative numbers.

Ordering Numbers

You'll already have had a lot of practice with ordering and comparing numbers.
In Year 5, you need to be confident doing it with numbers up to 1 000 000.

Example

Which of these numbers is the largest?

<u>8</u>37 426　　　<u>9</u>51 993　　　<u>9</u>58 236　　　<u>8</u>74 573　　　Look at the hundred thousands digit: 9 is the largest.

95<u>1</u> 993　　　95<u>8</u> 236　　　Both numbers have the same ten thousands digit.
　　　　　　　　　　　　　Look at the thousands digit: 8 is the largest. So **958 236** is the largest number.

Set A

Which is bigger:

1. 24 064 or 36 152?
2. 75 981 or 72 741?
3. 13 235 or 13 633?
4. 25 697 or 25 709?
5. 485 031 or 483 055?
6. 792 695 or 791 648?

Which is smallest:

7. 83 541 or 83 669?
8. 17 137 or 17 146?
9. 99 483 or 99 452?
10. 52 206 or 52 202?
11. 824 971 or 824 817?
12. 353 652 or 353 661?

13. Put these numbers in order starting with the largest:

92 046	71 551
88 672	72 931

14. Put these numbers in order starting with the smallest:

553 118	652 694
652 946	553 175

Set B

Which symbol (< or >) should go in each gap?

1. 54 613 ☐ 45 399
2. 12 096 ☐ 12 807
3. 38 107 ☐ 38 225
4. 411 925 ☐ 416 593
5. 979 371 ☐ 979 314
6. 152 683 ☐ 152 638

Find the second largest number in each list:

7. 155 233, 515 322, 551 232
8. 241 687, 214 876, 241 768
9. 783 119, 738 991, 738 919
10. 852 422, 852 242, 852 442
11. 439 265, 439 652, 439 526
12. 903 661, 930 161, 930 661

Look at the numbers below.

693 217	995 720
729 457	631 943
637 185	980 614

13. Put these numbers in order starting with the smallest.

14. Which of the numbers above is more than 860 000 but less than 985 000?

Set C

Find the second smallest number in each list:

1. 36 912, 34 709, 28 534
2. 55 748, 67 193, 55 842
3. 24 630, 54 318, 35 132, 26 654
4. 170 356, 181 639, 186 842, 173 115
5. 405 748, 405 425, 405 562, 405 583

Put these numbers in order starting with the largest:

6. 751 443, 751 343, 751 434
7. 488 365, 488 635, 488 563
8. 346 215, 364 512, 346 521, 364 251
9. 579 314, 597 341, 597 314, 579 341
10. 280 692, 280 622, 280 962, 280 926

11. The board below shows the top scorers in a video game:

LEADERBOARD

CoolCat51.............967 987
Zapperman..............967 879
Kickerz_99.............976 789
Points_Master.........967 978

Azi scored 10 less than the lowest score on the board. What was her score?

I can order and compare numbers up to 1 000 000.

Rounding Numbers

In Year 4, you learnt how to round numbers to the nearest 10, 100 and 1000.
This time, we'll be looking at rounding numbers to the nearest 10 000 and 100 000 too.

Example

Round 62 748 to the nearest 10 000.

The digit to the right of the place you're rounding to tells you whether to round up or down.

If the digit is 5 or more, round up.
If the digit is less than 5, round down.

TTh	Th	H	T	O
6	(2)	7	4	8

The digit to the right of the ten thousands place is 2. So you need to round down to **60 000**.

Set A

Round 72 189:

1. to the nearest 10
2. to the nearest 100
3. to the nearest 1000

Round 188 413:

4. to the nearest 10 000
5. to the nearest 100 000

Round 236 679:

6. to the nearest 1000
7. to the nearest 10 000
8. to the nearest 10

Round 417 536:

9. to the nearest 100 000
10. to the nearest 1000

11. Which number from the box below rounds to 450 000 when rounded to the nearest 10 000?

431 759	445 812
456 773	442 386

12. What is 82 163 rounded to the nearest 100 000?

Set B

Round 427 509:

1. to the nearest 10 000
2. to the nearest 1000
3. to the nearest 10

Round 638 746:

4. to the nearest 100
5. to the nearest 100 000

Round to the nearest 10 000:

6. 701 274
7. 865 935

Round to the nearest 100 000:

8. 529 441
9. 73 862
10. 945 621

Which power of 10 has each number been rounded to?

11. 275 746 ⟶ 300 000
12. 407 181 ⟶ 407 000
13. 653 924 ⟶ 650 000
14. 948 379 ⟶ 948 380
15. 555 423 ⟶ 555 400

Set C

Round to the nearest 10, 100 and 1000:

1. 219 538
2. 460 275

Round to the nearest 10 000 and 100 000:

3. 587 314
4. 929 252

5. Phillippe says, "325 065 rounded to the nearest 10 000 is 320 000." Explain why he is wrong.

6. 740 000 pebbles, to the nearest 10 000, are collected from a beach. What are the largest and smallest possible numbers of pebbles?

There are 300 000 litres of water in a tank, to the nearest 100 000 litres.

Which value in each list could be the exact number of litres in the tank?

7. | 238 452 | 351 561 | 308 579 |

8. | 354 173 | 267 498 | 248 502 |

9. | 360 265 | 349 431 | 249 977 |

I can round numbers to different powers of 10.

Solving Problems with Numbers

These questions put everything you've learnt in this section to the test. Make sure you have a look at the examples before getting stuck in — they'll show you how to tackle some of the questions.

Examples

The number of people travelling to three cities from an airport is listed below.

- four hundred and ninety-six thousand, one hundred and seventy-eight people travelled to Madrid.

- eight hundred and twenty-five thousand, four hundred and sixty-three people travelled to New York.

- seven hundred and fifteen thousand, four hundred and eighteen people travelled to Dubai.

Which city did the largest number of people travel to?

Write each number using digits: Madrid — 496 178, New York — 825 463, Dubai — 715 418.

The largest number is 825 463, so the answer is **New York**.

There are 332 419 locusts in a swarm.
With each mile it travels, the swarm grows by 100 000 locusts.
How many locusts are there after 5 miles?

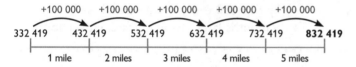

So there are **832 419** locusts after 5 miles.

Set A

Four CD barcodes are shown below:

| 48 366 | 38 964 | 51 753 | 47 747 |

The CDs are ordered in a pile by their barcodes, with the largest at the top.

1. Which barcode is at the bottom of the stack?

2. Which barcode is at the top of the stack?

A rocket is travelling to an unknown planet. It has travelled 67 000 miles, to the nearest 1000 miles.

3. Which of the numbers below could be the exact number of miles the rocket has travelled?

| 67 523 | 67 689 | 66 432 | 66 514 |

The temperature on the unknown planet is 8 °C in the sun. The temperature in the shade is 9 °C lower.

4. What is the temperature in the shade?

The rocket has used 12 642 litres of fuel so far. It uses 10 more litres every minute.

5. How many litres will it have used after 3 more minutes?

There are 90 000 poppies, to the nearest 10 000 poppies, at a flower show.

6. Which amount below is the highest possible number of poppies?

| 89 999 | 94 000 | 94 999 | 85 000 |

7. Which amount from the box above is the lowest possible number of poppies?

The tables below show how many fans went to see different sports at the Olympics.

| Hockey | 112 873 | Boxing | 143 295 |
| Cycling | 189 560 | Rowing | 102 873 |

8. Which sport was the most popular?

9. Which sport had 10 000 fewer fans than hockey?

10. Lyndon has a baking blog with six hundred and forty thousand followers. He gains one thousand more followers every month.

How many followers does Lyndon have after five months?

Set B

1. An ice cream company asked its customers to vote for their favourite ice cream flavour.

   129 742 people chose chocolate, 125 368 chose strawberry, and 126 082 chose vanilla. Which flavour was the least popular?

Three people won some money on the lottery.

- Jack won three hundred and fifteen thousand, seven hundred and seventy-one pounds.
- Sian won five hundred and sixty-two thousand, nine hundred and eighty-two pounds.
- Polly won seventy-eight thousand, one hundred and thirty-six pounds.

Answer using digits:

2. What was the largest amount of money won?

3. Round Jack's winnings to the nearest £10.

4. Polly already had £100 000. How much does she have now?

5. Pencils come in packs of 1000. A shop has 73 000 pencils. How many more packs does the shop need to have 81 000 pencils?

A glassblowing studio has made 572 987 baubles. The baubles are sold in batches of 10 and 100.

6. 7 customers buy a batch of 100 and 8 customers buy a batch of 10. How many baubles does the studio have left?

At the end of the day, the studio has 310 000 baubles left, to the nearest 10 000 baubles.

7. What are the largest and smallest possible numbers of baubles?

8. Some seals are diving to find food. The surface of the sea is at 0 m.

   A male seal dives to −17 m. A female seal dives to −25 m. How much further than the male seal does the female seal dive?

9. There are 4 houses for sale in a village. The prices for each house are:

   | £556 197 | £525 355 | £593 785 | £510 425 |

   The most expensive house is reduced by £10 000 every month until it sells 6 months later. How much did it sell for?

Set C

A company has 6 luxury boats for sale. Their prices are shown below.

Boat	Price
A	£863 469
B	£944 859
C	£943 763

Boat	Price
X	£892 565
Y	£951 993
Z	£872 264

1. Put the boats in order, starting with the cheapest.

The prices of boats B, X and Z are reduced by £10 000.

2. How much do boats B, X and Z cost now?

A castle gets nine hundred and seventy-nine thousand, three hundred and thirty-two visitors a year. A cathedral gets nine hundred and fifty-four thousand, four hundred and eighty-eight.

3. Which has the fewest visitors?

4. A radio advert for the cathedral attracts 1000 more visitors every month. How many visitors does the cathedral have after a year?

Marlon is comparing the temperature of different habitats in the world. A desert is 35 °C.

5. A mountain top is 39 °C colder than the desert. What is the temperature on the mountain top?

6. It's −27 °C in the Arctic. How many degrees does the temperature need to rise for it to be 1 °C warmer than the desert?

Jane works in a button factory. She records the number of buttons made in one day by three machines in the table below.

The numbers are rounded to the nearest 10 000. If the rounded number is less than 740 000, the machine needs to be restarted.

Machine	Buttons
1	735 880
2	736 621
3	734 596

7. Which machine needs to be restarted?

8. Another machine makes 742 850 buttons in one day. It makes 1000 fewer buttons each day. After how many days will it need to be restarted?

I can solve problems using numbers.

Number and Place Value — Review 2

Count forwards or backwards to work out:

1. $6 - 7$
2. $3 - 8$
3. $-2 - 9$
4. $-4 - 10$
5. $-8 + 6$
6. $-11 + 5$
7. $-5 + 9$
8. $-3 + 10$

What is:

9. $6 - 12$?
10. $14 - 20$?
11. $-9 - 3$?
12. $-3 - 20$?
13. $-28 + 5$?
14. $-25 + 10$?
15. $-4 + 17$?
16. $-7 + 15$?

Complete the sentences with the correct number:

17. -7 is ☐ less than 1
18. -9 is 5 more than ☐
19. ☐ is 10 less than 4
20. -4 is 12 less than ☐
21. 16 is ☐ more than -3

22. The surface of a lake is at 0 m. A fish is swimming at -12 m and a frog is swimming at -3 m. What is the distance between the frog and the fish?

Which is smaller:

23. 59 087 or 55 807?
24. 16 924 or 16 492?
25. 402 178 or 403 187?
26. 928 681 or 982 861?
27. 735 573 or 753 537?

Put these numbers in order starting with the largest:

28. 92 448, 57 366, 81 394
29. 271 512, 217 152, 271 251
30. 969 825, 984 575, 939 167, 947 254

Round:

31. 69 318 to the nearest 10
32. 28 170 to the nearest 1000
33. 73 044 to the nearest 10 000
34. 895 373 to the nearest 10
35. 127 531 to the nearest 100
36. 618 357 to the nearest 100
37. 779 912 to the nearest 1000
38. 966 056 to the nearest 10 000
39. 365 482 to the nearest 100 000
40. 932 609 to the nearest 100 000

Which power of 10 has each number been rounded to?

41. 346 753 ⟶ 346 750
42. 582 196 ⟶ 582 000
43. 409 378 ⟶ 409 400
44. 761 245 ⟶ 760 000
45. 883 950 ⟶ 900 000

46. There are 604 500 people, to the nearest 100 people, living on an island. What is the smallest possible number of people on the island?

Jasmine's pedometer records the number of steps she takes. So far, she's taken 347 161 steps. How many steps in total will Jasmine have taken after:

47. 2 more days, if she takes 10 000 steps per day?
48. 2 more months, if she takes 100 000 steps per month?

Alice has 251 768 songs on her music player. Boris has 252 356 and Samir has 252 294.

49. Who has the largest number of songs?

Alice adds 1000 songs to her music player. Samir adds 100 and Boris adds 10.

50. Who has the second largest number of songs now?

That was a mountain of questions — give yourself a well-deserved pat on the back!

Fractions and Decimals

Digits in decimals have a place value too, just like in whole numbers. Fractions can also be used to represent tenths, hundredths and thousandths. Have a look at the examples below...

Examples

What is the value of each digit in 2.853?

Ones	Tenths	Hundredths	Thousandths
2 .	8	5	3

2 is **2 ones**
8 is **8 tenths**
5 is **5 hundredths**
3 is **3 thousandths**

Write six thousandths as a fraction.

six thousandths = $\frac{6}{1000}$

Set A

What is the value of each underlined digit?

1) 4.3<u>2</u>

2) <u>6</u>.21

3) 1.8<u>2</u>9

4) 9.74<u>3</u>

5) 8.<u>5</u>76

6) 1.07<u>4</u>

A grid is made of 1000 identical squares. Write what fraction of the grid is shaded if:

7) 1 square is shaded

8) 3 squares are shaded

9) 10 squares are shaded

10) twelve squares are shaded

11) eighteen squares are shaded

12) Copy and complete the number line using the numbers in the box.

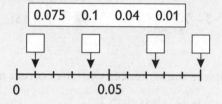

13) Is four hundredths bigger or smaller than four thousandths?

Set B

What is the value of the:

1) 7 in 8.73?

2) 6 in 4.265?

3) 2 in 2.947?

4) 3 in 8.163?

Write the value of each digit:

5) 3.972

6) 7.345

Write as a fraction:

7) nine hundredths

8) seven thousandths

9) nineteen thousandths

Complete the statements with 'hundredths' or 'thousandths':

10) 6 ☐ = 0.006

11) 8 ☐ = 0.08

12) Copy the number line below and fill in the gaps using the correct values from the box.

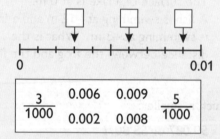

Set C

What is the value of the:

1) 1 in 9.314?

2) 4 in 4.562?

3) 2 in 34.288?

4) 7 in 3.097?

Write the value of each digit:

5) 2.386

6) 14.732

Write as a fraction:

7) fourteen thousandths

8) thirty thousandths

9) forty-two thousandths

Write as a decimal:

10) nine thousandths

11) eleven thousandths

12) seventeen thousandths

Copy the number line below and fill in the missing numbers.

13)

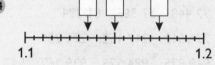

14)

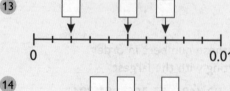

I know the value of fractions and decimals.

Sequences

Sequences are lists of numbers that follow a pattern.
Look at the gaps between each number to work out how much has been added or taken away.

Example

Look at this sequence: | 1   3   5   7   9 |

What is the rule for this sequence?

Write down the next term in the sequence.

$$9 + 2 = \mathbf{11}$$

1   3   5   7   9
+2   +2   +2   +2   The rule is **add two**.

Set A

Use the rules for these sequences to find the next term.

1. Add three:
   5   8   11   14   ☐

2. Subtract four:
   20   16   12   8   ☐

3. Add five:
   25   30   35   40   ☐

4. Subtract two:
   17   15   13   11   ☐

Write down the rule for each of these sequences:

5. 10, 20, 30, 40
6. 13, 10, 7, 4
7. 6, 10, 14, 18
8. 20, 15, 10, 5
9. 15, 11, 7, 3
10. 14, 16, 18, 20

Write down the next term in each of these sequences:

11. 0, 6, 12, 18
12. 28, 22, 16, 10
13. 9, 16, 23, 30
14. 37, 29, 21, 13
15. 14, 17, 20, 23
16. −20, −10, 0, 10

Set B

Use the rules for these sequences to find the next two terms.

1. Add four:
   1   5   9   13

2. Subtract three:
   29   26   23   20

3. Add five:
   −10   −5   0   5

4. Subtract two:
   22   20   18   16

Write down the rule for each of these sequences:

5. 30, 40, 50, 60
6. 62, 58, 54, 50

Write down the next term in each of these sequences:

7. 28, 31, 34, 37
8. 65, 57, 49, 41

Find the missing number in each of these sequences:

9. 54   57   ☐   63
10. 69   66   ☐   60
11. 3   ☐   13   18
12. ☐   30   36   42
13. 90   ☐   72   63
14. ☐   44   40   36

Set C

Find the 3rd term in each sequence described below:

1. The rule is subtract two. The first term is 27.

2. The rule is add seven. The first term is 3.

3. The rule is subtract fifty. The first term is 425.

4. The rule is add twenty-five. The first term is 30.

Write down the rule for each of these sequences:

5. 3, 9, 15, 21
6. 33, 66, 99, 132
7. 14, 26, 38, 50
8. 80, 55, 30, 5
9. 104, 54, 4, −46
10. −11, −14, −17, −20

Find the missing number in each of these sequences:

11. 22   44   66   88   ☐
12. −11   −9   −7   −5   ☐
13. 102   93   84   75   ☐
14. 0   −5   −10   ☐   −20
15. −4   ☐   0   2   4
16. 1   −2   ☐   −8   −11

I can recognise and use number sequences.

Roman Numerals

You'll have seen Roman numerals before, but in Year 5 you learn two new ones — D and M.
You'll also see how Roman numerals can be used to write years.

Examples

| I = 1 | V = 5 | X = 10 | L = 50 | C = 100 | D = 500 | M = 1000 |

Write 503 as a Roman numeral.

500 = D

3 = 1 + 1 + 1 = III ← A row of the same Roman numerals means they are added together.

503 = 500 + 3

503 = **DIII** ← Small numerals that are after big numerals are added on to the big numeral.

Write CMXL as a number.

CM = 1000 – 100 = 900

XL = 50 – 10 = 40

CMXL = 900 + 40

CMXL = **940**

Small numerals that are before big numerals are subtracted from the big numeral.

Write the year below as a number.

MMXV

M = 1000   X = 10   V = 5

1000 + 1000 + 10 + 5 = **2015**

Write the year below as a number.

M = 1000 → **MCMXCIV** ← IV = 5 – 1 = 4

CM = 1000 – 100 = 900   XC = 100 – 10 = 90

1000 + 900 + 90 + 4 = **1994**

Set A

Each of these cards has a Roman numeral on it.

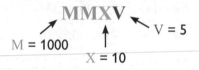

Pick two cards to make:

1. 55
2. 110
3. 400
4. 505
5. 600

Look at the cards below.

Use one of the cards to complete each Roman numeral:

6. 102 = C ☐ I
7. 410 = ☐ DX
8. 504 = DI ☐

Identify the correct number for each Roman numeral:

9. CC   250, 300, 200
10. LX   60, 40, 50
11. CL   550, 400, 150
12. MX   1010, 1100, 1001
13. DL   400, 550, 600

Copy and complete the tables below:

14.

C		D
100	300	

15.

	CDL	DCL
250		650

16.

DCCC		
	900	1000

Which is larger:

17. DLX or DXL?
18. DC or CD?

Which is smaller:

19. MD or MCD?
20. CM or MC?

21. Match the years to the correct Roman numerals.
One has been done for you.

2000	MMIX
2004	MMIII
2009	MMXVII
2011	MM
2003	MMXI
2017	MMIV

Set B

Write these Roman numerals as numbers:

1. LXX
2. CX
3. CCV
4. CLX
5. DXV

For each pair of soldiers, find the smaller Roman numeral.

6.
   CCXX   CCXV
7.
   CDX   CDV

Find the missing Roman numeral:

8. 850 = DCC☐L
9. 910 = ☐MX

Which is the correct Roman numeral?

10. 115 = CXV or CXIV?
11. 290 = CXCX or CCXC?
12. 402 = DCII or CDII?
13. 623 = DCXXIII or DCXIII?

Are the following true or false?

14. 360 = CCCL
15. 425 = CDXXV
16. 740 = DCCXL
17. 814 = DCCCV

Some houses have the year they were

In each pair, which was built most rece...?

18.
    A   B
    MCD   MDCL

19.
    C   D
    MMIX   MCMXCVI

Write these years in Roman numerals:

20. 1308
21. 2007

Set C

Find the missing Roman numerals:

1. 582 = D☐XXXI☐
2. 674 = ☐CLX☐IV
3. 1091 = M☐☐I

Write these numbers as Roman numerals:

4. 300
5. 514
6. 625
7. 870
8. 441
9. 992

Write these years as numbers:

10. MDCCCV
11. MCMXLV
12. MCMXCVIII

Write these years in Roman numerals:

13. 1066
14. 1509
15. 2017

16. Jonah is watching a film.

    At the end of the film, the year it was made is given in Roman numerals.

    THE END

    MCMLXXXVII

    When was the film made?

Are the following statements true or false?

17. CCCLXII < CDLXXXI
18. DCCCLV < DCCCXXXVIII

Each of these cards has a Roman numeral on it.

D X M L C

Use some of the cards to make:

19. a 3-digit number that is bigger than 450, but smaller than 500.

20. a 4-digit number that is bigger than 1100, but smaller than 1120.

21. Hassan and his grandma have the same birthday.

    The years they were born in are shown as Roman numerals below.

    MMVIII

    MCMXLVIII

    How many years older than Hassan is his grandma?

I can read and write Roman numerals up to and beyond 1000.

What is the value of the:

1. 1 in 3.12?
2. 3 in 6.83?
3. 4 in 76.413?
4. 5 in 2.875?
5. 6 in 8.462?
6. 9 in 27.659?

Write the value of each digit:

7. 8.34
8. 9.02
9. 4.098
10. 8.462

11. Copy the number line below and fill in the gaps using the correct values from the box.

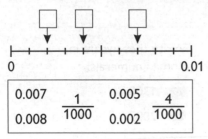

| 0.007 | 1/1000 | 0.005 | 4/1000 |
| 0.008 | | 0.002 | |

Write as a decimal:

12. three thousandths
13. seven thousandths
14. fifteen thousandths

Use the rules for these sequences to find the next term:

15. Add seven:
    0   7   14   21
16. Subtract four:
    40   36   32   28
17. Add two:
    −3   −1   1   3
18. Subtract six:
    90   84   78   72

Write down the rule for each of these sequences:

19. 17,   23,   29,   35
20. 59,   56,   53,   50
21. 34,   43,   52,   61
22. 100,   80,   60,   40

Find the missing number in each of these sequences:

23. 4   10   16   22   ☐
24. 28   31   34   37   ☐
25. 0   8   16   ☐   32
26. 72   70   ☐   66   64
27. ☐   55   45   35   25
28. −9   ☐   −3   0   3

29. Copy the numbers and Roman numerals below. Match each number with the Roman numeral it represents.

    78   MCMXCIII
    530   DXXX
    797   CCXXIV
    224   LXXVIII
    1993   DCCXCVII

Write these Roman numerals as numbers:

30. L
31. CI
32. CD
33. LXV
34. XCII
35. CXVIII
36. DLV
37. CDXCIX

Write these numbers as Roman numerals:

38. 19
39. 132
40. 501
41. 390
42. 560
43. 990
44. 645
45. 465

Write these years as numbers:

46. MM
47. MDCCC
48. MMVIII
49. MMX
50. MCM
51. MCMXCIX

That was a lot to work through — great job!

Number and Place Value — Challenges

 1 You will need to get into pairs for this sequence game.

a) With your partner, take it in turns to be
the sequence maker and the sequence guesser.

The sequence maker chooses a starting number
and a sequence rule from the box on the right
and writes down the first four terms of a sequence.
The guesser needs to work out which rule from the
box is being followed.

Sequence Rules:
• Add 5
• Subtract 4
• Subtract 10
• Add 15
• Subtract 9
• Add 7

b) When you have used all of the rules, make some of
your own sequence rules and play the game again.
Ask your partner to work out the rules you have used.

 2 This timeline has been written in Roman numerals. Some of the dates are missing.

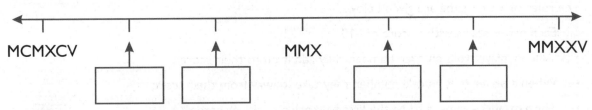

MCMXCV   MMX   MMXXV

a) Write the first and last dates shown on the timeline using digits.

b) Copy the timeline and fill in the missing years using Roman numerals.

c) Draw an arrow on your timeline pointing to the year you were born.
Label the arrow using Roman numerals.

d) Draw an arrow on your timeline pointing to the current year.
Label the arrow using Roman numerals.

 3 In this task you will need a group of 3 or more to play place value bingo.

• Nominate a player to be the game leader. All other players make
a 4 × 4 grid and write a five-digit number in each square.

• The game leader cuts a piece of paper into 14 pieces. Write 1-9 on 9 of them, and
on the other 5 write ten thousands, thousands, hundreds, tens and ones. Fold all
14 pieces up and put them in two piles — a pile of numbers and a pile of place values.

• The game leader chooses one piece of paper from each pile and reads out what they say.
For example, if 5 and tens are chosen, say "5 in the tens place". Put these back, then choose again.

How to play:

• Players with numbers that match what the leader reads out must mark their squares with an X.

• The person who matches all the numbers on their grid is the winner.

• If no one matches all their numbers, the player who has matched the most numbers wins.

4   Lexi is trying to remember the code for her alarm.

7 2 0 6 3 1	2 3 6 7 0 4	2 7 0 6 3 9	2 7 5 3 6 0	2 6 0 3 8 7
A	B	C	D	E

Here are some hints to help her work out which code is correct.

> **Hint 1:** The 3 should not be in the hundreds place.
>
> **Hint 2:** The 7 should not be in the ones or hundreds place.
>
> **Hint 3:** The digit in the hundred thousands place should be smaller than the digit in the ten thousands place.

Work out which code she should use.

5   The rules of a dice game are given below.

- Each player starts with a score of –10.
- When a player rolls an even number, they add it on to their score.
- When a player rolls an odd number, they take it away from their score.
- The aim of the game is to be the first to reach a positive score.

Suman is playing the dice game with a friend. Suman rolls 3, 4, 2, 5, 4.

a)   What is his total score?

b)   Work out the minimum number of times he needs to roll the dice again to reach a positive score.

c)   What is the lowest possible score you could get after rolling the dice 5 times?

d)   What is the highest possible score you could get after rolling the dice twice?

e)   With a partner, roll a dice ten times each and record your scores in a table like the one on the right.

Work out who has the highest score.

	Player 1	Player 2
1st roll		
2nd roll		
3rd roll		
4th roll		
5th roll		
6th roll		
7th roll		
8th roll		
9th roll		
10th roll		

6   Frances thinks of a number.
She adds 1000 to the number, then rounds the result to the nearest 100. She gets 16 800.

a)   Write down the smallest and largest possible numbers she could have been thinking of.

Liev thinks of another number.
He subtracts 10 000, adds 100, then rounds to the nearest 1000. He gets 420 000.

b)   What are the smallest and largest possible numbers that Liev could have been thinking of?

7   Summer is on a TV gameshow. She has spun a wheel 5 times.
The wheels below show the numbers she landed on.

a)   To get through to the next round, Summer needs to use the digits she spun on the wheel to make the smallest number possible. What number does she need to make?

b)   If Summer can use the digits she spun on the wheel to make the largest number possible, she will get extra time in the final round of the game. What number does she need to make?

c)   In a bonus round, Summer is given the written numbers below.
She needs to choose the numbers she could make using the digits she spun on the wheel.
Which numbers does she need to choose?

| Thirty-seven thousand, nine hundred and fifty-one. | Seventy thousand, three hundred and ninety-five. |

| Fifteen thousand, three hundred and ninety-seven. | One hundred thousand and ninety-five. | Nine hundred thousand, five hundred and seventy-three. |

You 1, challenges 0 — well done for solving these brainteasers!

Section 1 — Number and Place Value

Mental Addition — 1

Knowing about place value is really helpful for adding numbers together in your head.
The examples below show you how to do it.

Examples

What is 1300 + 1500?

1300 has 13 hundreds, and 1500 has 15 hundreds.

13 hundreds + 15 hundreds = 28 hundreds

So 1300 + 1500 = **2800**

What is 50 631 + 20 000?

50 631 has 50 thousands, and 20 000 has 20 thousands.

50 thousands + 20 thousands = 70 thousands

So 50 631 + 20 000 = **70 631**

Set A

Work out:

1. 1200 + 300
2. 2400 + 500
3. 1600 + 400
4. 3700 + 800
5. 5600 + 600
6. 4200 + 1300
7. 6200 + 1400

Work out:

8. 6870 + 2100
9. 14 000 + 2000
10. 10 200 + 6000
11. 12 500 + 13 000
12. 15 810 + 11 000
13. 370 800 + 200 000
14. 249 525 + 30 000

Find the missing number:

15. 12 000 + ☐ = 20 000
16. 11 700 + ☐ = 17 700
17. 28 500 + ☐ = 38 500
18. 44 450 + ☐ = 64 450
19. 100 000 + ☐ = 170 000
20. 235 000 + ☐ = 285 000
21. 200 000 + ☐ = 410 000

Set B

Work out:

1. 1100 + 1800
2. 4400 + 1600
3. 4210 + 2000
4. 5200 + 1200
5. 13 101 + 3000
6. 11 570 + 1000
7. 13 334 + 800

Work out:

8. 14 140 + 17 000
9. 16 420 + 30 000
10. 11 690 + 400
11. 15 582 + 12 000
12. 23 250 + 14 000
13. 44 935 + 8000
14. 112 320 + 200 000

Find the missing number:

15. 40 205 + ☐ = 55 205
16. 52 820 + ☐ = 56 820
17. 32 230 + ☐ = 32 730
18. 114 990 + ☐ = 130 990
19. 123 270 + ☐ = 213 270
20. 271 322 + ☐ = 341 322
21. 355 434 + ☐ = 475 434

Set C

Work out:

1. 4352 + 1600
2. 16 723 + 2100
3. 18 458 + 4800
4. 22 430 + 16 000
5. 35 820 + 11 000
6. 43 572 + 30 400
7. 120 000 + 37 000

Work out:

8. 10 750 + 4000 + 200
9. 16 320 + 2000 + 300
10. 24 645 + 30 000 + 4000
11. 33 564 + 10 000 + 5000
12. 42 811 + 21 000 + 600
13. 130 138 + 17 000 + 4000
14. 125 891 + 300 000 + 9000

Find the missing number:

15. 24 561 + ☐ = 31 561
16. 46 635 + ☐ = 76 635
17. 139 452 + ☐ = 155 452
18. 124 386 + ☐ = 174 386
19. 231 947 + ☐ = 252 947
20. 444 575 + ☐ = 584 575
21. 563 412 + ☐ = 592 412

I can do mental addition using place value.

Mental Addition — 2

There's another way to add big numbers together in your head — it's called partitioning. By splitting up big numbers into smaller numbers, it'll make it easier for you to add them up using place values.

Examples

What is 17 320 + 7600?

17 320 + 7000 + 600
= 24 320 + 600
= **24 920**

What is 142 947 + 42 700?

142 947 + 40 000 + 2000 + 700
= 182 947 + 2000 + 700
= 184 947 + 700
= **185 647**

Set A

Work out:

1. 1400 + 1050
2. 1550 + 1300
3. 2481 + 3100
4. 3195 + 2700
5. 5317 + 4080
6. 10 501 + 3002
7. 12 454 + 6100

Work out:

8. 11 294 + 7040
9. 14 450 + 10 800
10. 23 819 + 5070
11. 46 440 + 22 500
12. 102 000 + 4400
13. 110 200 + 40 009
14. 122 451 + 16 000

Find the missing number:

15. 18 500 + 1000 + ☐ = 19 900
16. 25 130 + 3000 + ☐ = 28 430
17. 33 823 + 8000 + ☐ = 41 829
18. 46 790 + 10 000 + ☐ = 59 790
19. 52 380 + 30 000 + ☐ = 82 780
20. 121 500 + 20 000 + ☐ = 146 500
21. 75 764 + 4000 + ☐ = 79 772

Set B

Work out:

1. 32 500 + 1700
2. 80 551 + 1600
3. 64 423 + 1030
4. 10 722 + 8100
5. 317 407 + 10 300
6. 88 934 + 20 050
7. 307 437 + 6009

Work out:

8. 111 310 + 3100
9. 53 288 + 400 400
10. 351 111 + 130 000
11. 122 835 + 600 040
12. 458 904 + 30 200
13. 231 941 + 50 009
14. 464 352 + 60 800

Find the missing number:

15. 22 535 + ☐ = 45 535
16. 32 140 + ☐ = 53 240
17. 68 160 + ☐ = 98 960
18. 43 745 + ☐ = 52 752
19. 132 431 + ☐ = 152 831
20. 164 868 + ☐ = 267 868
21. 361 513 + ☐ = 372 413

Set C

Work out:

1. 13 210 + 40 300
2. 26 289 + 200 700
3. 37 396 + 3800
4. 48 459 + 70 050
5. 52 894 + 400 008
6. 37 195 + 20 006
7. 79 755 + 830 000

Work out:

8. 145 612 + 4300
9. 162 574 + 8400
10. 236 427 + 6500
11. 125 862 + 300 090
12. 274 510 + 90 200
13. 441 431 + 130 009
14. 686 520 + 209 700

Find the missing number:

15. 37 512 + ☐ = 77 712
16. 53 195 + ☐ = 143 895
17. 153 298 + ☐ = 164 198
18. 942 443 + ☐ = 971 443
19. 497 534 + ☐ = 507 537
20. 653 186 + ☐ = 874 186
21. 761 428 + ☐ = 962 628

I can do mental addition using partitioning.

Mental Subtraction — 1

And now on to subtraction. You can also use place value to help you when subtracting numbers in your head.

Examples

What's 5730 – 3200?

5730 has 57 hundreds and 3200 = 32 hundreds.

57 hundreds – 32 hundreds = 25 hundreds

So 5730 – 3200 = **2530**

What's 77 450 – 40 000?

77 450 has 77 thousands and 40 000 = 40 thousands.

77 thousands – 40 thousands = 37 thousands.

So 77 450 – 40 000 = **37 450**

Set A

Work out:

1. 1800 – 200
2. 2400 – 700
3. 3600 – 800
4. 2500 – 1200
5. 4400 – 2200
6. 3650 – 1400
7. 5920 – 2800

Work out:

8. 34 530 – 100
9. 82 333 – 20 000
10. 15 800 – 8000
11. 120 000 – 5000
12. 14 620 – 6000
13. 280 400 – 60 000
14. 391 300 – 20 000

Find the missing number:

15. 12 700 – ☐ = 8700
16. 17 900 – ☐ = 14 900
17. 284 320 – ☐ = 84 320
18. 37 530 – ☐ = 29 530
19. 106 000 – ☐ = 66 000
20. 111 005 – ☐ = 106 005
21. 224 300 – ☐ = 223 800

Set B

Work out:

1. 2500 – 1400
2. 4950 – 2700
3. 8624 – 700
4. 71 498 – 30 000
5. 15 380 – 3000
6. 16 671 – 9000
7. 109 537 – 400

Work out:

8. 13 240 – 5000
9. 16 140 – 9000
10. 25 820 – 7000
11. 246 440 – 20 000
12. 848 201 – 300 000
13. 277 235 – 60 000
14. 142 538 – 4000

Find the missing numbers:

15. 23 350 – ☐ = 13 350
16. 60 070 – ☐ = 54 070
17. 344 219 – ☐ = 44 219
18. 59 255 – ☐ = 58 355
19. 421 126 – ☐ = 411 726
20. 713 920 – ☐ = 683 920
21. 216 252 – ☐ = 215 552

Set C

Work out:

1. 7404 – 1300
2. 8227 – 3400
3. 13 531 – 2000
4. 151 421 – 3000
5. 168 795 – 50 000
6. 417 354 – 80 000
7. 519 962 – 16 000

Work out:

8. 15 690 – 13 000
9. 31 614 – 20 000
10. 648 310 – 400 000
11. 361 473 – 90 000
12. 783 904 – 4000
13. 142 730 – 900
14. 232 210 – 70 000

Find the missing numbers:

15. 59 440 – ☐ = 39 440
16. 67 732 – ☐ = 67 662
17. 123 550 – ☐ = 103 550
18. 284 304 – ☐ = 84 304
19. 382 343 – ☐ = 381 543
20. 464 381 – ☐ = 456 381
21. 572 454 – ☐ = 571 744

I can do mental subtraction using place value.

Mental Subtraction — 2

Partitioning can help you with subtraction as well as addition. These questions will give you some practice at it.

Examples

What's 14 560 − 1300?

14 560 − 1000 − 300
= 13 560 − 300
= **13 260**

What's 45 680 − 20 400?

45 680 − 20 000 − 400
= 25 680 − 400
= **25 280**

Set A

Work out:

1. 2950 − 1800
2. 1791 − 1500
3. 2627 − 1010
4. 6401 − 2100
5. 7970 − 4050
6. 10 430 − 6002
7. 14 650 − 3500

Work out:

8. 19 764 − 8400
9. 22 542 − 10 300
10. 28 539 − 2020
11. 56 270 − 20 060
12. 129 710 − 5500
13. 138 497 − 20 005
14. 145 612 − 409

Find the missing number:

15. 24 940 − 3000 − ☐ = 21 240
16. 27 406 − 6000 − ☐ = 21 106
17. 38 490 − 8000 − ☐ = 30 460
18. 49 830 − ☐ − 500 = 39 330
19. 50 610 − ☐ − 400 = 30 210
20. 72 850 − 24 000 − ☐ = 48 150
21. 131 920 − ☐ = 121 420

Set B

Work out:

1. 5870 − 1600
2. 4921 − 2400
3. 7433 − 5030
4. 14 265 − 3200
5. 17 370 − 4100
6. 29 534 − 10 300
7. 137 867 − 20 050

Work out:

8. 59 214 − 40 010
9. 60 451 − 2300
10. 133 860 − 7600
11. 155 305 − 100 008
12. 298 940 − 70 003
13. 324 355 − 10 090
14. 331 577 − 280 000

Find the missing number:

15. 29 650 − ☐ = 24 350
16. 34 870 − ☐ = 28 870
17. 44 424 − ☐ = 36 420
18. 71 597 − ☐ = 42 597
19. 154 903 − ☐ = 123 103
20. 227 402 − ☐ = 57 402
21. 336 316 − ☐ = 256 256

Set C

Work out:

1. 24 641 − 17 000
2. 35 928 − 8008
3. 38 193 − 20 200
4. 47 240 − 40 060
5. 56 204 − 1005
6. 71 570 − 30 700
7. 83 325 − 5600

Work out:

8. 141 511 − 23 000
9. 476 396 − 190 000
10. 256 213 − 7010
11. 338 445 − 20 900
12. 382 018 − 100 040
13. 463 937 − 101 010
14. 589 190 − 250 600

Find the missing number:

15. 62 514 − ☐ = 42 314
16. 91 651 − ☐ = 87 351
17. 141 780 − ☐ = 125 780
18. 273 810 − ☐ = 242 910
19. 352 237 − ☐ = 231 237
20. 771 770 − ☐ = 504 770
21. 489 430 − ☐ = 281 130

I can do mental subtraction using partitioning.

...d way that you can do subtraction — by counting up to get back to the original number.
...l you reach a round number, then add on what's left over.

Examples

What's 2500 – 1291?

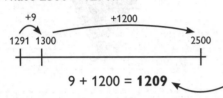

9 + 1200 = **1209**

Your knowledge of place values will help you to work these out.

What's 7040 – 2660?

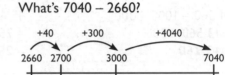

40 + 300 + 4040 = **4380**

Set A

Use the number lines to work out:

1 1200 – 690

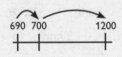

2 2800 – 1120

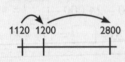

Work out, by counting up:

3 6300 – 6270
4 2800 – 1390
5 13 100 – 12 550
6 34 000 – 31 295
7 64 200 – 63 640
8 47 800 – 45 260
9 12 000 – 7970

Work out, by counting up:

10 14 000 – 7600
11 19 000 – 12 600
12 28 000 – 17 700
13 230 000 – 219 800
14 835 000 – 826 950
15 190 000 – 159 900
16 138 000 – 117 985

Set B

Use the number lines to work out:

1 1700 – 504

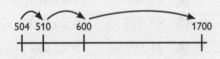

2 4500 – 2322

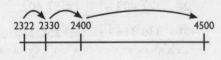

Work out, by counting up:

3 3800 – 2160
4 7510 – 4970
5 14 500 – 8490
6 10 000 – 3140
7 19 020 – 11 800
8 24 700 – 13 900
9 37 700 – 23 650

Work out, by counting up:

10 947 000 – 923 800
11 165 012 – 131 970
12 346 030 – 329 750
13 143 700 – 42 920
14 125 899 – 109 899
15 174 150 – 123 990
16 239 040 – 129 950

Set C

Use the number lines to work out:

1 14 560 – 12 880

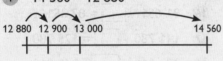

2 30 470 – 25 690

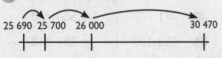

Work out, by counting up:

3 15 700 – 3680
4 17 000 – 11 820
5 19 200 – 10 980
6 18 900 – 14 630
7 20 222 – 12 850
8 35 312 – 24 950
9 49 179 – 37 880

Work out, by counting up:

10 133 300 – 115 007
11 142 702 – 127 920
12 149 230 – 131 680
13 267 300 – 136 750
14 372 100 – 249 955
15 360 090 – 343 870
16 471 890 – 439 843

I can do mental subtraction by counting up.

Addition and Subtraction — Review 1

Work out the following in your head:

1. $4300 + 500$
2. $6100 + 1200$
3. $5450 + 3000$
4. $7530 + 800$
5. $10\ 581 + 4000$
6. $16\ 725 + 20\ 000$
7. $19\ 940 + 70$
8. $18\ 803 + 21\ 000$
9. $32\ 486 + 8000$
10. $118\ 760 + 5000$
11. $54\ 940 + 90\ 000$
12. $135\ 130 + 24\ 000$
13. $120\ 470 + 800\ 000$
14. $44\ 820 + 30\ 000 + 100$
15. $213\ 240 + 40\ 000 + 4000$
16. $127\ 910 + 7000 + 100$

Work out the following in your head:

45. $3600 - 700$
46. $2800 - 1300$
47. $5500 - 2200$
48. $4650 - 3400$
49. $5195 - 600$
50. $16\ 870 - 5000$
51. $11\ 423 - 8000$
52. $27\ 482 - 20\ 000$
53. $48\ 790 - 800$
54. $56\ 841 - 7000$
55. $73\ 570 - 20\ 000$
56. $332\ 331 - 60\ 000$
57. $157\ 459 - 9000$
58. $163\ 023 - 40$
59. $254\ 290 - 600$
60. $911\ 584 - 30\ 000$

Find the missing number:

17. $7400 + \boxed{} = 7600$
18. $4590 + \boxed{} = 4640$
19. $16\ 305 + \boxed{} = 24\ 305$
20. $23\ 792 + \boxed{} = 24\ 592$
21. $72\ 213 + \boxed{} = 472\ 213$
22. $125\ 193 + \boxed{} = 205\ 193$

Find the missing number:

61. $8887 - \boxed{} = 8487$
62. $10\ 750 - \boxed{} = 6750$
63. $21\ 911 - \boxed{} = 12\ 911$
64. $34\ 192 - \boxed{} = 33\ 692$
65. $72\ 455 - \boxed{} = 72\ 375$
66. $727\ 110 - \boxed{} = 657\ 110$

Work out the following using partitioning:

23. $3220 + 2600$
24. $4580 + 2020$
25. $8671 + 4300$
26. $9157 + 7400$
27. $12\ 845 + 30\ 050$
28. $15\ 478 + 3700$
29. $27\ 243 + 120\ 000$
30. $33\ 812 + 809$
31. $48\ 125 + 16\ 000$
32. $67\ 509 + 20\ 700$
33. $134\ 596 + 20\ 006$
34. $172\ 972 + 80\ 050$
35. $155\ 305 + 106\ 000$
36. $248\ 231 + 690\ 000$
37. $336\ 548 + 21\ 400$
38. $486\ 022 + 308\ 009$

Work out the following using partitioning:

67. $3580 - 2300$
68. $7705 - 3400$
69. $9960 - 3090$
70. $11\ 449 - 4200$
71. $12\ 897 - 7900$
72. $16\ 530 - 10\ 010$
73. $27\ 419 - 18\ 000$
74. $32\ 933 - 4040$
75. $40\ 620 - 20\ 700$
76. $71\ 475 - 706$
77. $125\ 100 - 3700$
78. $147\ 322 - 38\ 000$
79. $231\ 245 - 55\ 000$
80. $323\ 830 - 100\ 050$
81. $345\ 583 - 90\ 700$
82. $406\ 105 - 10\ 400$

Find the missing number:

39. $4370 + 4000 + \boxed{} = 8770$
40. $34\ 872 + 5000 + \boxed{} = 39\ 972$
41. $19\ 546 + \boxed{} + 700 = 30\ 246$
42. $72\ 991 + \boxed{} = 81\ 291$
43. $145\ 405 + \boxed{} = 186\ 105$
44. $92\ 234 + \boxed{} = 298\ 234$

Work out the following by counting up:

83. $1800 - 710$
84. $2200 - 1450$
85. $2600 - 1210$
86. $13\ 100 - 7995$
87. $14\ 900 - 8870$
88. $23\ 400 - 15\ 700$
89. $35\ 050 - 14\ 800$
90. $20\ 330 - 13\ 940$
91. $45\ 210 - 37\ 190$
92. $141\ 650 - 129\ 850$
93. $168\ 107 - 123\ 070$
94. $234\ 500 - 132\ 890$

Nicely done – you've made your way through the first lot of review questions!

Written Addition — 1

It's really important that the numbers are lined up correctly when you're doing written addition.
If they're not, you might accidentally add the wrong numbers, so it's worth double checking before you start.

Examples

What is 31 419 + 18 233?

```
    3 1 4 1 9
  + 1 8 2 3 3
  ─────────────
    4 9 6 5 2
            1
```

103 829 people attended a music festival on Saturday. 81 207 people attended it on Sunday.

How many people attended the music festival in total?

```
    1 0 3 8 2 9
  +   8 1 2 0 7
  ───────────────
    1 8 5 0 3 6
          1   1
```

Set A

Work out:

1.   4 4 7 3
     + 2 5 2 5

2.   8 7 3 9
     + 1 1 6 0

3.   1 1 4 2 8
   + 2 4 2 5 4

Work out:

4.   1 3 5 2 5
   + 1 4 6 3 1

5.   2 1 4 1 1
   + 3 5 8 3 7

6.   3 2 6 8 4 0
   +   4 2 5 5 2

Answer the following:

7. 27 394 + 11 405

8. 34 176 + 12 515

9. 49 934 + 22 060

10. 26 507 + 31 223

11. 50 812 + 31 128

12. 132 104 + 154 792

13. 141 942 + 176 039

Set B

Work out:

1.   1 4 0 8 3
   + 2 2 5 1 4

2.   3 5 7 4 2
   + 3 1 8 0 7

3.   5 5 2 9 1
   + 4 7 1 6 6

Find the missing numbers:

4.
```
    3 ☐ 7 4 1 4
  + 2 7 0 ☐ 8 3
  ───────────────
  ☐ 9 7 8 9 ☐
```

5.
```
    4 5 ☐ 3 6
  + 3 8 6 1 5
  ─────────────
  ☐ 3 8 5 ☐
```

Answer the following:

6. 163 095 + 149 521

7. 332 634 + 240 187

8. 287 456 + 77 092

Jade's dress has 15 860 red sequins and 22 988 orange sequins.

9. How many sequins are there in total?

Set C

Answer the following:

1. 32 943 + 24 335

2. 51 830 + 29 501

3. 47 392 + 38 943

4. 123 556 + 45 391

5. 431 740 + 282 519

6. 559 453 + 316 262

7. 394 183 + 241 915

Find the number that is:

8. 23 139 more than 128 222

9. 44 503 more than 259 799

10. 193 471 more than 332 472

A spaceship flies 386 283 miles, then 135 544 miles home.

11. How far does it fly in total?

Here are the populations of three different islands:

Oxwater: 120 456
Kingbay: 98 524
Rivercliff: 165 308

Find the total population:

12. of Oxwater and Kingbay

13. of all three islands

I can do addition using written methods.

Written Addition — 2

Carrying on with addition, but let's throw some decimals in for fun. Like on the last page, make sure your numbers are lined up correctly — the decimal points should sit one on top of the other.

Examples

What's 134.631 + 342.284?

```
  1 3 4 . 6 3 1
+ 3 4 2 . 2 8 4
  4 7 6 . 9 1 5
            1
```

Salma weighs out 450.75 g of flour and 374.8 g of sugar. How much do the ingredients weigh in total?

```
  4 5 0 . 7 5
+ 3 7 4 . 8 0 ←  Put a zero here to
  8 2 5 . 5 5      make it easier to add.
      1   1
```

Set A

Work out:

1) 120.3
   +143.2

2) 204.2
   +162.7

3) 344.1
   +210.4

Work out:

4) 101.6
   +327.5

5) 19.478
   +20.171

6) 34.22
   +18.131

Answer the following:

7) 102.6 + 173.2

8) 223.4 + 111.8

9) 315.4 + 129.4

10) 241.45 + 165.13

11) 474.58 + 263.1

12) 384.92 + 102.4

Set B

Work out:

1) 146.9
   +141.8

2) 123.6
   +218.9

3) 345.73
   +443.18

Work out:

4) 612.49
   +245.51

5) 159.518
   +190.341

6) 287.32
   +118.455

Answer the following:

7) 249.471 + 304.28

8) 404 + 398.16

9) 714.55 + 194.884

Harriet took 550.752 seconds to finish a race. Quinn took 324.86 seconds.

10) How long did they take in total?

Set C

Work out:

1) 198.7 + 304.7

2) 273.3 + 219.91

3) 408.51 + 365.33

4) 539.74 + 249.16

5) 697.842 + 286.15

6) 736.651 + 127.19

7) 529 + 494.284

Work out:

8) 382.195 + 452.75

9) 553.6 + 389.901

10) 770.694 + 254.75

Angela ran a marathon in 453.576 minutes last year. This year, she took 464.89 minutes.

11) How long did it take her in total to run both marathons?

The table below shows how far Ralph travels in his car on three journeys.

Journey A	134.531 miles
Journey B	111.87 miles
Journey C	150.245 miles

12) Find the total distance of Journey A and Journey B.

13) Ralph can only go 400 miles before he runs out of fuel. Show that he can complete all three journeys.

I can add decimals using written methods.

Written Subtraction — 1

Have a go at some written subtraction. Just like with addition, make sure your numbers are correctly in line.

Examples

What's 24 522 – 12 381?

```
        4 12
    2 4 5̶ 2̶ 2
  –  1 2 3 8 1
  ─────────────
    1 2 1 4 1
```

1 hundred is exchanged for 10 tens.

132 391 people watched a documentary about penguins on TV. 84 150 watched a comedy show.

How many more people watched the documentary?

```
        12 12
    1̶ 3̶ 2̶ 3 9 1
  –     8 4 1 5 0
  ─────────────────
      4 8 2 4 1
```

Set A

Work out:

(1)
```
    4 9 8 7
  – 2 5 7 1
```

(2)
```
    5 6 2 4
  – 3 2 1 3
```

(3)
```
    8 9 5 0
  – 5 7 3 6
```

Work out:

(4)
```
   1 4 3 7 4
  –    3 2 6 0
```

(5)
```
   2 7 4 5 8
  –    4 1 8 8
```

(6)
```
   2 9 9 1 6 5
  – 1 7 8 0 1 4
```

Answer the following:

(7) 27 310 – 13 200

(8) 14 592 – 7233

(9) 31 294 – 17 071

(10) 48 585 – 24 191

(11) 56 940 – 33 728

(12) 283 617 – 71 406

(13) 374 922 – 211 380

Set B

Work out:

(1)
```
   3 7 2 4 2
  – 1 5 1 3 2
```

(2)
```
   4 2 5 9 9
  – 3 6 0 2 7
```

(3)
```
   5 1 7 0 5
  – 2 5 3 2 3
```

Work out:

(4)
```
   6 3 0 9 4
  – 2 2 4 1 9
```

(5)
```
   1 4 7 9 4 4
  –    3 6 2 7 1
```

(6)
```
   3 8 1 6 7 7
  – 1 9 0 0 9 3
```

Answer the following:

(7) 45 966 – 39 728

(8) 199 421 – 120 770

(9) 234 534 – 115 091

Jamal earned 123 743 points in a computer game. Georgia earned 90 981 points.

(10) How many more points did Jamal have?

Set C

Answer the following:

(1) 55 729 – 37 418

(2) 72 943 – 66 182

(3) 115 356 – 84 105

(4) 234 859 – 125 424

(5) 494 194 – 255 047

(6) 761 704 – 428 153

Find the number that is:

(7) 72 821 less than 193 450

(8) 132 874 less than 301 995

(9) 251 743 less than 521 461

(10) A factory makes 256 793 jars of jam and 179 822 jars of honey.

How much more jam does it make than honey?

A house costs £540 350. The price includes a garage worth £85 715 and a field worth £143 225.

Find out:

(11) how much more the field is worth than the garage.

(12) how much the house would cost without the garage or the field.

I can do subtraction using written methods.

Written Subtraction — 2

This page is similar to the last one, but this time you're going to practise subtracting decimals.
Like when adding decimals, make sure that the decimal points are lined up properly.

Examples

What's 187.9 – 66.2?

```
   187.9
 −  66.2
   121.7
```

Ayesha buys a new bike which costs £154.99.
How much change will she get from £180?

```
     7 9  9 10
   1 8 0 . 0 0
 − 1 5 4 . 9 9
   2 5 . 0 1
```

These zeros after the decimal point have been put in to make the subtraction easier.

Set A

Work out:

1) 141.6
   −110.3

2) 296.5
   −153.9

3) 339.4
   −218.7

Work out:

4) 441.9
   −325.8

5) 383.049
   −147.036

6) 451.572
   −220.23

Answer the following:

7) 371.3 – 190.1

8) 246.6 – 121.9

9) 425.93 – 202.15

10) 533.44 – 320.52

11) 487.15 – 273.41

12) 341.89 – 190.5

13) 682.71 – 326.2

Set B

Work out:

1) 237.8
   −129.4

2) 718.45
   −363.23

3) 588.194
   −291.472

Fill in the missing numbers:

4)
```
  4 ☐ 9 . 6 3
− 2 2 8 . ☐ 7
  2 3 1 . 0 ☐
```

5)
```
  3 9 3 . 5 4
−  2 1 ☐ . 2
  ☐ 7 5 . ☐☐
```

Answer the following:

6) 591.405 – 322.264

7) 749.852 – 277.14

8) 489 – 246.49

9) Patches the guinea pig weighs 952.413 g. Mabel the guinea pig weighs 791.27 g.

   How much more does Patches weigh than Mabel?

Set C

Answer the following:

1) 243.5 – 122.9

2) 401.82 – 255.7

3) 693.55 – 340.93

4) 485.12 – 201.86

5) 892.311 – 503.203

6) 742.48 – 524.146

7) 974 – 450.52

Find the number that is:

8) 340.86 less than 780.491

9) 434.7 less than 829.485

10) 321.042 less than 556.61

Diego ran 200 m in 27.84 seconds.
Lara ran 200 m in 31.931 seconds.

11) How much faster was Diego than Lara?

The table below shows the heights of the Smith children.

Maddie	142.59 cm
Jonathan	173.802 cm
Nina	125.651 cm

12) How much taller is Jonathan than Maddie?

13) How much taller is Maddie than Nina?

I can subtract decimals using written methods.

Addition and Subtraction — Review 2

Work out:

1. 6294
    $+2661$

2. 26843
    $+45346$

3. 53699
    $+35155$

4. 489377
    $+190480$

Answer the following:

5. 23 456 + 38 231
6. 35 505 + 53 616
7. 42 719 + 34 471
8. 77 826 + 19 342
9. 67 161 + 24 709
10. 138 024 + 51 866
11. 230 846 + 190 137
12. 472 557 + 214 628
13. 301 449 + 476 701
14. 511 872 + 349 309

A rainforest is home to 34 572 mammals, 45 635 birds and 153 792 insects.

Find the total number of:

15. mammals and birds.
16. birds and insects.

Work out:

17. 341.8
    $+224.1$

18. 258.47
    $+431.18$

19. 569.41
    $+316.73$

20. 485.635
    $+412.708$

Fred's Furniture Store is selling the following items.

Find out the total cost of:

Sofa	£451.45
Table	£287.09
Bed	£325.90

21. the sofa and table
22. the bed and table

Answer the following:

23. 731.6 + 124.7
24. 486.4 + 211.8
25. 425.87 + 462.1
26. 513.38 + 367.91
27. 308 + 229.51
28. 413.245 + 479.35
29. 257.76 + 623.511
30. 374.84 + 208.926
31. 804.219 + 137.29
32. 445 + 298.322

Work out:

33. 7394
    -2713

34. 25837
    -14752

35. 49410
    -36205

36. 654981
    -437642

Answer the following:

37. 56 389 – 38 141
38. 94 523 – 22 701
39. 159 674 – 72 822
40. 249 755 – 127 927
41. 385 352 – 237 910
42. 610 561 – 402 345
43. 725 840 – 341 921
44. 701 731 – 499 801

Find the number that is:

45. 14 952 less than 58 363
46. 54 732 less than 89 841
47. 176 855 less than 904 957
48. 462 942 less than 779 590

Work out:

49. 352.9
    -131.7

50. 548.3
    -225.8

51. 812.54
    -581.29

52. 735.74
    -411.561

Find the missing numbers:

53. 662.92 – ☐ = 381.21
54. 887.14 – ☐ = 593.83
55. 746.291 – ☐ = 228.19

56. Plane A is flying at a speed of 482.34 mph.
    Plane B is flying at a speed of 595.104 mph.
    How much faster is Plane B flying than Plane A?

Answer the following:

57. 347.45 – 212.3
58. 231.28 – 106.1
59. 585 – 241.46
60. 524.621 – 383.404
61. 785 – 441.19
62. 823.528 – 541.65

That's a whole page of questions on written addition and subtraction finished — nice one!

Checking Calculations

You know how to do addition and subtraction, but it's important to be able to check your answers too. One way to see if your answer is sensible is by rounding.

Examples

Lily is working out how many schoolchildren there are in her town.
There are 15 189 children in primary school and 19 702 in secondary school.
She thinks there are 34 891 schoolchildren in total.

What calculation could Lily use to check her answer?

15 000 + 20 000 = **35 000**

Round to the nearest thousand.

Work out the following calculation:

275 677 – 139 253

```
      6 15
  2 7̶ 5̶ 6 7 7
– 1 3 9 2 5 3
  1 3 6 4 2 4
```

Now round the values to the nearest ten thousand and calculate. What's the difference between this answer and the accurate answer?

Round 275 677 and 139 253 to the nearest ten thousand.

280 000 – 140 000 = 140 000

140 000 – 136 424 = 3576

So the difference between the two answers is **3576**.

Set A

Write down a calculation you could use to check:

1. 5123 + 2489 = 7612
2. 9516 – 4348 = 5168
3. 8413 + 6154 = 14 567
4. 10 426 + 11 530 = 21 956
5. 18 370 – 10 464 = 7906
6. 24 648 + 19 121 = 43 769
7. 31 856 – 15 557 = 16 299

8. Hope rounded the values of these calculations and found the answers, but they have been mixed up. Match the best rounded answer to each calculation:

4495 + 7132 = 11 627	6200
9745 – 3591 = 6154	16 000
14 934 – 7717 = 7217	26 000
12 875 + 13 363 = 26 238	14 000
27 554 – 12 202 = 15 352	11 600
24 714 – 10 779 = 13 935	7000

Four of the calculations below are incorrect. Use rounding to check which ones are wrong.

9. 7252 + 3663 = 10 915
10. 13 977 – 6218 = 7759
11. 14 254 + 13 910 = 32 164
12. 29 112 + 16 480 = 45 592
13. 44 503 – 26 197 = 28 306
14. 151 396 + 27 763 = 199 159
15. 139 123 – 117 835 = 21 288
16. 241 206 – 124 359 = 156 847

The table below shows the populations of two towns.

Great Highdale	28 712
Little Highdale	20 079

17. Work out the total population.
18. Now use rounding to check your calculation.
19. Is the rounded answer higher or lower than the accurate answer?

Write down a calculation you could use to check:

1. 14 823 + 28 141 = 42 964

2. 35 794 − 21 533 = 14 261

3. 45 365 + 49 277 = 94 642

4. 96 149 − 62 682 = 33 467

5. 106 229 + 32 541 = 138 770

6. 125 737 − 47 443 = 78 294

7. 156 924 + 132 468 = 289 392

Zaid has calculated how many points he has earned on a computer game.

> A. 49 672 + 36 707 = 86 379
>
> B. 83 194 + 12 888 = 99 082
>
> C. 29 053 + 66 556 = 95 609

8. What calculations could he use to check his answers?

9. One of Zaid's answers is incorrect. Identify which one is wrong.

Work out accurately and use rounding to check the following calculations:

10. 77 103 + 18 600

11. 58 715 + 85 040

12. 44 510 − 23 950

13. 81 195 − 46 009

14. 152 422 + 134 903

15. 324 115 + 278 817

16. 284 527 − 141 230

17. 445 976 − 226 184

18. Work out the following calculations accurately.

    85 409 + 36 090

    375 510 − 234 300

    212 957 + 143 231

19. Now round to the nearest thousand and calculate. What's the difference between these answers and the accurate answers?

Work out accurately and use rounding to check the following calculations:

1. 25 432 + 41 080

2. 76 300 − 38 190

3. 98 227 − 63 700

4. 85 814 + 47 050

5. 121 198 + 239 621

6. 272 854 − 116 513

7. 348 308 + 349 415

8. 642 943 − 231 487

Tilly wants to work out 326 793 + 135 625. She gets the answer 473 018.

9. What calculation could she use to check her answer?

10. Explain why this calculation shows her answer is not correct.

11. Work out the calculation accurately.

Work out accurately and use rounding to check the following calculations:

12. 165 614 + 213 300

13. 362 258 + 229 070

14. 486 400 − 241 975

15. 515 924 + 319 342

16. 585 104 − 299 043

17. 713 507 − 448 311

18. Round the following values to the nearest ten and calculate.

    134 114 + 152 723 = 286 837

    285 613 − 133 452 = 152 161

    330 538 + 484 747 = 815 285

19. Now round the values to the nearest hundred and calculate.

20. Compare your answers. What do you notice?

I can use rounding to check calculations and accuracy.

Addition and Subtraction Problems — 1

Now it's time to put your addition and subtraction skills to the test.
For these problems, you'll need to have a think about what to do to find the answer.

Examples

This year, 54 920 pupils took part in a national maths competition. Last year, 41 500 pupils took part.

How many more students took part this year than last year?

54 920 – 41 500

You can partition 41 500 into 41 000 and 500.

54 920 – 41 000 – 500 = 13 420

So **13 420** more students took part this year.

On a tropical island, there were 45 856 palm trees.
There were 26 321 more fruit trees than palm trees.

A storm wipes out 19 024 fruit trees. How many fruit trees are left after the storm?

First, calculate how many fruit trees there were before the storm.

```
   4 5 8 5 6
 +  2 6 3 2 1
   7 2 1 7 7
     1   1
```

So there were 72 177 fruit trees.

Then subtract the number of trees wiped out from the original number of fruit trees.

```
        6  12
   7  2  1 7 7
 - 1 9 0 2 4
   5 3 1 5 3
```

So there are **53 153** fruit trees left after the storm.

Set A

Uma cycled 10 000 m on Saturday and 15 143 m on Sunday.

1. How much farther did she cycle on Sunday than Saturday?

2. How far did she cycle in total?

3. Harris cycled 12 030 m in total. How much less did he cycle than Uma's total?

Riley, Amaya and Jason pull numbers out of a hat. Riley's number is 11 413. Amaya's number is 20 050 more than Riley's.

4. What is Amaya's number?

5. Jason's number is 11 420 less than Amaya's. What is Jason's number?

Horace the porcupine has 27 443 spines. George the porcupine has 5043 fewer spines.

6. How many spines do they have in total?

A blue train travelled 46 000 miles last year. A red train travelled 31 900 miles more.

7. How many miles did the red train travel last year?

8. The red train needs repairing when it reaches 110 000 miles. How many more miles can the red train travel before it must be repaired?

The table below shows the number of visitors to Amblemere Castle.

June	30 700
July	93 384
August	51 250

9. How many more people visited in July than in June?

10. How many fewer people visited in June than August?

11. How many more people visited in July than the total number for June and August?

Set B

Maisie is moving her cows into a new field. The old field was 17 934 m² and the new field is 5120 m² bigger.

① How big are the two fields in total?

Maisie puts her sheep in a field that is 15 671 m².

② How much smaller is the sheep field than the two cow fields combined?

The table below shows the prices of some cars.

Blue car	£31 890
Green car	£17 450

A silver car costs £13 020 more than the green car. A red car costs £19 700 more than the silver car.

③ Calculate the price of the red car.

④ How much more does the red car cost than the blue car?

⑤ A customer buys both the blue car and the silver car. How much do they spend in total?

The table below shows how many people voted in a survey about favourite dog breeds.

Dalmatian	74 851
Labrador	?
Pug	?

⑥ 13 324 more people voted for labrador than dalmatian. 21 283 more people voted for pug than labrador. How many people voted for pug?

Gillian is building a town on a computer game. She has £538 900 in the bank.

⑦ She builds a park costing £123 040, then earns £281 495. How much does she have in the bank now?

Another day she has £302 780 in the bank. She wins £555 555 in a competition, but spends £446 712 building a new town hall.

⑧ How much money does she have in the bank after building the new town hall?

Set C

The table below shows how many people entered a competition on TV and which answer they chose.

Answer A	34 600
Answer B	72 240
Answer C	?
Answer D	?

① 20 700 fewer people answered C than B. 42 600 more people answered D than C. Calculate how many people answered D.

Asma is trying to guess which number Luke is thinking of. He adds 134 800 to it, subtracts 81 700 and gets the answer 242 900.

② Asma guesses 192 800. Explain if her guess is correct or not.

This time, Asma thinks of a number. She subtracts 178 210 from it, then adds 55 078. She gets the answer 260 985.

③ Luke guesses 395 117. Show that his guess is wrong.

④ A female blue whale weighs 114 680 kg. A male blue whale weighs 132 350 kg.

The difference between the male and female's weights is 11 300 kg less than the weight of a young blue whale.

Calculate the young blue whale's weight.

Roger finds some buried treasure. The table shows how much the treasure is worth.

Crown	£254 896
Necklace	£161 962
Gold coins	£355 906
Ring	£121 868

⑤ Roger estimates the ring will be worth £20 000 more each year. Estimate how much the ring will be worth in 4 years.

⑥ A collector has a budget of £505 000. How much more money does she need to buy the necklace and the gold coins?

⑦ A museum buys the ring and the crown. They get a discount of £23 190. How much does the museum spend in total?

I can solve multi-step problems in addition and subtraction.

And just when you thought you'd solved all the problems, here are some more for you to do.
These numbers are decimals, so you'll need to pay extra close attention.

Examples

Gerald wants to book an adventure holiday. A rock climbing trip costs
£124.30. A canoeing trip costs £94.15 more than the rock climbing
trip. A skiing trip costs £128.25 more than the canoeing trip.

How much does the skiing trip cost?

```
    1 2 4 . 3 0
  +    9 4 . 1 5
  ─────────────
    2 1 8 . 4 5
      1
```
So the canoeing trip
costs £218.45.

```
    2 1 8 . 4 5
  + 1 2 8 . 2 5
  ─────────────
    3 4 6 . 7 0
      1       1
```
So the skiing trip costs **£346.70**.

Miranda needs to buy string for two plants in her garden.
She needs 521.78 cm for one plant and 312.62 cm for the other.

How much string will she need in total?

```
    5 2 1 . 7 8
  + 3 1 2 . 6 2
  ─────────────
    8 3 4 . 4 0
        1   1
```
So she'll need
834.4 cm of string.

The string is only sold in 100 cm pieces. If she buys
900 cm, how much string will Miranda have left over?

```
    8  9  9  10
    9̶  0̶  0̶ . 0̶
  - 8  3  4 . 4
  ──────────────
       6  5 . 6
```
So she'll have **65.6 cm**
of string left over.

Set A

Percy the pigeon is 325.6 mm long.
Barney the budgie is 205.2 mm long.

1 How much longer is Percy than Barney?

2 Find their total combined length.

3 Penny the parrot is 102.1 mm shorter
than Percy and Barney's combined
length. Find the length of Penny.

The table below shows the heights of
three different cakes.

Chocolate	202.11 mm
Vanilla	254.62 mm
Lemon	315.81 mm

4 How much taller is the lemon
cake than the chocolate cake?

5 How tall are the vanilla cake and
the chocolate cake in total?

6 How much smaller is the lemon
cake than the combined height of
the chocolate and vanilla cakes?

Theo wants to buy a new TV. He has to decide
between two — the first one costs £310.10.

7 The second TV is £117.55 more expensive
than the first. Calculate its price.

8 The sales assistant offers Theo a discount
of £90.25 on the more expensive TV.
What is the new price?

The table below shows how many points some
children have scored in a gymnastics competition.

Adrian	300.71
Olivia	250.11
Rhys	175.8

9 How much less did Adrian score than
the total points for Olivia and Rhys?

10 Olivia scores another 320 points,
and Adrian scores another 270 points.

Who has the highest overall
score, and by how much?

Set B

Hamish lives 344.5 miles away from London. Omar lives 161.3 miles from London.

1. How much farther does Hamish live from London than Omar?

2. Hamish, Omar and their friend Scott travel to London from their own houses. If they travel 748.2 miles in total, how far away does Scott live from London?

Leah is buying a snowboard. It costs £365.75 in the sale.

3. The original price was £405.95. How much cheaper is the snowboard in the sale?

4. She also buys some boots and a jacket. Their total cost is £114.50 less than the snowboard sale price. If the jacket costs £119.45, how much do the boots cost?

The table below shows the weights of three animals.

Alligator	115.84 kg
Polar bear	290.815 kg
Giant panda	102.711 kg

5. What is the total weight of the polar bear and the giant panda?

6. How much more does the polar bear weigh than the alligator?

7. Each animal is 5 kg heavier when they are weighed again. What is the total weight of the three animals now?

Chester has a red and a blue ribbon. The blue ribbon is 235.315 cm and the red ribbon is 460.52 cm.

8. How much longer is the red ribbon than the blue ribbon?

9. An orange ribbon is 202.919 cm longer than the blue ribbon. How much longer is the red ribbon than the orange ribbon?

Set C

A hotel room costs £118.40 on a Friday and £139.90 on a Saturday. A customer wants to book the room for Friday, Saturday and Sunday. It will cost £385.39 in total.

1. How much does the room cost on Sunday?

2. The customer decides just to book Saturday and Sunday. What is the new total price?

Carla is travelling. The table below shows how far she travels on each stage of her journey.

By bus	290.32 miles
By plane	482.485 miles

3. How much further did she travel by plane than by bus?

4. Carla travelled 594.305 miles less by car than the total miles travelled by bus and plane. How far did she travel by car?

5. Carla's brother travelled a total of 182.16 miles more than the distance Carla travelled by car. How far did Carla's brother travel in total?

Faisal and Tia timed how long it took for them to run around the park. Faisal took 337.45 seconds and Tia took 59.131 seconds less than Faisal.

6. How long did Faisal and Tia take in total?

7. Their friend Amy took 109.16 seconds less than their total time. Find Amy's time.

Grace lives in a village. The table below shows the distance from her village to two cities.

Benbridge	531.841 km
Cinfield	412.55 km
Susbrough	?
Westville	?

8. Susbrough is 152.95 km further away than Benridge. How far is it to Susbrough?

9. Westville is 372.966 km closer than the total distance to Benbridge and Cinfield. How far is it to Westville?

10. Grace has been to two cities. Their total distance from her village is 983.975 km. Which cities has she been to?

I can solve addition and subtraction problems with decimals.

Write down a calculation you could use to check:

(1) 7193 + 4567 = 11 760

(2) 14 523 + 12 289 = 26 812

(3) 28 331 − 15 839 = 12 492

(4) 41 956 − 25 309 = 16 647

(5) 58 773 + 31 428 = 90 201

(6) 105 871 + 215 703 = 321 574

(7) 245 983 − 122 490 = 123 493

Work out accurately and use rounding to check the following calculations:

(8) 8344 + 6700

(9) 19 543 − 11 100

(10) 17 308 + 14 600

(11) 24 213 − 12 095

(12) 28 415 + 31 800

(13) 39 726 − 24 900

(14) 45 336 + 39 400

(15) 54 154 + 39 631

(16) 78 435 − 39 215

(17) 112 186 + 143 973

(18) 214 595 − 105 111

(19) 309 204 + 282 377

(20) 556 647 + 348 184

(21) 772 788 − 499 537

(22) Work out the following calculation accurately.

73 143 + 49 487

(23) Now round the values to the nearest hundred and calculate. What's the difference between this answer and the estimated answer?

In a survey, people were asked how many portions of fruit and vegetables they eat on average in a day. The results were divided into categories. The table below shows the number of people in each category.

0-2 portions	11 203
3-4 portions	24 994
5-6 portions	58 538
7+ portions	11 404

(24) How many fewer people eat 7+ portions than 5-6 portions?

(25) How many people eat 4 portions or less?

(26) How many more people eat 5-6 portions than the total number of the other categories?

A cake factory employs 34 800 people.
A custard factory employs 29 000 people.

(27) The factories need to employ 85 550 people in total to keep up with demand. How many more people do they need to employ?

The table below shows how many people attended an arts and crafts fair.

April	47 825
May	65 399

(28) 11 300 fewer people attended in March than in April. 12 000 fewer people attended in February than in March. Calculate how many people attended the fair in February.

(29) The organisers expect the increase in visitors between May and June to be the same as the increase between April and May. Calculate how many people are expected in June.

Malia is making a sculpture. Currently it is 213.7 cm tall. She adds the final part, which is 128.2 cm tall, to the top of the sculpture.

(30) What is the total height of the sculpture?

(31) She needs to fit the sculpture through a door that's 310 cm tall. How much taller is the sculpture than the door?

Alek works out how much money it would cost for him to go on holiday.

Flight	£253.48
Hotel	?
Spending money	?

(32) Alek's spending money is £140.46 more than the flight. Calculate the value of the spending money.

(33) The total cost of the holiday is £995.70. How much does the hotel cost?

Sabrina, Eric and Jamie are set a challenge. Sabrina takes 124.49 seconds to complete the challenge. Eric takes 209.67 seconds longer than Sabrina. Jamie takes 118.065 seconds less than Eric.

(34) How long did Jamie take to complete the challenge?

(35) How long did they take in total?

Well done, that's the last review for this section done and dusted!

1 The calculations below are missing some numbers. Complete the calculations by using the numbers in the boxes beside each one.

a)
```
    ☐ 1 7 ☐ 3
  + 2 ☐ ☐ 6 ☐
  ─────────────
    4 9 2 8 1
```
2	7
5	8
1	

c)
```
    2 ☐ ☐ . 1 ☐
  + ☐ 2 3 . ☐ 8
  ───────────────
    3 7 1 . 6 7
```
4	8
4	9
1	

b)
```
    ☐ 3 ☐ 8 ☐
  − 3 ☐ ☐ ☐ 2
  ─────────────
    3 4 1 2 1
```
1	6
9	2
7	3

d)
```
    ☐ 0 3 . ☐ ☐
  − 4 ☐ ☐ . ☐ 1
  ───────────────
    2 8 7 . 1 3
```
6	2
3	7
1	4

 2 An adventure park is running a competition. To win, you need to work out the mystery number. Below are some things which have been given a number, and some others which you'll need to work out. Find the mystery number by using the calculations below.

Big wheel	28 105
Ghost train	73 740
Hot dog	59 516
Dodgems	35 932
Helter skelter	?
Popcorn	?
Roller coaster	?

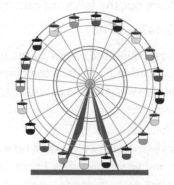

A. Hot dog − Big wheel = Helter skelter

B. Popcorn + eighteen thousand = Dodgems

C. Ghost train − 34 495 = Roller coaster

D. Helter skelter + Popcorn + Roller coaster = The Mystery Number

3. Randall the robot rounds 5-digit and 6-digit numbers before doing any calculations:

- for 5-digit even numbers, round to the nearest 10.
- for 5-digit odd numbers, round to the nearest 100.
- for all 6-digit numbers, round to the nearest 1000.

a) Work out the calculations below accurately, then
   check by rounding according to Randall's instructions.

| 21 312 + 24 187 | 49 390 + 34 209 | 78 113 + 63 485 |

| 134 123 + 345 613 | 33 871 + 41 438 | 129 841 + 65 072 |

b) Ricky the robot rounds all numbers to the nearest 100.
   He is used by a company to estimate how much stock they'll sell.

   Explain how Ricky could be improved and why.

4. Copy out the calculations below and work out the answers. If there are two
boxes which are the same colour, the same number should go in both boxes.

$$112.7 \ + \ 153.1 \ = \ \boxed{A} \atop \boxed{B} \ \over 508.95 \ +$$

$$\boxed{A} \ + \ 623.56 \ = \ \boxed{C} \atop \boxed{B} \over \boxed{D} \ -$$

$$\boxed{C} \ - \ 599.215 \ = \ \boxed{E} \atop \boxed{D} \over \boxed{F} \ +$$

5. For this task, you'll need a piece of paper, a coin and a friend to play with. Follow these instructions:

1. Fold a piece of A4 paper in half 4 times, then cut into 16 pieces — 8 for you, 8 for your friend.
   Write a number between 1 and 9 on each piece of paper. You can use numbers more than once.

2. Turn them face down and mix them. Now choose 5 numbers each and lay
   them out in the order you chose them — this is your 5-digit number.

3. Flip the coin to decide if you'll be adding or subtracting
   the numbers. Heads is addition, tails is subtraction.

   5 3 2 9 1

4. Using a pen and paper, do the calculation.
   Whoever completes it correctly first gets a point.

   3 8 1 7 5

5. When someone reaches 5 points, start choosing
   6 numbers each and play with 6-digit numbers.

6. The winner is the first person to get 10 points.

6 Copy and complete the diagram below.

- Each row and column should add up to the numbers in the blue boxes.
- The numbers in the green boxes should add up to 100 000.
- The numbers in the red boxes must be the same.

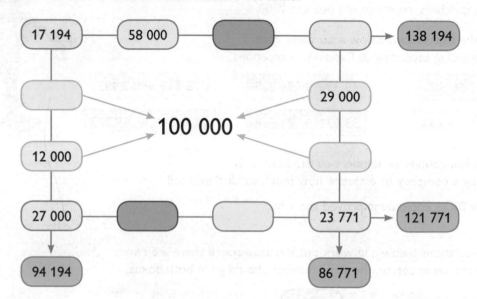

17 194 — 58 000 — [ ] — [ ] → 138 194

[ ] 29 000

100 000

12 000 [ ]

27 000 — [ ] — [ ] — 23 771 → 121 771

94 194 86 771

---

7 A troll only lets people cross his bridge if he is given a certain amount of coins.

Look at the statements below:

Alan: I wasn't allowed to cross the bridge. I had 10 500 fewer coins than Cali.

Brenda: I had 9200 more coins than Damon. The troll needed exactly 1200 fewer coins than the amount I had.

Cali: I had 20 700 coins, but the troll didn't let me cross the bridge.

Damon: I have the same amount of coins as Alan and Cali put together. I haven't tried to cross the bridge yet.

a) How many coins do you need to cross the bridge?

b) How many more coins does:

   i) Alan need?

   ii) Cali need?

   iii) Damon need?

And that's the end of those tricky challenges — good going!

Multiples

To work out multiples of things you need to know your times tables.
If something is a multiple of a number, that means it appears in its times table.

Example

Write out the first three multiples of 2.

2, 4, 6 ◄──── This just means write the first 3 numbers in the 2 times table.

Set A

Write out the first four multiples of each number below:

1. 3
2. 4
3. 5
4. 10
5. 50
6. 100

Which of the numbers in each box are a multiple of:

7. 2? | 15 | 18 | 22 | 25 |
8. 3? | 18 | 23 | 30 | 46 |
9. 4? | 14 | 20 | 38 | 44 |
10. 10? | 60 | 71 | 88 | 100 |
11. 11? | 33 | 50 | 74 | 99 |

Are the following true or false?

12. 56 is a multiple of 8.
13. 29 is a multiple of 3.
14. 54 is a multiple of 5.
15. 32 is a multiple of 4.
16. 60 is a multiple of 6.
17. 26 is a multiple of 7.

Set B

Write out the first five multiples of each number below:

1. 7
2. 9
3. 12
4. 25
5. 30
6. 250

Look at the numbers in this box:

| 36 | 42 | 56 | 60 | 54 | 63 |
| 85 | 77 | 121 | 72 | 80 | 96 |

Which of these numbers are multiples of:

7. 4?
8. 8?
9. 9?

Are the following true or false?

10. All multiples of 2 end in an even number.
11. There are 4 multiples of 10 between 80 and 100.
12. 32 is a multiple of 5.
13. All multiples of 3 end in 3, 6 or 9.

Set C

Write out the first six multiples of each number below:

1. 6
2. 20
3. 1000
4. 110
5. 45
6. 22

Find the missing digit to complete the sentences below:

7. 5☐ is a multiple of 7.
8. 6☐ is a multiple of 8.
9. 8☐ is a multiple of 9.
10. 12☐ is a multiple of 10.
11. 8☐ is a multiple of 11.
12. 1☐8 is a multiple of 12.

Are the following true or false?

13. All multiples of 5 end in 0 or 5.
14. Multiples of 4 are always even numbers.
15. 675 is a multiple of 25.
16. All multiples of 3 are also multiples of 9.

I can identify multiples of numbers.

Factors

Factors of a number are the numbers that can be multiplied together to give that number.
If two numbers have the same factor, it's called a common factor.

Examples

Find the missing factor of 36
in this factor pair.

36 ⟶ 3 and ☐

You can just divide 36 by 3 ⟶ 36 ÷ 3 = **12**
to find the missing factor.

Find a common factor of 12 and 16.

Factors of 12. ⟶ 1 2 3 4 6 12

Factors of 16. ⟶ 1 2 4 8 16

The common factors of
12 and 16 are **1**, **2** and **4**.

Set A

The boxes show the factors of each
number. Find the missing factors.

1. 6 | 1 2 ? 6 |
2. 8 | 1 ? 4 8 |
3. 10 | 1 2 ? 10 |
4. 14 | 1 2 7 ? |
5. 15 | 1 3 ? 15 |

Find the missing values to give
all the factor pairs of 28:

6. 1 × ☐ = 28
7. 2 × ☐ = 28
8. 4 × ☐ = 28

Find the missing factors:

9. ☐ × ☐ = 13
10. ☐ × ☐ = 11

The box shows the factors of 30.

| 1 | 2 | 3 | 5 |
| 6 | 10 | 15 | 30 |

Which of these numbers
are also factors of:

11. 33?
12. 50?
13. 24?

Set B

The boxes show the factors of each
number. Find the missing factors.

1. 12 | 1 2 3 4 ? 12 |
2. 16 | 1 2 ? 8 16 |
3. 18 | 1 2 ? 6 9 18 |
4. 20 | 1 2 ? ? 10 20 |
5. 81 | 1 3 ? 27 81 |

Find the missing values to give
all the factor pairs of 48:

6. 1 × ☐ = 48
7. 2 × ☐ = 48
8. 3 × ☐ = 48
9. 4 × ☐ = 48
10. 6 × ☐ = 48
11. Find the common factors
    of 48 and 12.

Look at the numbers in the box.

| 2 | 4 | 5 | 7 |
| | 8 | 9 | 10 |

Find two numbers that
are common factors of:

12. 35 and 70
13. 54 and 18
14. 42 and 56

Set C

Find the factors of
these numbers:

1. 36
2. 33
3. 40
4. 24
5. 27

Which has more factors:

6. 42 or 28?
7. 18 or 21?
   What are their
   common factors?
8. 30 or 45?
   What are their
   common factors?

Find all the common factors of
each pair of numbers below:

9. 18 and 12
10. 48 and 36
11. 28 and 24
12. 35 and 70
13. 32 and 16

I can identify factors and find common factors of two numbers.

Prime Numbers

A prime number is a number that can only be divided by itself and 1.
Numbers that <u>can</u> be divided by other numbers are called composite numbers.

Example

Answer true or false: 4 is a prime number.

False ← 4 can be divided by 1, 4 and 2,
so it is not a prime number.

Set A

Write down the next prime number after:

1. 2
2. 10
3. 15
4. 18
5. 20
6. 25

Find the prime number in each list.

7. 6 7 8 9 10
8. 12 13 14 15 16
9. 30 31 32 33 34
10. 44 45 47 48 50
11. 60 61 62 63 64
12. 68 69 70 71 72

Are the following true or false?

13. 19 is a prime number.
14. 33 is a prime number.
15. 18 is a composite number.
16. 41 is a composite number.
17. 9 is a prime number.
18. 12 is a composite number.

Set B

Write down the next prime number after:

1. 0
2. 4
3. 12
4. 30
5. 42
6. 63

Find a prime number between each pair of numbers below.

7. 14 and 18
8. 25 and 30
9. 33 and 40
10. 50 and 55
11. 85 and 90
12. 90 and 100

Are the following true or false?

13. 39 is a composite number.
14. 2 is the only even prime number.
15. 11 is a prime number.
16. There are 5 prime numbers between 0 and 10.
17. 1 is the smallest prime number.

Set C

Find two prime numbers between each pair of numbers below.

1. 4 and 10
2. 20 and 30
3. 40 and 45
4. 75 and 85
5. 50 and 60
6. 85 and 100

Are the following true or false?

7. There are 3 prime numbers less than 5.
8. There are 2 prime numbers between 80 and 90.
9. 73 is a prime number.
10. 85 is a composite number.
11. 28 is a prime number.

12. Rasul says that 2 is the only even prime number. Is he right or wrong? Explain your answer.
13. Lacey says that every prime number over 10 ends in 1, 3, 7 or 9. Explain why she is correct.
14. Ryan says that every number over 10 that ends in 1, 3, 7 or 9 is prime. Explain why he is wrong.

I know and can use prime numbers up to 100.

Prime Factors

The factors of a number that are prime numbers are called prime factors.
You can use a factor tree to help you work out a number's prime factors.

Example

Which prime numbers multiply together to make 50?

A factor tree breaks up a number
to show its prime factors.

So, 50 = **2 × 5 × 5**

The numbers at the ends of
the branches are the prime
factors of the number.

Set A

Find the missing numbers to show
the prime factors of each number.

1. 6 = 2 × ☐
2. 9 = 3 × ☐
3. 10 = 2 × ☐
4. 15 = 3 × ☐
5. 8 = 2 × 2 × ☐

Copy and complete the factor trees to find the prime factors:

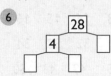

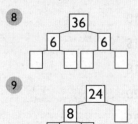

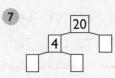

Set B

Find the missing numbers to show
the prime factors of each number.

1. 21 = ☐ × 3
2. 22 = 2 × ☐
3. 16 = 2 × 2 × 2 × ☐
4. 18 = 2 × 3 × ☐
5. 32 = 2 × 2 × 2 × 2 × ☐
6. 33 = ☐ × ☐

Copy and complete the factor trees to find the prime factors:

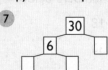

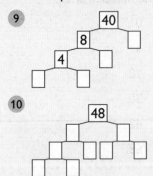

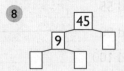

Set C

Copy and complete the factor trees to find the prime factors:

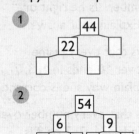

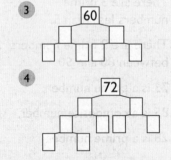

Find the prime factors of
the following numbers.

5. 35 = ☐ × ☐
6. 49 = ☐ × ☐
7. 56 = ☐ × ☐ × ☐ × ☐
8. 63 = ☐ × ☐ × ☐
9. 66 = ☐ × ☐ × ☐

I can find the prime factors of a number.

Multiplication and Division — Review 1

Write out the first 3 multiples of each number below:

1. 2
2. 1
3. 8
4. 11
5. 15
6. 200

Find the missing multiples in each sequence.

7. 3   6   ☐   12   15
8. 10   20   30   40   ☐
9. ☐   24   36   48   60

Which of the numbers in each box are multiples of:

10. 7? | 42 43 44 45 46 47 48 |
11. 8? | 52 53 54 55 56 57 58 |
12. 9? | 62 63 64 65 66 67 68 |

Are the following true or false?

13. 8 is a multiple of 16.
14. 34 is a multiple of 8.
15. 18 is a multiple of 9.

Find the missing factors in each box.

16. 34 | 1 2 ? 34 |
17. 28 | 1 2 4 ? 14 28 |
18. 35 | 1 5 ? 35 |

Find the missing values to give all the factor pairs of 32.

19. 1 × ☐ = 32
20. 2 × ☐ = 32
21. 4 × ☐ = 32

Find the factors of the following numbers.

22. 15
23. 12
24. 21
25. 14
26. 16
27. 20

Look at the numbers in the box below:

| 4   7   10   14 |
| 18   20   36 |

Find the numbers in the box that are common factors of:

28. 60 and 40
29. 72 and 36
30. 28 and 42

Find the next prime number after:

31. 6
32. 14
33. 21
34. 26
35. 29
36. 35

Find all the prime numbers between each pair of numbers below:

37. 1 and 6
38. 10 and 15
39. 45 and 50
40. 60 and 65
41. 65 and 70
42. 70 and 75

Are the following true or false?

43. 45 is a prime number.
44. There are 3 prime numbers between 10 and 20.
45. 20 is a composite number.
46. 5 is a prime number.
47. 19 is a composite number.

Find the prime factors of these numbers by copying and filling in the factor trees.

48.
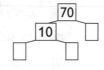

49.
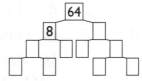

Some of those questions were pretty tough but you've made it to the end — good job!

Multiplying by 10, 100 and 1000

You can multiply by 10, 100 and even 1000 in your head by thinking about place value.

Example

Work out the answer to 3.4 × 1000.

1000 has <u>3 zeros</u>, so you need to move each digit 3 places to the left.

If there are only zeros after the decimal point, you don't need to write them.

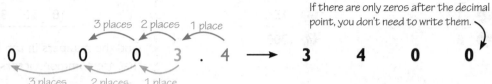

| Thousands | Hundreds | Tens | Ones | Tenths | | Thousands | Hundreds | Tens | Ones |

0   0   0   3 . 4 ⟶ 3   4   0   0

Set A

Work out:

1. 4.1 × 10
2. 30.7 × 10
3. 100 × 10
4. 20 × 100
5. 60.4 × 100
6. 40.6 × 1000
7. 500 × 1000

What is:

8. seventeen times ten?
9. fifty times ten?
10. three times one hundred?
11. seven hundred times one hundred?
12. four times one thousand?
13. eighty times one thousand?

14. Copy and complete the table. The first row has been done.

Start Number	× 100	× 1000
2.3	230	2300
9		
5.71		
40.68		

Set B

Work out:

1. 9 × 10
2. 40.83 × 10
3. 70.26 × 100
4. 120 × 100
5. 3.72 × 1000
6. 63 × 1000

Find the missing numbers:

7. 8.23 × ☐ = 82.3
8. 5 × ☐ = 5000
9. 92 × ☐ = 9200
10. 8.047 × ☐ = 804.7
11. 370 × ☐ = 3700
12. 45.092 × ☐ = 45 092

Look at this box of numbers.

601 520	620.3	6420
6203	64.2	6015.2

Which number is:

13. 10 times bigger than 6.42?
14. 100 times bigger than 62.03?
15. 1000 times bigger than 601.52?

Set C

Find the missing numbers:

1. ☐ × 10 = 39.24
2. 182 × ☐ = 1820
3. 7.628 × ☐ = 762.8
4. 736 × ☐ = 736 000
5. ☐ × 1000 = 4800
6. ☐ × 1000 = 9023
7. ☐ × 100 = 90.7

How many times bigger is:

8. 73.7 than 0.737?
9. 8290 than 8.29?
10. 75 300 than 753?
11. 4180 than 418?
12. 12 000 than 120?
13. 530 000 than 530?
14. 4278 than 4.278?

Are the following true or false?

15. 65.81 × 10 is bigger than 6.581 × 1000.
16. 58.28 × 100 is smaller than 5828 × 10.
17. 907 × 10 is bigger than 9.07 × 100.
18. 4.563 × 1000 = 45 630.

I can multiply whole numbers and decimals by 10, 100 and 1000.

Dividing by 10, 100 and 1000

Dividing by 10, 100 and 1000 may look scary but it's not — just move digits to the right.

Example

Work out the answer to 230 ÷ 1000.

1000 has <u>3 zeros</u>, so you need to move each digit 3 places to the right.

Set A

Work out:

1. 2000 ÷ 10
2. 30 ÷ 100
3. 9000 ÷ 1000
4. 80 ÷ 1000
5. 40.5 ÷ 10
6. 200.6 ÷ 100
7. 500.7 ÷ 100

What is:

8. seven hundred divided by ten?
9. five thousand divided by one hundred?
10. thirty divided by one hundred?
11. eight hundred divided by one thousand?
12. six divided by ten?
13. fifty divided by one thousand?

Find the missing numbers:

14. 500 ÷ ☐ = 5
15. 402 ÷ 10 = ☐
16. 6030 ÷ ☐ = 6.030
17. 21 000 ÷ 100 = ☐
18. 800.3 ÷ ☐ = 80.03
19. 18 000 ÷ 1000 = ☐
20. 50.9 ÷ ☐ = 0.509

Set B

Work out:

1. 4710.3 ÷ 10
2. 230 ÷ 10
3. 130.4 ÷ 100
4. 52 ÷ 100
5. 2300 ÷ 1000
6. 180.9 ÷ 1000
7. 91.3 ÷ 100

Find the missing numbers:

8. 1400 ÷ ☐ = 140
9. 750.6 ÷ ☐ = 7.506
10. 8400.5 ÷ ☐ = 84.005
11. 86 ÷ ☐ = 0.086
12. 64.3 ÷ ☐ = 6.43
13. 530 ÷ ☐ = 0.53
14. 980 ÷ ☐ = 9.8

Look at this box of numbers:

5.48	548	5.21
0.521	0.502	5.02

Which number is:

15. ten times smaller than 54.8?
16. one hundred times smaller than 52.1?
17. one thousand times smaller than 502?

Set C

Find the missing numbers:

1. 4530 ÷ ☐ = 453
2. ☐ ÷ 100 = 0.93
3. ☐ ÷ 1000 = 0.182
4. 2290 ÷ ☐ = 2.29
5. ☐ ÷ 10 = 3.62
6. 5870.5 ÷ ☐ = 58.705
7. 321 ÷ ☐ = 3.21

Are the following true or false?

8. 654 ÷ 10 is equal to 6540 ÷ 100.
9. 7830 ÷ 1000 is less than 78 ÷ 100.
10. 4500 ÷ 1000 is bigger than 45 ÷ 10.
11. 7.83 ÷ 10 = 0.783

How many times smaller is:

12. 3.32 than 332?
13. 65.82 than 658.2?
14. 9.504 than 9504
15. 0.044 than 44?
16. 2.4 than 24?
17. 8.73 than 873?
18. 89 than 8900?

I can divide whole numbers and decimals by 10, 100 and 1000.

Mental Multiplication — 1

If you know your times tables you can use them to help you work out harder multiplication questions.

Examples

Work out 60 × 20.

$$\underline{6}0 \times \underline{2}0 = 1200 \longleftarrow$$ Break the number down to something easier, then add the zeros at the end.

$$(\underline{6} \times \underline{2} = \underline{12})$$

Work out 14 × 6.

$$14 = 7 \times 2$$

So $\underline{14} \times 6 = \underline{7 \times 2} \times 6$
$$= 7 \times 12 = \mathbf{84}$$

Set A

Answer the following:

1. 4 × 30
2. 3 × 50
3. 40 × 6
4. 7 × 900
5. 5 × 700
6. 600 × 2

Work out:

7. 12 × 15, starting with 12 × 5.
8. 6 × 120, starting with 6 × 12.
9. 5 × 24, starting with 5 × 4.
10. 3 × 36, starting with 3 × 4.
11. 8 × 45, starting with 8 × 9.
12. 7 × 22, starting with 7 × 11.

Work out the missing number.

13. 6000 × ☐ = 42 000
14. 9 × ☐ = 180 000
15. 2 × ☐ = 8000
16. 7000 × ☐ = 21 000
17. 4 × ☐ = 320 000
18. 5 × ☐ = 1500

Set B

Answer the following:

1. 50 × 200
2. 400 × 30
3. 600 × 40
4. 7000 × 20
5. 300 × 900
6. 1100 × 70

Work out the missing number.

7. 20 × ☐ = 24 000
8. 500 × ☐ = 250 000
9. 400 × ☐ = 16 000
10. 1100 × ☐ = 66 000
11. 60 × ☐ = 48 000
12. 3000 × ☐ = 360 000

13. An apple tree is 320 cm tall. A pear tree is three times as tall as the apple tree. How tall is the pear tree?

14. Sachin uses 5 scoops of ice cream to make one milkshake. How many scoops would he need to make 80 milkshakes?

Set C

Answer the following:

1. 1100 × 30
2. 80 × 900
3. 120 × 500
4. 600 × 600
5. 90 × 5000
6. 1000 × 400

Jayden is filling bags of sweets to sell in his shop. How many sweets will he need to fill:

7. 700 bags with 30 sweets?
8. 300 bags with 25 sweets?
9. 500 bags with 40 sweets?
10. 450 bags with 20 sweets?
11. 180 bags with 30 sweets?

12. Poppy runs 2200 m. Stanley runs four times as far as Poppy. How far does Stanley run?

13. Kian wants to work out 48 × 40. Break the calculation down into easier calculations and work out the answer.

I can multiply using times tables facts.

Mental Multiplication — 2

If you've got some tricky numbers to multiply, try breaking up the question into simpler multiplications. It'll be much easier than trying to do the whole calculation all at once.

Examples

Calculate 58 × 4.

58 = 60 − 2

60 × 4 = 240

2 × 4 = 8

So 58 × 4 = 240 − 8 = **232**

You can make calculations like these easier by using a number that is close to the original number.

Calculate 72 × 3.

72 = 70 + 2

70 × 3 = 210

2 × 3 = 6

So 72 × 3 = 210 + 6 = **216**

Set A

Find the missing values:

1. 39 × 8
40 × ☐ = 320, and
1 × 8 = ☐,
so 39 × 8 = 320 − 8 = ☐

2. 21 × 5
20 × ☐ = 100, and
1 × 5 = ☐,
so 21 × 5 = 100 + 5 = ☐

Find the missing values:

3. 78 × 5
80 × ☐ = 400, and
2 × 5 = ☐,
so 78 × 5 = 400 − 10 = ☐

4. 52 × 6
50 × ☐ = 300, and
2 × 6 = ☐,
so 52 × 6 = 300 + 12 = ☐

Calculate the following:

5. 32 × 3
6. 29 × 4
7. 48 × 2
8. 51 × 3
9. 63 × 4
10. 101 × 5

Set B

Find the missing values:

1. 47 × 6
50 × ☐ = 300, and
☐ × 6 = ☐,
so 47 × 6 = 300 − ☐ = ☐

2. 52 × 7
50 × ☐ = 350, and
☐ × 7 = ☐,
so 52 × 7 = 350 + ☐ = ☐

Calculate the following:

3. 87 × 5
4. 59 × 6
5. 43 × 7
6. 78 × 6
7. 92 × 3
8. 61 × 4

Comics in a shop cost 98p each.

9. Jared wants to buy 6 comics. How much will it cost him?

10. 12 comics have been damaged and reduced to 62p. How much would it cost if Jared bought all of them?

Set C

Calculate the following:

1. 67 × 8
2. 49 × 4
3. 83 × 9
4. 58 × 7
5. 96 × 6
6. 75 × 9

Calculate the following:

7. 76 × 5
8. 84 × 7
9. 902 × 6
10. 590 × 8
11. 63 × 90
12. 28 × 70

A shop sells skipping ropes that are 132 cm long.

13. The shop also sells giant skipping ropes that are 3 times longer than the normal ones. How long are the giant ropes?

14. Hallie buys 6 normal ropes. How long are they in total?

I can multiply using partitioning.

Mental Division — 1

You can work out divisions of big numbers in your head too, you just need to remember those handy times tables.

Example

Work out 288 ÷ 24.

288 ÷ 24
288 ÷ 2 = 144 ← Try breaking the numbers down into simpler calculations
144 ÷ 12 = **12**   so that you can still work them out in your head.

Set A

Find the missing values:

(1) 84 ÷ 14
84 ÷ ☐ = 12
12 ÷ 2 = ☐

(2) 1200 ÷ 20
1200 ÷ ☐ = 600
600 ÷ 10 = ☐

(3) 72 ÷ 18
72 ÷ ☐ = 12
12 ÷ 3 = ☐

Find the missing values:

(4) 3000 ÷ 30
3000 ÷ ☐ = 1000
1000 ÷ 10 = ☐

(5) 80 ÷ 16
80 ÷ ☐ = 10
10 ÷ 2 = ☐

(6) 96 ÷ 24
96 ÷ ☐ = 8
8 ÷ 2 = ☐

Work out the missing number.

(7) 1500 ÷ ☐ = 500

(8) 2800 ÷ ☐ = 700

(9) 3600 ÷ ☐ = 120

(10) 1600 ÷ ☐ = 40

Calculate the following:

(11) 56 ÷ 14

(12) 132 ÷ 22

Set B

Find the missing values:

(1) 54 ÷ 18
54 ÷ 6 = ☐
☐ ÷ 3 = ☐

(2) 450 ÷ 90
450 ÷ 10 = ☐
☐ ÷ 9 = ☐

(3) 72 ÷ 24
72 ÷ 6 = ☐
☐ ÷ 4 = ☐

Find the missing values:

(4) 70 ÷ 14
70 ÷ 7 = ☐
☐ ÷ 2 = ☐

(5) 60 000 ÷ 120
60 000 ÷ 10 = ☐
☐ ÷ 12 = ☐

(6) 128 ÷ 16
128 ÷ 2 = ☐
☐ ÷ 8 = ☐

Calculate the following:

(7) 90 ÷ 18

(8) 1320 ÷ 120

(9) 96 ÷ 16

(10) Harry has 180 flowers. He wants to divide them into 12 equal bunches. How many flowers should he put in each bunch?

Set C

Calculate the following:

(1) 144 ÷ 24

(2) 88 000 ÷ 110

(3) 98 ÷ 14

(4) 110 ÷ 22

(5) 192 ÷ 16

(6) 162 ÷ 18

(7) 64 000 ÷ 800

Calculate the following:

(8) 264 ÷ 24

(9) 5600 ÷ 70

(10) 154 ÷ 14

(11) Posy has 216 lollipops. She wants to share them out between 18 people. How many lollipops will each person have?

A car washing company can wash 22 cars an hour. How long would it take them to wash:

(12) 132 cars?

(13) 242 cars?

(14) When they clean the inside of the car too, the company can wash 16 cars an hour. How long would it take them to wash 192 cars in this way?

I can divide using times table facts.

Mental Division — 2

You can work out division calculations in your head by splitting the question up into easier calculations.

Example

Work out the answer to 189 ÷ 9.

189 = 180 + 9 ← First, split the number up so that it is easier.

180 ÷ 9 = 20

(18 ÷ 9 = 2)

9 ÷ 9 = 1

20 + 1 = **21** ← Then, add the answers to both of your calculations together.

Set A

Find the missing values:

1. 275 ÷ 5
   250 ÷ ☐ = 50, and
   25 ÷ ☐ = 5,
   so 275 ÷ 5 = 50 + 5 = ☐

2. 216 ÷ 4
   200 ÷ ☐ = 50, and
   16 ÷ ☐ = 4,
   so 216 ÷ 4 = 50 + 4 = ☐

Find the missing values:

3. 189 ÷ 3
   180 ÷ ☐ = 60, and
   9 ÷ ☐ = 3,
   so 189 ÷ 3 = 60 + 3 = ☐

4. 808 ÷ 4
   800 ÷ ☐ = 200, and
   8 ÷ ☐ = 2,
   so 808 ÷ 4 = 200 + 2 = ☐

Calculate the following:

5. 126 ÷ 3
6. 176 ÷ 8
7. 312 ÷ 6
8. 154 ÷ 7
9. 365 ÷ 5
10. 412 ÷ 4

Set B

Find the missing values:

1. 340 ÷ 4
   320 ÷ ☐ = 80, and
   ☐ ÷ 4 = ☐,
   So 340 ÷ 4 = 80 + ☐ = ☐

2. 297 ÷ 9
   270 ÷ ☐ = 30, and
   ☐ ÷ 9 = ☐,
   so 297 ÷ 9 = 30 + ☐ = ☐

Calculate the following:

3. 372 ÷ 4
4. 294 ÷ 7
5. 584 ÷ 8
6. 861 ÷ 7
7. 1331 ÷ 11
8. 515 ÷ 5

A paint shop has 520 tins of paint. They have the same amount of 8 different colours.

9. How many tins of each colour does the shop have?

10. The shop sells one fifth of their paint in one day. How many tins of paint do they sell?

Set C

Find the missing values:

1. 780 ÷ 12
   720 ÷ ☐ = ☐, and
   ☐ ÷ 12 = ☐,
   so 780 ÷ 12 = ☐ + ☐ = ☐

2. 855 ÷ 9
   810 ÷ ☐ = ☐, and
   ☐ ÷ 9 = ☐,
   so 855 ÷ 9 = ☐ + ☐ = ☐

Calculate the following:

3. 456 ÷ 4
4. 774 ÷ 6
5. 485 ÷ 5
6. 912 ÷ 8
7. 511 ÷ 7
8. 3627 ÷ 3

Bobby has 2436 apples and 3 lorries.

9. How many apples can he put in each lorry so that they each have the same number of apples?

10. One quarter of the apples are red. How many of the apples are red?

I can divide using partitioning.

Multiplication and Division — Review 2

Calculate the following:

(1) 21.84 × 10

(2) 715 × 10

(3) 9.56 × 100

(4) 638 × 100

(5) 8.28 × 1000

(6) 70.5 × 1000

Find the missing numbers:

(7) 6.32 × ☐ = 63.2

(8) 300.9 × ☐ = 30 090

(9) 800.6 × ☐ = 800 600

How many times bigger is:

(10) 52 850 than 52.85?

(11) 63 272 than 632.72?

(12) 70 050 than 700.5?

Calculate the following:

(13) 3100.6 ÷ 10

(14) 36 ÷ 10

(15) 2400.6 ÷ 100

(16) 40 ÷ 100

(17) 8400 ÷ 1000

(18) 54 ÷ 1000

Find the missing numbers:

(19) 2190.4 ÷ ☐ = 219.04

(20) 285.7 ÷ ☐ = 2.857

(21) 60.8 ÷ ☐ = 0.608

How many times smaller is:

(22) 20.08 than 200.8?

(23) 0.49 than 490?

(24) 287 than 2870?

Calculate the following:

(25) 6 × 20

(26) 50 × 70

(27) 40 × 50

(28) 40 × 800

(29) 300 × 500

(30) 200 × 700

Find the missing numbers:

(31) 43 × 6
40 × ☐ = 240 and 3 × ☐ = 18,
so 43 × 6 = 240 + 18 = ☐

(32) 68 × 4
70 × ☐ = 280 and 2 × 4 = ☐,
so 68 × 4 = 280 − ☐ = ☐

(33) 33 × 9
30 × 9 = ☐ and 3 × 9 = ☐,
so 33 × 9 = ☐ + ☐ = ☐

Calculate the following:

(34) 72 × 3

(35) 59 × 4

(36) 37 × 6

(37) 62 × 5

(38) 88 × 7

(39) 44 × 9

Find the missing values:

(40) 64 ÷ 16
64 ÷ 8 = ☐
☐ ÷ 2 = ☐

(41) 90 ÷ 15
90 ÷ 3 = ☐
☐ ÷ 5 = ☐

Calculate the following:

(42) 440 ÷ 11

(43) 180 ÷ 60

(44) 4000 ÷ 800

(45) 3600 ÷ 30

(46) 10 800 ÷ 120

(47) 12 000 ÷ 400

Find the missing numbers:

(48) 172 ÷ 4
160 ÷ ☐ = 40 and 12 ÷ 4 = ☐,
so 172 ÷ 4 = 40 + 3 = ☐

(49) 364 ÷ 4
320 ÷ ☐ = 80 and 44 ÷ 4 = ☐,
so 364 ÷ 4 = 80 + ☐ = ☐

(50) 378 ÷ 7
350 ÷ 7 = ☐ and 28 ÷ 7 = ☐,
so 378 ÷ 7 = ☐ + ☐ = ☐

Calculate the following:

(51) 225 ÷ 3

(52) 280 ÷ 5

(53) 456 ÷ 6

(54) 296 ÷ 8

(55) 374 ÷ 11

(56) 192 ÷ 12

Finish all of these questions to multiply those mental maths skills!

Grid Method Multiplication

If you need to multiply two numbers together that are too big to do in your head then you can use the grid method.

Example

Work out the answer to 64 × 34.

First, split the numbers into tens and ones.

×	30	4
60	1800	240
4	120	16
	1920	256
	2176	

← Multiply to fill in the grid and add up the columns.

← Then, add the answers to both columns together.

Set A

Copy and complete the grid to work out:

1 84 × 9

×	9
80	
4	

2 96 × 8

×	8
90	
6	

3 267 × 7

×	7
200	
60	
7	

4 473 × 6

×	6
400	
70	
3	

5 58 × 23

×	20	3
50		
8		

Use the grid method to work out:

6 68 × 7   **7** 94 × 6   **8** 325 × 5   **9** 562 × 4   **10** 36 × 24

Set B

Copy and complete the grid to work out:

1 56 × 6

×	6
50	
6	

2 781 × 5

×	5
700	
80	
1	

3 342 × 4

×	4
300	
40	
2	

4 36 × 72

×	70	2
30		
6		

5 52 × 35

×	30	5
50		
2		

Use the grid method to work out:

6 83 × 84   **7** 327 × 5   **8** 356 × 6   **9** 82 × 34   **10** 163 × 42

Set C

Copy and complete the grid to work out:

1 437 × 4

×		

2 723 × 3

×		

3 67 × 23

×		

4 81 × 68

×		

5 386 × 79

×		

Use the grid method to work out:

6 283 × 3   **7** 472 × 4   **8** 82 × 63   **9** 421 × 65   **10** 845 × 37

I can multiply using the grid method.

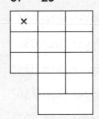 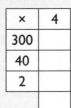 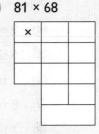

Short multiplication is a written method you can use to multiply two numbers together.

Examples

Work out 836 × 4.

Line up the digits in columns according to their place value.

```
    8 3 6
  ×     4
  3 3 4 4
    1 2
```

Work out 224 × 3.

```
    2 2 4
  ×     3
    6 7 2
      1
```

Set A

Work out:

1)
```
    3 2 1
  ×     3
```

2)
```
    4 1 5
  ×     4
```

3)
```
    1 4 3
  ×     5
```

Work out:

4)
```
    2 5 3
  ×     5
```

5)
```
    5 0 2
  ×     4
```

6)
```
    3 1 4
  ×     2
```

Use short multiplication to work out:

7) 243 × 6

8) 423 × 5

9) 140 × 3

10) four lots of two hundred and fourteen

11) two lots of five hundred and twenty four

Set B

Work out:

1)
```
    4 5 3
  ×     4
```

2)
```
    5 3 6
  ×     5
```

3)
```
    6 0 4
  ×     3
```

Work out:

4)
```
    7 4 6
  ×     7
```

5)
```
    5 3 7
  ×     6
```

6)
```
    4 7 5
  ×     5
```

What number is:

7) 6 times bigger than 376?

8) 5 times bigger than 783?

9) 7 times bigger than 582?

10) 3 times bigger than 474?

11) 4 times bigger than 673?

12) 6 times bigger than 524?

Set C

Work out:

1)
```
    8 2 4
  ×     6
```

2)
```
    7 9 5
  ×     7
```

3)
```
    9 6 7
  ×     8
```

What number is:

4) 9 times bigger than 694?

5) 6 times bigger than 856?

6) 5 times bigger than 934?

7) 8 times bigger than 758?

8) 7 times bigger than 592?

9) 5 times bigger than 684?

Maria's cafe sells 927 cups of tea every day. How many does she sell:

10) over 4 days?

11) over 9 days?

Kelly plays 785 songs a week on her radio show. How many does she play:

12) in 6 weeks?

13) in 8 weeks?

I can use short multiplication.

Short Multiplication — 2

You can use the same method for multiplying a 4-digit number — just give it a go.

Example

Use a formal written method to work out 3645 × 4.

Line up the digits in columns according to their place value.

$$\begin{array}{r} 3\,6\,4\,5 \\ \times \qquad 4 \\ \hline \mathbf{1\,4\,5\,8\,0} \\ \scriptstyle 2\ \ 1\ \ 2 \end{array}$$

Set A

Work out:

1. $\begin{array}{r} 2\,5\,3\,1 \\ \times \qquad 3 \\ \hline \end{array}$

2. $\begin{array}{r} 3\,6\,2\,3 \\ \times \qquad 4 \\ \hline \end{array}$

3. $\begin{array}{r} 4\,0\,3\,1 \\ \times \qquad 2 \\ \hline \end{array}$

Work out:

4. $\begin{array}{r} 5\,3\,2\,4 \\ \times \qquad 5 \\ \hline \end{array}$

5. $\begin{array}{r} 2\,7\,3\,5 \\ \times \qquad 3 \\ \hline \end{array}$

6. $\begin{array}{r} 3\,5\,3\,0 \\ \times \qquad 4 \\ \hline \end{array}$

Use short multiplication to work out:

7. 1832 × 3
8. 3425 × 2
9. 5261 × 4
10. 2414 multiplied by 5
11. 4523 multiplied by 2
12. 4251 multiplied by 3

Set B

Work out:

1. $\begin{array}{r} 5\,6\,8\,2 \\ \times \qquad 4 \\ \hline \end{array}$

2. $\begin{array}{r} 3\,6\,3\,7 \\ \times \qquad 5 \\ \hline \end{array}$

3. $\begin{array}{r} 4\,7\,3\,5 \\ \times \qquad 6 \\ \hline \end{array}$

Work out:

4. $\begin{array}{r} 7\,6\,3\,5 \\ \times \qquad 7 \\ \hline \end{array}$

5. $\begin{array}{r} 5\,3\,7\,2 \\ \times \qquad 6 \\ \hline \end{array}$

6. $\begin{array}{r} 7\,4\,6\,7 \\ \times \qquad 5 \\ \hline \end{array}$

What number is:

7. 4 times bigger than 6372?
8. 5 times bigger than 7365?
9. 6 times bigger than 6356?
10. 7 times bigger than 2854?
11. 5 times bigger than 3548?
12. 7 times bigger than 5684?

Set C

Work out:

1. $\begin{array}{r} 7\,3\,8\,6 \\ \times \qquad 6 \\ \hline \end{array}$

2. $\begin{array}{r} 7\,4\,8\,2 \\ \times \qquad 8 \\ \hline \end{array}$

3. $\begin{array}{r} 9\,4\,7\,6 \\ \times \qquad 7 \\ \hline \end{array}$

What number is:

4. 9 times bigger than 8376?
5. 8 times bigger than 6749?
6. 6 times bigger than 7847?
7. 8 times bigger than 5847?
8. 7 times bigger than 8473?
9. 6 times bigger than 9652?

Dylan counts 7839 daisies and 3457 dandelions in a field.

10. Raniya counts six times as many daisies in a different field. How many daisies does she count?

11. Raniya counts 8 times as many dandelions as Dylan. How many dandelions does she count?

I am confident using short multiplication.

Long Multiplication — 1

Long multiplication uses partitioning to make those tricky calculations a bit easier.

Example

Using long multiplication, work out 328 × 32.

$$
\begin{array}{r}
3\ 2\ 8 \\
\times \quad 3\ 2 \\
\hline
6\ 5\ 6 \\
{\scriptstyle 1} \\
9\ 8\ 4\ 0 \\
{\scriptstyle 2} \\
\hline
\mathbf{1\ 0\ 4\ 9\ 6} \\
{\scriptstyle 1}
\end{array}
$$

First, find 328 × 2 and put the answer here. →

Then, find 328 × 30 and put the answer here. →

Now, add your two answers together. →

Set A

Work out:

1.
   2 0 1
×   2 0

2.
   4 2 3
×   3 4

3.
   3 5 2
×   4 1

Work out:

4.
   5 1 3
×   2 2

5.
   3 1 4
×   4 3

6.
   2 2 5
×   4 0

Use long multiplication to work out:

7. 534 × 34
8. 311 × 46
9. 253 × 52
10. 412 multiplied by 21
11. 405 multiplied by 32
12. 234 multiplied by 45

Set B

Work out:

1.
   3 7 5
×   2 6

2.
   4 5 2
×   3 5

3.
   5 6 2
×   6 1

Work out:

4.
   6 1 4
×   5 2

5.
   7 3 4
×   2 4

6.
   5 2 4
×   4 1

What number is:

7. 62 times bigger than 471?
8. 53 times bigger than 734?
9. 48 times bigger than 673?
10. 71 times bigger than 562?
11. 32 times bigger than 727?
12. 46 times bigger than 639?

Set C

Work out:

1.
   7 3 5
×   6 3

2.
   8 2 7
×   5 4

3.
   9 7 8
×   7 4

Work out:

4. 745 × 94
5. 857 × 64
6. 925 × 46
7. 639 × 21
8. 485 × 93
9. 759 × 45

What number is:

10. 65 times bigger than 673?
11. 58 times bigger than 793?
12. 47 times bigger than 836?
13. 62 times bigger than 907?
14. 73 times bigger than 538?
15. 83 times bigger than 694?

I can use long multiplication.

Long Multiplication — 2

Now you've had some practice, let's try the same method with some 4-digit numbers.

Example

Use long multiplication to work out the answer to 5321 × 52.

```
            5 3 2 1
      ×         5 2
```

First, find 5321 × 2 and put the answer here. ⟶ `1 0 6 4 2`

Then, find 5321 × 50 and put the answer here. ⟶ `2 6 6 0 5 0`
                                                  `1 1`
Now, add your two answers together. ⟶ **`2 7 6 6 9 2`**

Set A

Work out:

1.   2 3 1 5
    ×   3 2

2.   1 5 2 1
    ×   2 4

3.   3 4 0 2
    ×   3 1

Work out:

4.   4 0 2 1
    ×   2 5

5.   5 2 0 3
    ×   4 1

6.   2 4 4 2
    ×   5 1

Use long multiplication to work out:

7. 1325 × 32

8. 2503 × 41

9. 3423 × 24

10. 4214 multiplied by 53

11. 5241 multiplied by 21

12. 3521 multiplied by 31

Set B

Work out:

1.   4 2 3 4
    ×   4 2

2.   5 3 2 6
    ×   3 3

3.   6 4 5 2
    ×   5 4

Work out:

4.   3 7 2 5
    ×   4 1

5.   5 6 2 8
    ×   5 4

6.   4 7 3 2
    ×   6 4

What number is:

7. 63 times bigger than 3645?

8. 32 times bigger than 4573?

9. 42 times bigger than 5724?

10. 55 times bigger than 6023?

11. 36 times bigger than 7302?

12. 67 times bigger than 6354?

Set C

Work out:

1.   6 5 8 3
    ×   6 2

2.   7 2 0 7
    ×   5 3

3.   8 0 2 1
    ×   4 5

Work out:

4. 9376 × 74

5. 5987 × 83

6. 4785 × 95

7. 6348 × 76

8. 7385 × 92

9. 8264 × 58

What number is:

10. 78 times bigger than 5826?

11. 54 times bigger than 6932?

12. 82 times bigger than 9406?

13. 91 times bigger than 8205?

14. 67 times bigger than 7334?

15. 98 times bigger than 4598?

I am confident using long multiplication.

Copy and complete the grids to work out:

1 86 × 4

×	4
80	
6	

2 58 × 7

×	7
50	
8	

3 347 × 8

×	8
300	
40	
7	

4 623 × 6

×	6
600	
20	
3	

5 54 × 82

×	80	2
50		
4		

6 93 × 37

×	30	7
90		
3		

Use the grid method to work out the answers to these questions:

7 68 × 4

8 75 × 8

9 361 × 5

10 729 × 3

11 67 × 44

12 58 × 42

Use short multiplication to work out the answers to these questions:

13
```
  4 1 3
×     5
```

14
```
  3 5 1
×     4
```

15
```
  7 2 8
×     6
```

16
```
  5 9 4
×     8
```

What number is:

17 7 times bigger than 532?

18 4 times bigger than 482?

19 5 times bigger than 624?

20 6 times bigger than 708?

Use short multiplication to work out the answers to these questions:

21
```
  2 4 3 5
×       3
```

22
```
  6 2 4 8
×       5
```

23
```
  7 9 3 1
×       6
```

24
```
  8 4 6 2
×       7
```

What number is:

25 4 times bigger than 5482?

26 5 times bigger than 3861?

27 6 times bigger than 8263?

28 3 times bigger than 3926?

Use long multiplication to work out the answers to these questions:

29
```
  4 7 2
×   5 1
```

30
```
  6 3 9
×   3 7
```

31
```
  5 8 2
×   2 6
```

32
```
  7 0 6
×   7 4
```

What number is:

33 21 times bigger than 749?

34 82 times bigger than 638?

35 58 times bigger than 385?

36 64 times bigger than 729?

Use long multiplication to work out the answers to these questions:

37
```
  6 5 2 8
×     4 3
```

38
```
  4 9 5 1
×     6 3
```

39
```
  8 2 9 4
×     5 8
```

40
```
  7 2 0 5
×     7 5
```

What number is:

41 74 times bigger than 8392?

42 45 times bigger than 6721?

43 67 times bigger than 6436?

44 53 times bigger than 7328?

Great work on making it through this page!

Short Division — 1

Short division can help you divide by 1-digit numbers. All you have to do is split the number you want to divide into thousands, hundreds, tens and ones and then divide each number individually. Take a look at how it's done ...

Example

What is 4164 ÷ 4?

$$\begin{array}{r} 1\ 0\ 4\ 1 \\ 4\overline{)4\ 1\ {}^16\ 4} \end{array}$$

So 4164 ÷ 4 = **1041**.

1 ten is exchanged for 10 ones.

Set A

Work out:

1 6 | 8 4 6

2 5 | 6 9 0

3 8 | 4 9 6

4 7 | 5 6 7

Work out:

5 3 | 6 9 0 3

6 5 | 5 6 4 5

7 4 | 8 2 4 8

8 6 | 6 3 1 2

Use short division to work out:

9 834 ÷ 6

10 558 ÷ 9

11 8632 ÷ 2

12 9363 ÷ 3

13 4824 ÷ 4

14 5245 ÷ 5

Set B

Work out:

1 3 | 7 2 6

2 4 | 6 2 4

3 5 | 8 0 2 5

4 6 | 7 2 3 6

Work out:

5 7 | 7 1 8 2

6 4 | 2 8 6 4

7 5 | 3 4 4 0

8 9 | 4 7 5 2

Use short division to work out:

9 3246 divided by 2

10 4398 divided by 3

11 3744 divided by 4

12 2150 divided by 5

13 1883 divided by 7

14 6144 divided by 8

Set C

Work out:

1 6 | 9 6 4 2

2 8 | 9 6 4 0

3 7 | 2 7 8 6

4 6 | 5 4 4 8

Work out:

5 1071 divided by 9

6 2835 divided by 5

7 3296 divided by 4

8 3465 divided by 7

9 3168 divided by 8

10 5886 divided by 6

Akilah is making bunches of flowers. She has 5310 flowers in total. How many bunches can she make if she:

11 puts 5 flowers in each bunch?

12 puts 3 flowers in each bunch?

13 puts 9 flowers in each bunch?

14 puts 6 flowers in each bunch?

I can use short division without remainders.

Short Division — 2

Not all numbers divide by each other exactly. When you have numbers left over they are called remainders.

Examples

What is 841 ÷ 7?

$$\begin{array}{r} \mathbf{1\ 2\ 0}\ \mathbf{r\ 1} \\ 7\,\overline{|8\ ^14\ 1} \end{array}$$

← Sometimes you will have numbers left over. They should be written like this next to the answer.

What is 2234 ÷ 4?

$$\begin{array}{r} \mathbf{5\ 5\ 8}\ \mathbf{r\ 2} \\ 4\,\overline{|2\ 2\ ^23\ ^34} \end{array}$$

Set A

Work out:

1. 3 | 6 9 7
2. 2 | 5 6 1
3. 4 | 8 5 9
4. 5 | 3 9 4

Work out:

5. 2 | 6 3 9
6. 3 | 7 4 5
7. 4 | 6 3 1
8. 5 | 4 7 8

Work out:

9. 457 ÷ 2
10. 121 ÷ 3
11. 587 ÷ 4
12. 323 ÷ 4
13. 6241 ÷ 3
14. 2962 ÷ 5

Set B

Work out:

1. 4 | 2 7 5
2. 5 | 8 9 3
3. 6 | 8 2 7
4. 7 | 5 4 4

Work out:

5. 2 | 7 4 3 7
6. 3 | 2 3 7 4
7. 4 | 3 4 7 4
8. 5 | 4 7 3 9

Work out:

9. 743 divided by 5
10. 385 divided by 6
11. 649 divided by 7
12. 8353 divided by 2
13. 4627 divided by 3
14. 8294 divided by 4

Set C

Work out:

1. 8 | 7 4 7
2. 9 | 6 3 5
3. 3 | 5 2 4 2
4. 4 | 3 7 7 0

Work out:

5. 5 | 8 3 4 6
6. 6 | 4 2 7 7
7. 7 | 1 3 6 2
8. 8 | 4 3 5 6

Mia collects 4931 leaves and divides them into piles. How many leaves are left over if she divides them into:

9. 2 piles?
10. 7 piles?
11. 5 piles?
12. 6 piles?
13. 9 piles?

I can use short division with remainders.

Interpreting Remainders

Once you've divided a number and you're left with a remainder, you have to decide what to do with the remainder in your answer. This will often depend on what you're dividing — you've just got to use your common sense.

Examples

What is 439 ÷ 4?

First, work out the answer ⟶ **1 0 9 r 3** and <u>find the remainder</u>.

4 |4 3³9

You can write remainders as <u>numbers</u>, <u>fractions</u> or <u>decimals</u>.
439 ÷ 4 =
109 r 3 = $109\frac{3}{4}$ = 109.75

Sometimes you might be asked to round your answer to a whole number.

A taxi can carry 5 people. There are 11 people.

How many taxis do you need for all of the people?

11 ÷ 5 = 2 r 1, so you would need **3 taxis** for everyone. ⟵ For this question, you need to round up.

How many taxis can be filled?

11 ÷ 5 = 2 r 1, so **2 taxis** can be filled. ⟵ For this question, you need to round down.

Set A

Write the remainders in your answers as fractions:

① 3 |3 6 5

② 2 |5 6 7

③ 4 |7 2 5 3

④ 3 |2 5 1 0

⑤ 583 ÷ 2

⑥ 247 ÷ 3

⑦ 533 ÷ 4

⑧ 4555 ÷ 2

⑨ 1271 ÷ 4

⑩ 3197 ÷ 3

Write the remainders in your answers as decimals:

⑪ 5 |6 5 2

⑫ 4 |5 7 1

⑬ 2 |8 3 5

⑭ 4 |5 2 1 0

⑮ 2 |6 4 3 1

⑯ 437 ÷ 4

⑰ 575 ÷ 2

⑱ 399 ÷ 2

⑲ 546 ÷ 4

⑳ 463 ÷ 4

㉑ 2841 ÷ 5

㉒ 5477 ÷ 2

㉓ 6343 ÷ 4

Work out the answers then decide whether you should write the remainder as a number, a decimal, or round to a whole number.

㉔ Padma has 351 monster cards. She shares them out equally to 4 friends. How many monster cards does each friend have and how many are left over?

㉕ Lewis has 187 carrots. He wants to split them equally into 3 sacks. How many should he put in each sack?

㉖ The school canteen has 454 roast potatoes. How many students can they give 3 potatoes to?

㉗ Li wants to share 1645 ml of lemonade out equally between 4 glasses. How much should she put in each glass?

㉘ A library has 3634 books. The library staff want to split them equally between 4 rooms. How many books will be in each room?

Set B

Write the remainders in your answers as fractions:

1. 6 | 8 4 3
2. 8 | 7 7 3
3. 5 | 4 3 6 3
4. 4 | 3 8 7 1
5. 3 | 2 5 9 1

6. 659 ÷ 7
7. 984 ÷ 9
8. 281 ÷ 6
9. 2564 ÷ 3
10. 5825 ÷ 4
11. 4704 ÷ 5
12. 5089 ÷ 2

Write the remainders in your answers as decimals:

13. 2 | 8 0 3
14. 5 | 9 7 3
15. 4 | 3 2 8 3
16. 4 | 2 9 8 6
17. 5 | 4 7 3 9

18. 765 ÷ 2
19. 683 ÷ 5
20. 5637 ÷ 4
21. 6283 ÷ 5
22. 4502 ÷ 5
23. 3285 ÷ 2
24. 2987 ÷ 4

Work out the answers then decide whether you should write the remainder as a number, a fraction, or round to a whole number.

25. April has 732 beads. She makes 8 necklaces with an equal number of beads. How many beads does each necklace have? How many are left over?

26. There are 206 children going on a school trip to a farm. There must be at least one adult for every 4 children. How many adults should go with the children?

27. Ilyas has 346 biscuits. He splits them equally between 5 friends. If he shares out all of the biscuits, how many biscuits does each of his friends get?

28. Danni wants to build 3 walls that have an equal number of bricks. She has 6724 bricks. How many bricks can she use for each wall?

29. Roger wants to split 3407 sheets of paper into 6 equal piles. How many sheets should he put in each pile?

Set C

Write the remainders in your answers as fractions:

1. 7 | 9 8 6
2. 9 | 8 5 4
3. 7 | 6 7 8 4
4. 6 | 8 4 3 9

5. 7468 ÷ 8
6. 9483 ÷ 5
7. 8497 ÷ 9
8. 6837 ÷ 7
9. 5487 ÷ 6
10. 8293 ÷ 5

Write the remainders in your answers as decimals:

11. 2 | 7 3 5
12. 5 | 9 4 2
13. 5 | 7 6 8 9
14. 4 | 8 3 2 7
15. 4 | 8 0 3 4

16. 754 ÷ 5
17. 873 ÷ 4
18. 4871 ÷ 4
19. 5639 ÷ 2
20. 6704 ÷ 5
21. 9075 ÷ 4
22. 7497 ÷ 2

Work out the answers then decide whether you should write the remainder as a number, a decimal, or round to a whole number.

23. It is 874 miles from Land's End to John o'Groats. Yawen sets off from Land's End and walks 9 miles a day. How many days will it take her to reach John o'Groats?

24. Elliot has 6387 screws. He needs 4 screws to put up 1 shelf. How many shelves can he put up?

25. Samir has a giant bag of 5438 jelly beans. He wants to share them out equally between 9 people. How many will they get each and how many will be left over?

26. 1094 kg of oats are transported. The oats are split equally between 5 lorries. How many kg of oats are in each lorry?

I can interpret remainders in different situations.

Multiplication and Division — Review 4

Use short division to work out:

1 3] 7 2 0

2 4] 6 8 8

3 5] 6 5 5

4 6] 3 7 2

5 7] 5 6 7

6 3] 6 5 4 6

7 4] 4 5 8 4

8 5] 5 6 8 5

9 6] 2 6 4 0

10 7] 1 3 5 1

Use short division to work out:

11 981 ÷ 3

12 485 ÷ 5

13 738 ÷ 6

14 994 ÷ 7

15 756 ÷ 9

16 6544 ÷ 2

17 7124 ÷ 4

18 3258 ÷ 6

19 3654 ÷ 7

20 5416 ÷ 8

Use short division to work out:

21 432 divided by 6

22 357 divided by 7

23 428 divided by 2

24 456 divided by 8

25 2770 divided by 5

26 5344 divided by 4

27 1368 divided by 9

28 8451 divided by 3

Use short division to work out the answers.
Write any remainders as a number.

29 2] 7 6 3

30 3] 4 5 4

31 7] 8 4 5

32 5] 1 3 5 6

33 6] 4 5 3 1

34 7] 1 0 9 4

Use short division to work out the answer.
Write any remainders as a number.

35 546 ÷ 4

36 782 ÷ 5

37 926 ÷ 6

38 235 ÷ 8

39 460 ÷ 9

40 2315 ÷ 2

41 7624 ÷ 3

42 3043 ÷ 4

43 5629 ÷ 8

44 2384 ÷ 9

Use short division to work out the answers.
Write any remainders as a fraction.

45 4] 5 4 9

46 6] 8 7 2

47 3] 2 5 4 2

48 5] 5 4 3 2

Use short division to work out the answer.
Write any remainders as a fraction.

49 365 ÷ 2

50 563 ÷ 5

51 642 ÷ 7

52 5402 ÷ 4

53 1093 ÷ 6

54 2461 ÷ 8

Use short division to work out the answers.
Write any remainders as a decimal.

55 4] 5 6 2

56 5] 3 0 4

57 5] 8 4 2 1

58 2] 2 0 4 1

Use short division to work out the answer.
Write any remainders as a decimal.

59 787 ÷ 2

60 583 ÷ 4

61 632 ÷ 5

62 1094 ÷ 4

63 2736 ÷ 5

64 3485 ÷ 2

Work out the answers then decide whether
you should write the remainder as a number,
a decimal, or round to a whole number.

65 Aseem has 325 g of sweets. He wants to
share them out equally between 3 people.
How many grams of sweets will they get each?
How many will be left over?

66 Fraser has 875 ml of water and 4 plants.
He wants to share the water equally
between the 4 plants. How much
water should he give to each plant?

67 School shirts are sold in packs of 5.
A factory has made 2364 shirts.
How many packs of 5 can they make?

You've made it to the end of the page — fantastic!

Square and Cube Numbers

When you multiply a number by itself you get a square number, and when you multiply a number by itself twice, you get a cubed number. There's lots of square and cube number practice on this page.

Examples

What is 2^2?

$2^2 = 2 \text{ squared} = 2 \times 2 = \textbf{4}$

$2 \times 2 = 4$

What is 2^3?

$2^3 = 2 \text{ cubed} = 2 \times 2 \times 2 = \textbf{8}$

$2 \times 2 \times 2 = 8$

Set A

Find the missing numbers:

1. $1^2 = 1 \times 1 = \square$
2. $5^2 = 5 \times 5 = \square$
3. $6^2 = 6 \times 6 = \square$
4. $2^3 = 2 \times 2 \times 2 = \square$
5. $3^3 = 3 \times 3 \times 3 = \square$
6. $4^3 = 4 \times 4 \times 4 = \square$

Look at the numbers in this box:

125	64	121
100	81	250
200	78	216

7. Find and list all the square numbers.

8. Find and list all the cube numbers.

Find the missing number in the sequences:

9. 100   81 $\square$ 49   36

10. 1   8 $\square$ 64   125

Are the following true or false?

11. 55 is a square number.

12. $6^3 = 18$.

Set B

Find the missing numbers:

1. $7^2 = \square \times \square = \square$
2. $9^2 = \square \times \square = \square$
3. $5^3 = \square \times \square \times \square = \square$

Choose the correct answer for four cubed:

4.   12   16   40   64   80

Work out:

5. $2^2 + 5^2$
6. $6^2 + 3^2$
7. $8^2 + 1^2$
8. $2^3 + 3^3$
9. $4^3 + 2^3$
10. $5^3 + 1^3$

Find all the square numbers between:

11. 0 and 5

12. 5 and 20

Find the missing square numbers:

13. $7^3 = 343 = \square \times 7$

14. $8^3 = 512 = \square \times 8$

Set C

Work out:

1. $5^2 + 7^2$
2. $6^2 + 4^2$
3. $9^2 - 8^2$
4. $4^3 - 2^3$
5. $5^3 + 9^2$
6. $7^2 - 3^3$

The prime factors that multiply to give 24 can be written as $2^3 \times 3$. In a similar way, write the prime factors that multiply to give:

7. 49

8. 44

9. 100

10. 63

Are the following true or false?

11. $3^2 + 4^2 = 5^2$

12. $3^3 = 10 - 1$

13. $4^3 = 2 \times 2 \times 4 \times 4$

14. $9^2 \div 3 = 3^3$

15. There are 3 cube numbers between 10 and 100.

I recognise and can use square and cube numbers.

Multiplication and Division Problems

This topic gives you a chance to have a go at working out some problems using multiplication and division.
Spend some time thinking about what the question is asking you to do before you give it a go.

Examples

Cassie has a necklace made of 24 beads. Gavin has a necklace
made out of 4 times as many beads as Cassie's necklace.
How many beads is Gavin's necklace made from?

$$12 \times 4 = 48. \quad 48 \times 2 = \mathbf{96}.$$

So Gavin's necklace is made of **96 beads**.

There are 328 children at a primary school.
They are being split into teams for sports day.

How many teams would there be if the children were split into teams of 8?

$$\begin{array}{r} 4\ 1 \\ 8\,\overline{)3\ \ 2\ \ 8} \end{array}$$ So there would be **41 teams**.

The teachers split the pupils into 4 teams.
How many pupils are there in each team?

$$\begin{array}{r} 8\ 2 \\ 4\,\overline{)3\ \ 2\ \ 8} \end{array}$$ So there would be **82 pupils in each team**.

Set A

A building has 90 floors with 20 windows
on each floor.

1. How many windows does the building
   have in total?

2. Six of the windows on every floor
   have blinds. How many windows have
   blinds in the whole building?

Sasha buys a pack of hair bobbles.
There are 5 blue bobbles, 7 yellow bobbles,
3 purple bobbles and 2 green bobbles
in a pack.

3. How many of each colour bobble
   would there be in 70 packs?

Frances has 300 fairy lights. 4 in every 50
lights are red and 3 in every 50 lights are
blue. How many of the 300 lights are:

4. red?

5. blue?

A bakery sells birthday cakes with either icing,
chocolate or butter-cream on the top.
They sell their cakes in 5 different flavours.

6. How many different cakes does the bakery offer?

7. The bakery receives an order for 436 cakes.
   The customer wants an equal number of
   cakes in 4 different flavours. How many
   of each flavour should the bakery make?

There are 747 people on a train.
The train has 9 carriages.

8. The same number of people are in each carriage.
   How many people are in each carriage?

9. Another train has four times as many passengers.
   How many passengers does it have?

10. Over 5 days, a ship travels 3765 km.
    It travels the same distance every day.
    How far does it travel each day?

Set B

Marina has 104 hens.
One month, each hen lays 18 eggs.

1. How many eggs did the hens lay in total?

2. Marina can fit 6 eggs in a box.
   If Marina has 1666 eggs, how many
   boxes can she fill with eggs?

Caleb buys 32 packs of crayons.
Each pack has 5 different colours
and contains 2 of each colour.

3. How many of each colour crayon
   does Caleb have in total?

4. How many crayons are there in total?

5. Caleb shares the crayons out equally
   into 8 pots at school. How many
   crayons are in each pot?

6. A sweet shop has 729 sweets.
   They have 9 different types of sweet and
   an equal number of each type of sweet.
   How many of each sweet do they have?

Minnie the monkey eats 1825 bananas a year.

7. Marcel eats 4 times as many bananas a year
   as Minnie. How many does he eat a year?

8. Harvey the monkey eats 5 times less
   bananas a year than Minnie.
   How many does he eat?

Erin finds 60 spiders in her garden.
Each spider has 8 legs.

9. How many legs do the
   spiders have in total?

10. Erin finds 7 of every 10 spiders on the
    lawn. How many of the 60 spiders
    did she find on the lawn?

Each cake at a fair has been cut into 12 pieces.
There are 612 pieces in total.

11. How many cakes are there?

12. There is enough cake for everyone at the
    fair to have 4 pieces with no cake left over.
    How many people are at the fair?

Set C

Amita wants to decorate some
cupcakes with chocolate buttons.
She has 8 bags of chocolate buttons,
and there are 29 buttons in each bag.

1. How many chocolate buttons
   does Amita have in total?

2. If Amita decorates 18 cupcakes with
   8 chocolate buttons each, how
   many buttons will she have left?

3. If Amita puts 6 buttons on each
   cupcake, how many cupcakes
   can she decorate before she
   runs out of buttons?

A normal bus can carry 80 people.
A double decker bus can carry 134 people.

4. How many people can 4 normal buses
   and 8 double deckers carry?

5. 3 in every 10 seats on a normal bus are red.
   How many red seats are there on 2 normal buses?

Burgers are sold in packs of 8.
Burger buns are sold in packs of 6.

6. What is the smallest number of burgers
   and buns that can be bought to have
   the same number of both?

7. 113 people are coming to Dylan's
   barbecue. How many packs of
   burgers and buns should Dylan
   buy to make sure that everyone
   has a burger and a bun each?

On another planet, all aliens have
3 heads and 6 arms.

If there were 5340 aliens, how many:

8. arms would there be?

9. heads would there be?

2500 enemy aliens arrive on the planet.
6 in every 100 of these aliens have purple eyes.

10. How many enemy aliens have purple eyes?

I can solve multiplication and division problems.

Calculation Problems

Sometimes you'll need to use addition, subtraction, multiplication and division to work out the answer to a problem. These pages have got lots of questions for you to have a go at.

Examples

There are 7 chocolate biscuits in the biscuit tin and 9 times as many ginger biscuits. How many ginger biscuits are there?

$7 \times 9 = 63$. So there are **63 ginger biscuits** in the tin.

There are 87 biscuits in total in the tin. How many biscuits are not ginger or chocolate biscuits?

There are $7 + 63 = 70$ chocolate and ginger biscuits in total.

$87 - 70 = 17$. So **17 biscuits** are not ginger or chocolate.

A lighthouse is made of 8 cm tall bricks and is 1272 cm tall. How many bricks tall is the lighthouse?

$$8 \overline{)1\ 2\ ^47\ ^72}$$
$$\quad \mathbf{1\ 5\ 9}$$

So the lighthouse is **159 bricks tall**.

A new lighthouse is being built. It will be 372 bricks tall when completed. How many bricks taller will it be than the first lighthouse?

$$\begin{array}{r} 3\ \overset{6}{\cancel{7}}\ \overset{12}{\cancel{2}} \\ -\ 1\ 5\ 9 \\ \hline 2\ 1\ 3 \end{array}$$

So the new lighthouse will be **213 bricks taller** than the first lighthouse.

Set A

Hettie buys 7 packs of bubblegum. Each pack has 12 pieces.

1. How many pieces of bubblegum does Hettie have in total?

2. Hettie chews 6 pieces of bubblegum. How many pieces does she have left?

3. A post office has collected 1489 letters. 123 of the letters are for people in Scotland. 9 times as many of the letters are for people in England. How many letters are not for people in Scotland or England?

In a fish tank there are 16 green fish. There are three times as many purple fish as green fish.

4. How many purple fish are prohere?

5. There are 40 fewer blue fish than purple fish. How many blue fish are there?

Rachel has 9 guinea pigs. Every day, she gives each of them 3 pieces of cucumber and 2 pieces of carrot.

6. How many pieces of cucumber does one guinea pig eat in 15 days?

7. Rachel has 180 pieces of carrot. How many days does she have enough carrot for?

It takes Hannah 33 minutes to travel from her house to a theme park. It takes Joseph four times as long as Hannah to get to the theme park.

8. How long does it take Joseph to get to the theme park?

9. How many minutes quicker is the journey for Hannah than Joseph?

10. Manish runs 3 laps of the park and then walks 400 m home. 1 lap of the park is 1015 m. How far does Manish travel in total?

Set B

Joshua and Mina are having a competition to see who can stand on one leg for the longest. Joshua stood on one leg for 152 seconds. Mina stood on one leg for 4 times longer than Joshua.

1. How long did Mina stand on one leg for?

2. Liam stood on one leg for 54 seconds longer than Joshua. How long did he stand on one leg for?

5436 people are queuing to get tickets to see their favourite band. The band is performing on 6 different nights and there is a queue for each night.

3. If the same number of people wanted to see the band on each night, how many people would be in each queue?

654 people want to see the band on Monday. 3 times as many people want to see the band on Tuesday.

4. How many people want to see the band on Tuesday?

5. How many of the people queuing don't want to see the band on Monday or Tuesday?

8653 people voted in a council election. 812 people voted for Nanda. 5 times as many people voted for Julia.

6. How many people voted for Julia?

7. How many people didn't vote for Nanda or Julia?

8. 635 fewer people voted for Toby than Julia. How many people voted for Toby?

9. Libbie thought of a number. She multiplied it by 8, and then subtracted 403. The number she arrived at was 245. What was her original number?

Tyler is selling bowls of strawberries. He has 7832 strawberries.

10. If Tyler puts 9 strawberries in each bowl, how many bowls can he fill?

11. Tyler puts 50 ml of cream in each bowl. How much cream would he need for 683 bowls?

Set C

A tile is made up of 24 coloured squares. Each tile has 12 blue squares, 5 green squares and 7 grey squares. The tiles are sold in packs of 15.

1. How many of each colour square would there be in one pack of tiles?

2. How many grey squares would there be on 18 tiles?

3. Darcey counts all of the blue squares on the tiles that she has. There are 1320 blue squares. How many tiles does she have?

There are 53 wind turbines on top of a hill.

4. One day, each turbine turns 562 times. How many times do all of the turbines turn in total?

5. On another day, 44 of the turbines were turned off to be repaired. The remaining turbines turned 4203 times in total. How many times did each turbine turn?

A museum has 531 paintings and 9 rooms to put them in.

6. How many paintings should they put in each room to share them out equally?

7. 252 of the paintings are stolen. How many fewer paintings will there be in each room if an equal number is stolen from each room?

Sammy is making a book of maths questions. The book will have 722 pages and 45 questions on each page.

8. How many questions will there be in the finished book?

9. It takes Sammy 3 days to write 2 pages of questions. He has already written 264 pages. How long will it take him to finish the book?

10. Simone wrote answers for 810 questions from Sammy's book. How many pages of questions is this?

I can identify and carry out the correct calculations.

Multiplication and Division — Review 5

Find the missing numbers:

1 $4^2 = 4 \times 4 = \square$

2 $2^2 = \square \times \square = \square$

3 $5^2 = \square \times \square = \square$

4 $5^3 = 5 \times 5 \times 5 = \square$

5 $6^3 = 216 = 6 \times 6 \times \square$

6 $7^3 = 343 = \square \times \square \times \square$

Work out:

7 3^2

8 6^2

9 9^2

10 10^2

11 1^3

12 2^3

13 3^3

14 4^3

Work out:

15 $8^2 + 4^2$

16 $6^2 + 5^2$

17 $4^2 + 9^2$

18 $3^3 + 1^3$

19 $2^3 + 5^3$

20 $4^3 + 3^3$

21 $6^2 + 4^3$

22 $10^2 + 1^3$

Are the following true or false?

23 $3^2 = 3 \times 2$

24 $10^3 = 900 + 10^2$

25 $8^2 = 4^3$

26 $5^3 = 10^2 + 5^2$

27 $7^2 = 50 - 1$

28 $4^3 = 14 \times 4$

The prime factors that multiply to give 50 can be written as 2×5^2. In a similar way, write the prime factors that multiply to give:

29 12

30 18

31 28

32 40

33 56

An evil alien has 1875 robots and wants to invade 5 planets.

34 If he divides all his robots equally and sends them to the planets, how many robots would go to each planet?

35 The alien decides to send 245 robots to each planet. How many robots does he have left to protect his ship?

36 Riley has 276 pictures of her cat. She wants to use them to make a 12-month calendar with an equal number of pictures for each month. How many pictures will there be for each month?

Every day, Harrison takes his pet ferret for a walk. Harrison takes 2 steps for every metre that he walks. The ferret takes 10 times as many steps as Harrison.

37 How many steps would they each take if they walked 346 m?

38 If the ferret takes 8920 steps, how many steps does Harrison take?

Kitchen Magician sells tubs of ice cream in 300 ml tubs.

39 They have made 3900 ml of chocolate ice cream and 1200 ml of banana ice cream. How many tubs of each flavour can they make?

40 They have 3600 ml of mint ice cream in the freezer. How many tubs of mint ice cream do they have?

A radio station has 495 free tickets to give away to a festival over 9 days. They give away the same number of tickets each day.

41 How many tickets do they give away each day?

42 The station sold 5 times as many tickets as they gave away. How many tickets did they sell?

43 652 of the tickets cost £18 each. How much did these 652 tickets cost in total?

44 Shayma wants to give a leaflet to every house in her village. She has 267 leaflets, and there are 3 times as many houses in her village. How many more leaflets does she need?

Finished already? You're a maths superstar!

Multiplication and Division — Challenges

1 A group of aliens have been trying to tell us about three of their favourite planets, but the aliens only speak maths.

a) Work out the calculations for each letter in the table, and then use them to work out the names of each of the three planets.

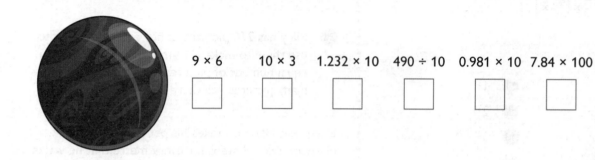

9 × 6	10 × 3	1.232 × 10	490 ÷ 10	0.981 × 10	7.84 × 100	4^3
□	□	□	□	□	□	□

0.37 × 10	120 × 5	320 ÷ 40	108 × 5	5.4 × 100	2400 ÷ 2	7840 ÷ 10	$10^2 + 5^2$
□	□	□	□	□	□	□	□

12.5 × 10	1.1 × 100	37 ÷ 10	64 ÷ 8	500 ÷ 5	60 × 9	14 × 100
□	□	□	□	□	□	□

A	B	C	D	E	F	G	H	I
5^3	2.89 × 100	270 ÷ 9	30 × 40	8^2	762 ÷ 3	1800 ÷ 3	981 ÷ 100	78.4 × 10
J	**K**	**L**	**M**	**N**	**O**	**P**	**Q**	**R**
80 × 7	320 ÷ 4	2^3	7825 ÷ 5	70 × 20	90 × 6	7^2	2.8 × 10	97 ÷ 10
S	**T**	**U**	**V**	**W**	**X**	**Y**	**Z**	
324 ÷ 6	10^2	370 ÷ 100	2.4 × 100	1^3	80 ÷ 4	1232 ÷ 100	1210 ÷ 11	

b) Now have a go at making up your own planet name, and use the code to write a clue. Give it to a friend to see if they can work out the name of your planet.

2 Bobby and Georgie have 36 cards, each with a number from 1 to 36 on it.

a) Georgie only wants the cards that are factors of 36. How many cards does this leave Bobby with?

b) Georgie sorts her cards into factor pairs.
Which card doesn't have a factor pair? Can you explain why?

c) Georgie takes away two of her cards, which when multiplied together give 27.
Which two cards does she take away?

3 A zoo keeper is trying to work out how much fish to order to feed his animals.
The diagrams below show how many kg of fish each animal eats in one day.

The zoo has 5 times as many penguins as sea lions.
There are half as many sea lions as giant otters.
The zoo has 5 baby penguins. The total number of penguins
is 5 times the number of baby penguins.

Penguins: 6 kg per day   Giant Otters: 8 kg per day   Sea Lions: 15 kg per day

How much fish would the zoo keeper need to feed his animals for 5 days?

4 When the difference between two prime numbers is 2, they are known as **twin primes**.

When the difference between two prime numbers is 4, they are known as **cousin primes**.

Jalil writes out the numbers from 0 to 20 and puts a box around the prime numbers.

a) Find all of the twin primes.

b) Find all of the cousin primes.

c) Can you find any numbers that have both a twin and a cousin prime?

5   Find the missing numbers in these calculations.

a)

b)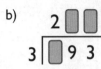

c)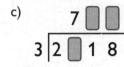

d)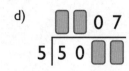

6   Rani has between 200 and 250 sweets. When she shares them out equally into 4 jars, she has 3 sweets left over. When she shares them out equally into 7 jars, she has 5 sweets left over.

a) Work out how many sweets Rani could have.

b) Can you find more than one possible answer?

7   The aim of this game is to get from a number in the START column to the FINISH column by following the rules.

You can only move forwards on the grid, as shown by the diagram. You can't move up, down or backwards.

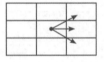

Rules:
1. If you land on a multiple of 9, you must move to a square number.

2. You cannot move from a multiple of 5 to a multiple of 4.

3. You cannot move from a prime number to another prime number.

4. If you land on 15 or less, you must move to a bigger number.

5. If you land on an even number, stop. Circle the number — this is now a dead end.

START   FINISH

58	1	32	17	62	39	61	64
41	55	13	51	45	24	14	36
52	12	23	2	26	25	5	53
7	31	11	46	6	30	44	16
56	63	42	18	34	20	54	81
21	2	32	8	49	19	4	3
43	28	50	9	33	37	15	69
15	57	27	38	59	10	47	48

a) Can you find a route across the grid?

b) How many dead ends can you find?

Hint: if you land on a multiple of 9 and there's no square number to move to next, it becomes a dead end too.

Wow, those challenges were pretty tricky! Well done for making it to the end.

Equivalent Fractions

Don't be fooled by equivalent fractions — they might look different but they're just showing the same number. Take a look at these examples and it'll all become clear.

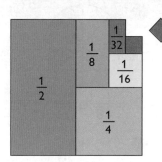

Examples

Complete the equivalent fractions to show the fraction of the shape which is shaded:

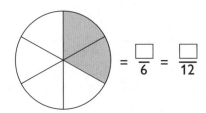 $= \dfrac{\square}{6} = \dfrac{\square}{12}$

2 out of the 6 parts are shaded.

$$\dfrac{2}{6} = \dfrac{4}{12}$$

×2 ... ×2

Complete this equivalent fraction to show the fraction of the shape which is shaded:

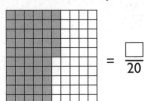 $= \dfrac{\square}{20}$

55 out of the 100 parts are shaded.

÷5

$$\dfrac{55}{100} = \dfrac{11}{20}$$

÷5

Set A

Complete the equivalent fractions to show the fraction of each shape that is shaded:

1

$\dfrac{\square}{4} = \dfrac{\square}{2}$

4

$\dfrac{\square}{8} = \dfrac{\square}{24}$

2

$\dfrac{\square}{6} = \dfrac{\square}{3}$

5

$\dfrac{\square}{5} = \dfrac{\square}{10}$

3

$\dfrac{\square}{8} = \dfrac{\square}{4}$

6

$\dfrac{\square}{9} = \dfrac{\square}{3} = \dfrac{\square}{6}$

Complete these equivalent fractions:

7 $\dfrac{1}{4} = \dfrac{\square}{12}$

8 $\dfrac{4}{5} = \dfrac{\square}{15}$

9 $\dfrac{5}{7} = \dfrac{10}{\square}$

10 $\dfrac{9}{12} = \dfrac{\square}{4}$

11 $\dfrac{7}{21} = \dfrac{1}{\square}$

12 $\dfrac{1}{10} = \dfrac{\square}{100}$

13 Draw lines to match each fraction on the left to an equivalent fraction on the right:

$\dfrac{30}{100}$	$\dfrac{9}{10}$
$\dfrac{90}{100}$	$\dfrac{3}{50}$
$\dfrac{6}{100}$	$\dfrac{3}{10}$

Complete the equivalent fractions to show the fraction of each shape that is shaded:

1
$$\frac{\square}{8} = \frac{\square}{24}$$

4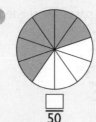
$$\frac{\square}{8}$$

2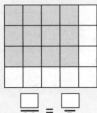
$$\frac{\square}{10} = \frac{\square}{100}$$

5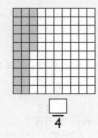
$$\frac{\square}{50}$$

3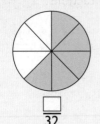
$$\frac{\square}{20} = \frac{\square}{5}$$

6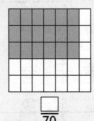
$$\frac{\square}{4}$$

Complete these equivalent fractions:

7 $\frac{2}{3} = \frac{\square}{9} = \frac{\square}{18}$

8 $\frac{5}{6} = \frac{\square}{12} = \frac{\square}{24}$

9 $\frac{3}{8} = \frac{\square}{16} = \frac{\square}{32}$

10 $\frac{70}{100} = \frac{\square}{50} = \frac{7}{\square}$

11 $\frac{16}{28} = \frac{8}{\square} = \frac{\square}{7}$

12 $\frac{9}{10} = \frac{27}{\square} = \frac{\square}{50}$

13 $\frac{44}{100} = \frac{22}{\square} = \frac{\square}{25}$

Which fraction is not equivalent to the others?

14 $\frac{3}{4}$ $\frac{30}{40}$ $\frac{60}{100}$

15 $\frac{10}{100}$ $\frac{2}{5}$ $\frac{5}{50}$

Complete the equivalent fractions to show the fraction of each shape that is shaded:

1
$$\frac{\square}{32}$$

4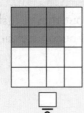
$$\frac{\square}{70}$$

2
$$\frac{\square}{100}$$

5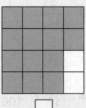
$$\frac{\square}{32}$$

3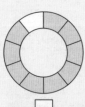
$$\frac{\square}{10}$$

6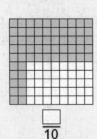
$$\frac{\square}{50}$$

Complete these equivalent fractions:

7 $\frac{3}{5} = \frac{\square}{15} = \frac{15}{\square}$

8 $\frac{6}{7} = \frac{18}{\square} = \frac{\square}{35}$

9 $\frac{30}{100} = \frac{\square}{20} = \frac{3}{\square}$

10 $\frac{\square}{12} = \frac{40}{60} = \frac{48}{\square}$

11 $\frac{\square}{14} = \frac{33}{42} = \frac{22}{\square}$

12 Which fractions in the box below are equivalent to $\frac{8}{10}$?

$$\frac{4}{5} \quad \frac{45}{50} \quad \frac{20}{25} \quad \frac{25}{30} \quad \frac{12}{15} \quad \frac{88}{100}$$

Which fraction is not equivalent to the others?

13 $\frac{5}{6}$ $\frac{15}{18}$ $\frac{55}{60}$ $\frac{25}{30}$

14 $\frac{3}{5}$ $\frac{15}{20}$ $\frac{30}{50}$ $\frac{18}{30}$

I can recognise and show equivalent fractions.

Ordering Fractions

Ordering fractions is a piece of cake when all the denominators are the same — just compare the numerators. If the denominators are different then you'll have to do a bit more work using equivalent fractions.

Example

Put the fractions below in order. Start with the smallest.

$$\frac{7}{8} \quad \frac{1}{2} \quad \frac{5}{8} \quad \frac{3}{4}$$

All the denominators are factors of 8.

Find equivalent fractions with denominators of 8.

$$\frac{7}{8} \qquad \frac{1}{2} = \frac{4}{8} \qquad \frac{5}{8} \qquad \frac{3}{4} = \frac{6}{8}$$

So the correct order is:

$$\frac{1}{2} \quad \frac{5}{8} \quad \frac{3}{4} \quad \frac{7}{8}$$

Check the order using fraction bars.

Set A

Find the equivalent fraction to help you decide which is larger:

1. $\frac{1}{2} = \frac{\square}{6}$, or $\frac{4}{6}$?

2. $\frac{2}{5} = \frac{\square}{10}$, or $\frac{3}{10}$?

3. $\frac{4}{8} = \frac{\square}{4}$, or $\frac{1}{4}$?

4. $\frac{1}{3} = \frac{\square}{9}$, or $\frac{4}{9}$?

Which fraction is smaller:

5. $\frac{5}{8}$ or $\frac{1}{2}$?

6. $\frac{3}{5}$ or $\frac{7}{10}$?

7. $\frac{11}{12}$ or $\frac{5}{6}$?

8. $\frac{3}{4}$ or $\frac{7}{12}$?

9. $\frac{1}{5}$ or $\frac{4}{15}$?

Put these fractions in order. Start with the smallest:

10. $\frac{1}{3} \quad \frac{5}{6} \quad \frac{2}{3}$

11. $\frac{3}{12} \quad \frac{1}{6} \quad \frac{1}{12}$

12. $\frac{2}{5} \quad \frac{5}{10} \quad \frac{7}{10} \quad \frac{3}{5}$

13. $\frac{3}{4} \quad \frac{8}{12} \quad \frac{10}{12} \quad \frac{1}{4}$

Set B

Which fraction is smaller:

1. $\frac{2}{3}$ or $\frac{8}{9}$?

2. $\frac{3}{10}$ or $\frac{1}{5}$?

3. $\frac{6}{7}$ or $\frac{11}{14}$?

4. $\frac{1}{4}$ or $\frac{6}{20}$?

5. $\frac{5}{9}$ or $\frac{22}{36}$?

Find the largest fraction in each list:

6. $\frac{4}{5} \quad \frac{9}{10} \quad \frac{7}{10}$

7. $\frac{3}{8} \quad \frac{5}{8} \quad \frac{17}{24}$

8. $\frac{1}{2} \quad \frac{3}{8} \quad \frac{3}{4}$

9. $\frac{3}{10} \quad \frac{7}{20} \quad \frac{11}{40}$

Put these fractions in order. Start with the smallest:

10. $\frac{3}{8} \quad \frac{5}{16} \quad \frac{1}{4}$

11. $\frac{1}{10} \quad \frac{19}{100} \quad \frac{2}{10} \quad \frac{23}{100}$

12. $\frac{5}{12} \quad \frac{1}{3} \quad \frac{5}{6} \quad \frac{1}{6}$

13. $\frac{13}{18} \quad \frac{5}{9} \quad \frac{1}{3} \quad \frac{2}{9}$

Set C

Find the smallest fraction in each list:

1. $\frac{2}{3} \quad \frac{8}{9} \quad \frac{15}{18}$

2. $\frac{9}{16} \quad \frac{1}{2} \quad \frac{3}{8} \quad \frac{5}{8}$

3. $\frac{2}{5} \quad \frac{6}{20} \quad \frac{1}{5} \quad \frac{3}{10}$

4. $\frac{19}{24} \quad \frac{7}{12} \quad \frac{5}{6} \quad \frac{11}{12}$

Put these fractions in order. Start with the largest:

5. $\frac{1}{3} \quad \frac{4}{6} \quad \frac{7}{18} \quad \frac{11}{18}$

6. $\frac{5}{10} \quad \frac{59}{100} \quad \frac{31}{50} \quad \frac{63}{100}$

7. $\frac{5}{8} \quad \frac{1}{2} \quad \frac{5}{6} \quad \frac{17}{24}$

8. $\frac{4}{5} \quad \frac{3}{10} \quad \frac{7}{10} \quad \frac{2}{5} \quad \frac{11}{20}$

9. Aki is knitting a scarf. She knits $\frac{3}{10}$ on Sunday, $\frac{7}{20}$ on Monday and $\frac{13}{40}$ on Tuesday. On which day did she knit the most?

10. Three friends each order a medium pizza. Leo eats $\frac{15}{18}$, Jane eats $\frac{7}{9}$ and Andy eats $\frac{2}{3}$. Who has the most pizza left?

I can compare and order fractions.

Mixed Numbers

When you need to write a fraction greater than 1, you can use a mixed number. They're called mixed numbers because they have a whole number part and a fraction part — so they're a mix!

Examples

Convert $\frac{9}{5}$ to a mixed number.

$$\frac{9}{5} = 9 \div 5 = 1 \text{ r } 4$$
So $\frac{9}{5} = \mathbf{1\frac{4}{5}}$

Which number is this arrow pointing to? Give your answer as a mixed number.

The number line is split into eighths.

The arrow is pointing to 5 eighths after 4 so $\mathbf{4\frac{5}{8}}$.

Set A

Write the amount of shaded circles as a mixed number:

1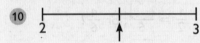

2

3

4

Convert to mixed numbers:

5 $\frac{3}{2}$

6 $\frac{7}{4}$

7 $\frac{6}{5}$

8 $\frac{7}{3}$

9 $\frac{13}{6}$

Which numbers are the arrows below pointing to? Write your answers as mixed numbers.

10
11
12

Set B

Convert to mixed numbers:

1 $\frac{8}{5}$

2 $\frac{13}{8}$

3 $\frac{11}{4}$

4 $\frac{27}{10}$

5 $\frac{23}{6}$

Write these amounts as mixed numbers:

6 8 thirds

7 9 fifths

8 11 sixths

9 9 halves

10 19 quarters

11 21 eighths

Which numbers are the arrows below pointing to? Write your answers as mixed numbers.

12
13
14

Set C

Convert to mixed numbers:

1 $\frac{13}{7}$

2 $\frac{14}{3}$

3 $\frac{29}{6}$

4 $\frac{53}{10}$

5 $\frac{203}{100}$

Write these amounts as mixed numbers:

6 ten thirds

7 fourteen fifths

8 nineteen sixths

9 seventeen halves

10 thirty-one eighths

11 forty-three quarters

Which numbers are the arrows below pointing to? Write your answers as mixed numbers.

12
13
14

I can recognise and use mixed numbers.

Improper Fractions

Improper fractions are another way that you can show fractions greater than 1.
They're really easy to spot because the numerator will always be bigger than the denominator.

Examples

Find the missing number: $4\frac{2}{3} = \boxed{}$ thirds.

There are $4 \times 3 = 12$ thirds in 4.
$12 + 2 = 14$

So $4\frac{2}{3} = \boxed{14}$ thirds.

Which number is this arrow pointing to?
Give your answer as an improper fraction.

The number line is split into fifths.

The arrow is pointing to $1\frac{3}{5} = \frac{8}{5}$.

Set A

Write the amount of shaded squares as an improper fraction:

1

2

3

4

Convert to improper fractions:

5 $1\frac{1}{3}$

6 $1\frac{2}{5}$

7 $1\frac{3}{8}$

8 $2\frac{4}{5}$

9 $3\frac{1}{2}$

Which numbers are the arrows below pointing to? Write your answers as improper fractions.

10

11

12

Set B

Find the missing numbers:

1 $1\frac{2}{3} = \boxed{}$ thirds

2 $1\frac{7}{8} = \boxed{}$ eighths

3 $3\frac{3}{4} = \boxed{}$ quarters

4 $3\frac{4}{5} = \boxed{}$ fifths

5 $4\frac{6}{7} = \boxed{}$ sevenths

Convert to improper fractions:

6 $1\frac{2}{7}$

7 $1\frac{8}{9}$

8 $2\frac{2}{3}$

9 $2\frac{5}{8}$

10 $3\frac{3}{7}$

Which numbers are the arrows below pointing to? Write your answers as improper fractions.

11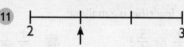

12

13

Set C

Convert to improper fractions:

1 $2\frac{5}{7}$

2 $7\frac{1}{2}$

3 $3\frac{5}{6}$

4 $4\frac{2}{9}$

5 $4\frac{29}{100}$

Find the missing numbers:

6 $3\frac{2}{7} = 2 + \boxed{}\frac{2}{7} = 2 + \frac{\boxed{}}{7}$

7 $5\frac{4}{5} = 1 + \boxed{}\frac{4}{5} = 1 + \frac{\boxed{}}{5}$

8 $7\frac{1}{2} = 3 + \frac{\boxed{}}{2}$

9 $8\frac{1}{6} = 5 + \frac{\boxed{}}{6}$

10 $9\frac{7}{10} = 6 + \frac{\boxed{}}{10}$

Which numbers are the arrows below pointing to? Write your answers as improper fractions.

11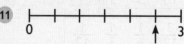

12

13

I can recognise and use improper fractions.

Complete the equivalent fractions to show the fraction of each shape that is shaded:

(1)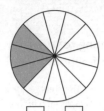

(3)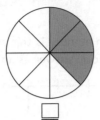

$$\frac{\square}{12} = \frac{\square}{4}$$

$$\frac{\square}{16}$$

(2)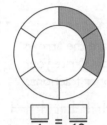

(4)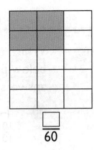

$$\frac{\square}{6} = \frac{\square}{18}$$

$$\frac{\square}{60}$$

Find the missing numbers in these equivalent fractions:

(5) $\frac{5}{6} = \frac{\square}{18}$

(8) $\frac{6}{10} = \frac{\square}{30} = \frac{60}{\square}$

(6) $\frac{10}{15} = \frac{\square}{3}$

(9) $\frac{3}{8} = \frac{9}{\square} = \frac{\square}{40}$

(7) $\frac{12}{20} = \frac{\square}{10} = \frac{3}{\square}$

(10) $\frac{\square}{13} = \frac{10}{26} = \frac{\square}{52}$

Which fraction is smallest:

(11) $\frac{2}{3}$ or $\frac{5}{6}$?

(15) $\frac{1}{3}$ or $\frac{4}{18}$?

(12) $\frac{7}{8}$ or $\frac{3}{4}$?

(16) $\frac{3}{12}$, $\frac{10}{36}$ or $\frac{17}{36}$?

(13) $\frac{11}{15}$ or $\frac{3}{5}$?

(17) $\frac{9}{15}$, $\frac{2}{5}$ or $\frac{2}{3}$?

(14) $\frac{5}{8}$ or $\frac{11}{16}$?

(18) $\frac{3}{4}$, $\frac{7}{8}$ or $\frac{13}{16}$?

Put these fractions in order. Start with the smallest:

(19) $\frac{3}{10}$ $\frac{3}{5}$ $\frac{1}{5}$

(20) $\frac{3}{12}$ $\frac{1}{6}$ $\frac{1}{3}$ $\frac{1}{12}$

(21) $\frac{3}{4}$ $\frac{9}{16}$ $\frac{5}{8}$ $\frac{3}{8}$

(22) $\frac{3}{10}$ $\frac{11}{50}$ $\frac{27}{100}$ $\frac{5}{20}$

Convert to mixed numbers:

(23) $\frac{5}{4}$

(29) $\frac{18}{7}$

(24) $\frac{9}{8}$

(30) $\frac{20}{9}$

(25) $\frac{11}{5}$

(31) $\frac{14}{3}$

(26) $\frac{16}{9}$

(32) $\frac{17}{6}$

(27) $\frac{14}{5}$

(33) $\frac{22}{3}$

(28) $\frac{10}{3}$

(34) $\frac{27}{4}$

Which numbers are the arrows below pointing to? Write your answers as mixed numbers.

(35)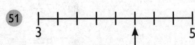

(36)

(37)

Convert to improper fractions:

(38) $1\frac{1}{5}$

(44) $3\frac{3}{4}$

(39) $1\frac{5}{6}$

(45) $3\frac{1}{8}$

(40) $1\frac{4}{5}$

(46) $9\frac{1}{3}$

(41) $4\frac{1}{2}$

(47) $4\frac{6}{7}$

(42) $2\frac{4}{6}$

(48) $5\frac{8}{9}$

(43) $2\frac{4}{9}$

(49) $6\frac{1}{10}$

Which numbers are the arrows below pointing to? Write your answers as improper fractions.

(50)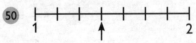

(51)

(52)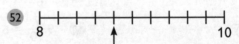

There were some tricky questions in that exercise — well done for getting to the end!

Adding and subtracting fractions is easy when the denominators are the same.
You just add or subtract the numerators and leave the denominator as it was.

Examples

What is $\frac{7}{12} + \frac{6}{12}$?

$\frac{7}{12} + \frac{6}{12} = \frac{13}{12}$ or $1\frac{1}{12}$

Work out $4\frac{2}{10} - \frac{3}{10}$. Give your answer as a mixed number.

$4\frac{2}{10} = \frac{42}{10}$ $\frac{42}{10} - \frac{3}{10} = \frac{39}{10} = 3\frac{9}{10}$

Set A

Work out:

1. $\frac{3}{7} + \frac{2}{7}$

2. $\frac{8}{10} - \frac{4}{10}$

3. $\frac{4}{11} + \frac{6}{11}$

4. $\frac{12}{14} - \frac{7}{14}$

5. $\frac{8}{17} + \frac{8}{17}$

Work out, giving your answers as improper fractions:

6. $\frac{7}{10} + \frac{6}{10}$

7. $\frac{23}{8} - \frac{8}{8}$

Write down the rule for each of these sequences:

8. $\frac{1}{2}$, 1, $\frac{3}{2}$, 2

9. 1, $\frac{3}{4}$, $\frac{1}{2}$, $\frac{1}{4}$

Find the missing digits:

10. $\frac{7}{8} + \frac{6}{8} = \frac{\Box}{8} = 1\frac{\Box}{8}$

11. $\frac{19}{7} - \frac{10}{7} = \frac{\Box}{7} = 1\frac{\Box}{7}$

12. $\frac{7}{9} + \frac{6}{9} = \Box\frac{4}{9}$

13. $\frac{19}{6} - \frac{2}{6} = \Box\frac{5}{6}$

14. $\frac{4}{13} + \frac{11}{13} = \Box\frac{\Box}{13}$

Set B

Work out, giving your answers as improper fractions:

1. $\frac{9}{10} + \frac{4}{10}$

2. $\frac{22}{7} - \frac{9}{7}$

3. $\frac{32}{20} - \frac{9}{20}$

4. $\frac{21}{18} + \frac{16}{18}$

5. $\frac{90}{100} + \frac{37}{100}$

Find the missing digits:

6. $\frac{8}{9} + \frac{7}{9} = 1\frac{\Box}{9}$

7. $\frac{42}{5} - \frac{25}{5} = \Box\frac{\Box}{5}$

Write down the rule for each of these sequences:

8. $\frac{1}{5}$, $\frac{3}{5}$, 1, $\frac{7}{5}$

9. 3, $2\frac{1}{3}$, $1\frac{2}{3}$, 1

Work out, giving your answers as mixed numbers:

10. $\frac{17}{6} - \frac{6}{6}$

11. $\frac{15}{10} + \frac{16}{10}$

12. $4\frac{7}{9} - \frac{5}{9}$

13. $3\frac{3}{5} + \frac{4}{5}$

14. $6\frac{2}{7} - \frac{5}{7}$

Set C

Find the missing digits:

1. $\frac{15}{4} - \frac{9}{4} = \Box\frac{\Box}{4}$

2. $\frac{8}{5} + \frac{13}{5} = \Box\frac{\Box}{5}$

3. $\frac{5}{3} + \frac{\Box}{3} = 4\frac{1}{3}$

4. $\frac{\Box}{6} - \frac{14}{6} = 1\frac{1}{6}$

5. $7\frac{1}{7} + \frac{\Box}{7} = 9\frac{2}{7}$

Write down the rule for each of these sequences:

6. $1\frac{2}{7}$, $1\frac{4}{7}$, $1\frac{6}{7}$, $2\frac{1}{7}$

7. 6, $4\frac{3}{4}$, $3\frac{1}{2}$, $2\frac{1}{4}$

Work out, giving your answers as mixed numbers:

8. $3 - \frac{7}{10}$

9. $1\frac{4}{7} + \frac{6}{7}$

Work out, giving your answers as mixed numbers:

10. $3 + \frac{9}{4}$

11. $5 - \frac{10}{3}$

12. $1\frac{2}{5} + \frac{9}{5}$

13. $4\frac{3}{8} + \frac{12}{8}$

14. $4\frac{2}{6} - \frac{9}{6}$

I can add and subtract fractions with the same denominator.

Adding and Subtracting Fractions — 2

Remember that to add or subtract fractions the denominators must be the same. Here you'll have to use equivalent fractions to make the denominators equal before you do any adding or subtracting.

Example

What is $\frac{1}{4} + \frac{5}{8}$?   Write $\frac{1}{4}$ as a number of eighths. $\frac{1}{4} = \frac{2}{8}$

Now you can add them together. $\frac{1}{4} + \frac{5}{8} = \frac{2}{8} + \frac{5}{8} = \frac{7}{8}$

Set A

Find the missing digits:

1. $\frac{1}{2} + \frac{1}{4} = \frac{\square}{4} + \frac{1}{4} = \frac{\square}{4}$

2. $\frac{1}{3} + \frac{1}{6} = \frac{\square}{6} + \frac{1}{6} = \frac{\square}{6}$

3. $\frac{3}{8} + \frac{1}{4} = \frac{3}{8} + \frac{\square}{8} = \frac{\square}{8}$

4. $\frac{5}{6} - \frac{1}{2} = \frac{5}{6} - \frac{\square}{6} = \frac{\square}{6}$

5. $\frac{9}{10} - \frac{3}{5} = \frac{9}{10} - \frac{\square}{10} = \frac{\square}{10}$

Work out:

6. $\frac{7}{9} - \frac{1}{3}$

7. $\frac{1}{2} + \frac{1}{10}$

Write down the rule for each of these sequences:

8. $0, \quad \frac{1}{6}, \quad \frac{1}{3}, \quad \frac{3}{6}$

9. $1, \quad \frac{3}{4}, \quad \frac{1}{2}, \quad \frac{1}{4}$

Work out, giving your answers as improper fractions:

10. $\frac{1}{2} + \frac{7}{8}$

11. $\frac{2}{3} + \frac{3}{6}$

12. $\frac{15}{4} - \frac{1}{2}$

13. $\frac{4}{5} + \frac{9}{10}$

14. $\frac{19}{8} - \frac{3}{4}$

Set B

Find the missing digits:

1. $\frac{3}{4} - \frac{5}{8} = \frac{\square}{8}$

2. $\frac{2}{5} + \frac{3}{10} = \frac{\square}{10}$

3. $\frac{2}{3} + \frac{1}{9} = \frac{\square}{9}$

4. $\frac{10}{12} - \frac{1}{4} = \frac{\square}{12}$

5. $\frac{1}{2} - \frac{3}{10} = \frac{\square}{10}$

Work out:

6. $\frac{7}{8} - \frac{1}{2}$

7. $\frac{2}{6} + \frac{7}{12}$

Write down the rule for each of these sequences:

8. $\frac{1}{8}, \quad \frac{1}{4}, \quad \frac{3}{8}, \quad \frac{2}{4}$

9. $\frac{7}{10}, \quad \frac{1}{2}, \quad \frac{3}{10}, \quad \frac{1}{10}$

Work out, giving your answers as mixed numbers:

10. $\frac{5}{6} + \frac{1}{2}$

11. $\frac{7}{9} + \frac{2}{3}$

12. $\frac{7}{12} + \frac{3}{4}$

13. $1\frac{3}{8} - \frac{1}{4}$

14. $3\frac{7}{10} - \frac{3}{5}$

Set C

Work out:

1. $\frac{11}{15} - \frac{1}{5}$

2. $\frac{3}{8} + \frac{9}{16}$

3. $\frac{2}{3} - \frac{7}{12}$

4. $\frac{3}{10} + \frac{37}{100}$

5. $\frac{7}{10} - \frac{21}{100}$

Write down the rule for each of these sequences:

6. $\frac{1}{6}, \quad \frac{5}{12}, \quad \frac{2}{3}, \quad \frac{11}{12}$

7. $\frac{13}{16}, \quad \frac{5}{8}, \quad \frac{7}{16}, \quad \frac{1}{4}$

Work out, giving your answers as mixed numbers:

8. $\frac{7}{14} + \frac{5}{7}$

9. $4\frac{1}{6} - \frac{2}{3}$

Find the missing digits:

10. $\frac{9}{6} - \frac{\square}{3} = \frac{5}{6}$

11. $\frac{2}{9} + \frac{\square}{27} = \frac{11}{27}$

12. $1\frac{\square}{8} - \frac{1}{4} = 1\frac{1}{8}$

13. $1\frac{9}{10} - \frac{\square}{5} = 1\frac{3}{10}$

14. $2\frac{11}{12} + \frac{\square}{6} = 3\frac{5}{12}$

I can add and subtract fractions with different denominators.

Multiplying by Fractions

Multiplying a whole-number amount by a fraction is the same as finding the fraction of the amount.
So doing $\frac{1}{2} \times 10$ is the same as finding $\frac{1}{2}$ of 10. Here are some examples of how to tackle different questions.

Examples

What number is $2\frac{2}{5}$ times as big as 50?

Multiply each part of the mixed number separately.
Then add the answers together.

$2 \times 50 = 100$

$\frac{2}{5} \times 50 = 50 \div 5 \times 2$
$= 10 \times 2 = 20$ $\qquad 100 + 20 = \mathbf{120}$

Work out $\frac{3}{4} \times 7$. Give your answer as a mixed number.

$7 \div 4$ doesn't give a whole number, so this time multiply the numerator by the whole number then convert to a mixed number.

$\frac{3}{4} \times 7 = \frac{3 \times 7}{4} = \frac{21}{4} = 5\frac{1}{4}$

Felix the cat eats $1\frac{2}{3}$ bowls of food every day. How many bowls of food will he eat in 4 days?

Convert the mixed number to an improper fraction before multiplying.

$1\frac{2}{3} = \frac{5}{3}$ $\qquad 4 \times \frac{5}{3} = \frac{4 \times 5}{3} = \frac{20}{3} = \mathbf{6\frac{2}{3}}$

So Felix eats $\mathbf{6\frac{2}{3}}$ **bowls** of food in 4 days.

Set A

Use the diagrams below to help you work out:

1. $\frac{1}{6} \times 5$

2. $\frac{3}{10} \times 3$

Work out:

3. $\frac{2}{7} \times 2$

4. $\frac{7}{100} \times 9$

Work out, giving your answers as mixed numbers:

5. $\frac{1}{2} \times 5$

6. $\frac{4}{5} \times 2$

7. $\frac{3}{4} \times 3$

8. $\frac{2}{3} \times 4$

Katya knits $\frac{2}{5}$ of a scarf each week.

9. How much of the scarf will Katya knit in 2 weeks?

10. How many scarves could Katya knit in 10 weeks?

Each day, Gordon eats $\frac{1}{8}$ of a box of cereal. Giving your answers as mixed numbers, how many boxes of cereal will he eat in:

11. 8 days?

12. 15 days?

13. A baker uses $\frac{2}{5}$ of a bag of flour for each loaf of bread. How much flour will he need for 8 loaves? Give your answer as a mixed number.

Find the missing numbers:

14. $1\frac{1}{4} \times 3 = 3 + \frac{\square}{4} = \square\frac{\square}{4}$

15. $2\frac{1}{7} \times 4 = \square + \frac{4}{7} = \square\frac{\square}{7}$

Set B

Use the diagram below to help you work out the calculation. Give your answer as a mixed number.

1 $\frac{2}{5} \times 6$

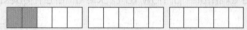

Work out, giving your answers as mixed numbers:

2 $\frac{1}{3} \times 7$

3 $\frac{3}{4} \times 5$

4 $\frac{7}{10} \times 8$

Find the missing numbers:

5 $1\frac{1}{5} \times 3 = 3 + \frac{\square}{5} = \square\frac{\square}{5}$

6 $3\frac{1}{8} \times 5 = \square + \frac{5}{8} = \square\frac{\square}{8}$

Work out, giving your answers as mixed numbers:

7 $3\frac{1}{3} \times 2$

8 $2\frac{2}{5} \times 4$

Give your answers as mixed numbers:

9 Greg's hamster drinks $\frac{3}{10}$ of its water bottle each day. How many bottles of water will it drink in 6 days?

10 A chef can chop $3\frac{1}{6}$ carrots in a minute. How many can he chop in 5 minutes?

11 Jodie can do $1\frac{1}{2}$ turns when diving off the highest diving board. How many turns will she have done after 7 dives?

What number is:

12 $1\frac{1}{2}$ times as big as 80?

13 $1\frac{2}{5}$ times as big as 15?

14 $2\frac{3}{4}$ times as big as 20?

15 Fran's daisy chain is 30 cm long. Lucy's daisy chain is $1\frac{5}{6}$ times as long. How long is Lucy's daisy chain?

Set C

Work out, giving your answers as mixed numbers:

1 $\frac{3}{5} \times 4$

2 $\frac{3}{4} \times 9$

3 $\frac{2}{7} \times 10$

4 $\frac{4}{9} \times 12$

Work out, giving your answers as mixed numbers:

5 $1\frac{1}{8} \times 5$

6 $1\frac{2}{7} \times 4$

7 $2\frac{2}{5} \times 9$

8 $4\frac{1}{6} \times 10$

What number is:

9 $3\frac{1}{4}$ times as big as 60?

10 $5\frac{4}{7}$ times as big as 70?

11 Naveen's rose bush is 60 cm tall. His sunflower is $1\frac{4}{5}$ as tall. How tall is his sunflower?

Give your answers as mixed numbers:
Uri runs $4\frac{1}{4}$ laps of the playground every day. How many laps does he run in:

12 6 days?

13 10 days?

14 Suma puts $2\frac{1}{2}$ teaspoons of sugar in her cup of coffee. She drinks 9 cups of coffee in a week. How many teaspoons of sugar does she use?

15 Demi drinks $3\frac{2}{3}$ bottles of water every day. How many bottles will she drink in 7 days?

16 Kim can make $4\frac{5}{6}$ dresses with one roll of fabric. How many dresses can she make with 5 rolls of fabric?

I can multiply whole numbers by fractions.

Solving Problems with Fractions

To solve these fraction problems you'll need to use all of the fraction skills you've already learnt. Make sure you're confident with all the different skills before you have a go at these.

Examples

Harry has a full bottle of milk.
He uses $\frac{1}{10}$ in his tea and $\frac{1}{5}$ on his cereal.
What fraction of the milk has he used?

Harry uses $\frac{1}{5} = \frac{2}{10}$ on his cereal.
So in total he uses $\frac{1}{10} + \frac{2}{10} = \frac{3}{10}$ of the milk.

What fraction of milk is left in the bottle?

$1 - \frac{3}{10} = \frac{7}{10}$ of the milk is left.

Kamal has a bowl containing 20 g of sugar.
He increases the amount of sugar by $\frac{3}{5}$.
How much sugar is in the bowl now?

Kamal adds $\frac{3}{5} \times 20 = 20 \div 5 \times 3$
$= 4 \times 3 = 12$ g of sugar.
So in total there is 20 + 12 = **32 g** of sugar.

Kim has 7 pages left in her diary.
She writes $1\frac{1}{3}$ pages each day. Does she have enough space for the next 5 days?

$1 \times 5 = 5$ and $\frac{1}{3} \times 5 = \frac{5}{3} = 1\frac{2}{3}$
She will fill $5 + 1\frac{2}{3} = 6\frac{2}{3}$ pages in 5 days.
So **yes**, she will have enough space.

Set A

Remi has $\frac{4}{5}$ of a fruit cake and $\frac{3}{5}$ of a sponge cake.
How much cake does he have in total?
Give your answer as:

1. an improper fraction.

2. a mixed number.

3. A bottle of juice was $\frac{7}{9}$ full.
   Ben drank $\frac{2}{9}$ of the capacity of the bottle.
   What fraction of juice is left in the bottle?

4. Fiona got 50 cards at Christmas.
   She got $\frac{4}{5}$ as many cards on her birthday.
   How many cards did she get in total?

Julie walks $\frac{3}{8}$ of a mile to school
and Shaun walks $\frac{1}{2}$ of a mile.

5. How much further does Shaun walk than Julie?

6. How far do they walk in total?

Anna and Yusuf are packing a suitcase.
Anna fills $\frac{2}{7}$ of the suitcase and Yusuf fills $\frac{5}{14}$.

7. Who has filled more of the suitcase?

8. What fraction of the suitcase is empty?

Each night, Petra burns $\frac{1}{2}$ of a candle
and Oli burns $\frac{5}{6}$ of a candle.

9. Who burns less of their candle each night?

10. How many candles will Petra burn in 5 nights? Give your answer as an improper fraction.

At a buffet there are 7 eighths of vegetarian pizza and half a pepperoni pizza left.

11. How much more vegetarian pizza is there than pepperoni?

12. How much pizza is left in total? Give your answer as a mixed number.

A painter mixes $\frac{11}{12}$ litres of blue paint with $\frac{6}{12}$ litres of yellow paint to make green paint. How many litres of green paint does he have? Give your answer as:

1. an improper fraction.

2. a mixed number.

3. Keris has 30 chocolate buttons. Jen has $1\frac{1}{2}$ times as many. How many chocolate buttons does Jen have?

4. Mike is standing $3\frac{4}{5}$ m from a camera. Heather is standing $\frac{3}{5}$ m closer than Mike. How far is Heather from the camera? Give your answer as a mixed number.

Two friends are sharing a pot of peanuts. Justin has eaten $\frac{1}{3}$ of the peanuts and Lucy has eaten $\frac{5}{12}$.

5. Who has eaten fewer peanuts?

6. What fraction of the peanuts are left in the pot?

7. A bug climbs up $\frac{2}{5}$ of a tree in the morning and $\frac{7}{15}$ in the afternoon. How far is the bug up the tree?

A farmer's barn is filled with three grains. $\frac{4}{9}$ is oats, $\frac{1}{3}$ is barley and the rest is wheat.

8. What fraction of the grain is wheat?

9. Put the grains in order. Start with the one the farmer has most of.

10. A chef has $3\frac{5}{6}$ tubs of butter. She uses $\frac{2}{3}$ of a tub making breakfast. How many tubs does she have left?

11. Zara says, "I have 3 chocolate bars. If I give $1\frac{1}{10}$ bars away and eat $\frac{4}{5}$ of a bar, I'll have $1\frac{3}{10}$ bars left". Is she correct? Explain your answer.

Anna's rabbit weighs $\frac{12}{10}$ kg and her guinea pig weighs $\frac{9}{10}$ kg.

1. How many kg heavier is the rabbit than the guinea pig?

2. What is their total weight? Give your answer as a mixed number.

3. A small pot can hold $\frac{3}{8}$ of a bag of rice. How many bags of rice can 10 small pots hold? Give your answer as a mixed number.

This table shows how far Monib jogs on three days of the week.

Monday	Friday	Sunday
$\frac{3}{4}$ km	$2\frac{7}{8}$ km	$1\frac{1}{4}$ km

How much further did he jog:

4. on Sunday than on Monday?

5. on Friday than on Monday? Give your answer as a mixed number.

6. How far did he jog in total on Monday and Friday? Give your answer as a mixed number.

7. Fiona got 20 marks on her maths test. She got $2\frac{4}{5}$ as many marks on her English test as her maths test. How many marks did she get in total?

Joey has a bag of sweets. $\frac{2}{5}$ are blue, $\frac{8}{25}$ are red and the rest are green.

8. What fraction of the sweets are green?

9. Put the colours in order. Start with the colour that there is fewest of.

10. A bakery cut their pies into quarters or eighths. At lunch time there are three quarters and eleven eighths left. How many pies are left in total? Give your answer as a mixed number.

11. Mrs Reid gave out $3\frac{7}{12}$ packs of crayons to her class. When she collected them, $\frac{3}{4}$ of a pack had gone missing. How many packs of crayons did she collect?

I can solve problems with fractions.

Work out, giving your answers as improper fractions:

① $\frac{3}{6} + \frac{4}{6}$

④ $\frac{15}{16} + \frac{15}{16}$

② $\frac{12}{5} - \frac{3}{5}$

⑤ $\frac{67}{40} - \frac{14}{40}$

③ $\frac{8}{10} + \frac{13}{10}$

⑥ $\frac{53}{100} + \frac{64}{100}$

Find the missing digits:

⑦ $\frac{12}{3} - \frac{8}{3} = \square\frac{1}{3}$

⑩ $\frac{17}{5} - \frac{10}{5} = \square\frac{\square}{5}$

⑧ $\frac{11}{6} + \frac{2}{6} = 2\frac{\square}{6}$

⑪ $3\frac{3}{4} + \frac{2}{4} = \square\frac{\square}{4}$

⑨ $3\frac{1}{3} + \frac{1}{3} = \square\frac{\square}{3}$

⑫ $2\frac{4}{7} - \frac{5}{7} = \square\frac{\square}{7}$

Work out, giving your answers as mixed numbers:

⑬ $\frac{9}{5} - \frac{2}{5}$

⑯ $6 - \frac{3}{4}$

⑭ $\frac{5}{7} + \frac{6}{7}$

⑰ $1\frac{4}{6} + \frac{3}{6}$

⑮ $4\frac{8}{9} - \frac{4}{9}$

⑱ $3\frac{1}{8} - \frac{6}{8}$

Work out, giving your answers as improper fractions where appropriate:

⑲ $\frac{1}{5} + \frac{5}{10}$

㉓ $\frac{2}{3} + \frac{5}{9}$

⑳ $\frac{3}{4} - \frac{1}{8}$

㉔ $\frac{15}{16} - \frac{1}{2}$

㉑ $\frac{4}{12} + \frac{1}{4}$

㉕ $\frac{2}{3} + \frac{9}{12}$

㉒ $\frac{11}{16} - \frac{3}{8}$

㉖ $\frac{14}{20} + \frac{3}{4}$

Work out, giving your answers as mixed numbers:

㉗ $\frac{5}{6} + \frac{5}{12}$

㉛ $1\frac{1}{16} + \frac{1}{2}$

㉘ $\frac{1}{2} + \frac{8}{10}$

㉜ $3\frac{8}{15} - \frac{2}{5}$

㉙ $1\frac{8}{9} - \frac{2}{3}$

㉝ $2\frac{63}{100} + \frac{2}{10}$

㉚ $2\frac{7}{8} - \frac{1}{4}$

㉞ $5\frac{1}{4} - \frac{1}{2}$

Work out, giving your answers as mixed numbers:

㉟ $\frac{1}{2} \times 3$

㊳ $\frac{3}{4} \times 7$

㊱ $\frac{2}{3} \times 2$

㊴ $\frac{5}{8} \times 5$

㊲ $\frac{4}{7} \times 3$

㊵ $\frac{2}{5} \times 13$

Work out, giving your answers as mixed numbers:

㊶ $1\frac{2}{5} \times 2$

㊹ $1\frac{1}{3} \times 5$

㊷ $3\frac{1}{4} \times 3$

㊺ $2\frac{3}{7} \times 4$

㊸ $2\frac{2}{3} \times 2$

㊻ $1\frac{4}{5} \times 6$

What number is:

㊼ $2\frac{1}{3}$ times as big as 30?

㊽ $4\frac{3}{5}$ times as big as 100?

㊾ $3\frac{2}{7}$ times as big as 35?

Una uses $1\frac{3}{10}$ of a bar of chocolate to make one batch of muffins. How many bars of chocolate would she need to make:

㊿ three batches of muffins?

51 eight batches of muffins?

Gwen has two bags of spaghetti. One bag has $\frac{7}{8}$ of the spaghetti left and the other bag has $\frac{3}{8}$ left. How many bags of spaghetti are left in total? Give your answer as:

52 an improper fraction.

53 a mixed number.

After Zoe's party there is $\frac{1}{3}$ of a bag of ready salted crisps left, $\frac{5}{12}$ of a bag of prawn cocktail crisps and $\frac{3}{4}$ of a bag of cheese and onion crisps.

54 Which flavour has the least left?

Give your answers as mixed numbers:

55 How many bags of crisps were left in total?

56 There was 1 bag of each flavour of crisps before the party. How many bags of ready salted and prawn cocktail crisps were eaten in total?

Give yourself a round of applause — that was a lot of tricky fraction questions to tackle.

Tenths, Hundredths and Thousandths

Remember that the thousandths place is the 3rd place to the right of the decimal point.
There are 10 thousandths in 1 hundredth and 100 thousandths in 1 tenth.

Examples

Write $\frac{185}{1000}$ as a decimal.

0	.	1	8	5
Ones		Tenths	Hundredths	Thousandths

185 thousandths is the same as
1 tenth, 8 hundredths and 5 thousandths.

Write $\frac{9}{10} + \frac{5}{100} + \frac{7}{1000}$ as a decimal.

9 tenths
+ 5 hundredths $0.9 + 0.05 + 0.007 = \mathbf{0.957}$
+ 7 thousandths

Set A

Write as a decimal:

1. $\frac{3}{10}$
2. $\frac{9}{100}$
3. $\frac{57}{100}$
4. $\frac{145}{1000}$
5. $\frac{678}{1000}$

Find the missing numbers:

6. $\frac{300}{1000} = \frac{\square}{100}$
7. $\frac{40}{1000} = \frac{\square}{100}$
8. $\frac{50}{100} = \frac{\square}{1000}$
9. $\frac{1}{10} = \frac{\square}{100} = \frac{\square}{1000}$
10. $\frac{700}{1000} = \frac{\square}{100} = \frac{\square}{10}$

Write the answers as decimals:

11. $\frac{1}{10} + \frac{4}{100}$
12. $\frac{3}{10} + \frac{6}{100} + \frac{1}{1000}$
13. $\frac{8}{10} + \frac{5}{100} + \frac{2}{1000}$
14. $\frac{9}{100} + \frac{4}{1000}$
15. $\frac{3}{10} + \frac{2}{1000}$

Set B

Write as a decimal:

1. $\frac{37}{100}$
2. $\frac{3}{100}$
3. $\frac{302}{1000}$
4. $\frac{8}{1000}$
5. $\frac{97}{1000}$

Write the answers as decimals:

6. $\frac{1}{10} + \frac{4}{100} + \frac{8}{1000}$
7. $\frac{5}{10} + \frac{3}{1000}$
8. $\frac{9}{100} + \frac{6}{1000}$
9. $\frac{7}{100} + \frac{9}{1000}$
10. $\frac{2}{10} + \frac{4}{1000}$

Write these as decimals:

11. $4\frac{24}{100}$
12. $9\frac{49}{100}$
13. $12\frac{980}{1000}$
14. $45\frac{67}{1000}$
15. $73\frac{4}{1000}$

Set C

Write these as decimals:

1. $\frac{777}{1000}$
2. $\frac{51}{1000}$
3. $3\frac{647}{1000}$
4. $47\frac{7}{1000}$
5. $88\frac{80}{1000}$

Write the answers as decimals:

6. $\frac{1}{10} + \frac{68}{1000}$
7. $\frac{8}{10} + \frac{99}{1000}$
8. $\frac{60}{100} + \frac{7}{1000}$
9. $\frac{2}{10} + \frac{52}{100}$
10. $\frac{8}{100} + \frac{19}{1000}$

Look at the number line below.

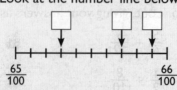

Write the number that
each arrow is pointing to:

11. as a fraction
12. as a decimal

I understand the relationship between
tenths, hundredths and thousandths.

Counting in Decimals

You can do mental calculations and count in decimals by using place value.
Just keep track of the decimal places and you'll fly through this lot.

Examples

Count forward 5 steps of 0.001 from 0.574.

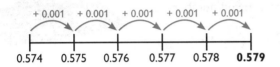

0.574 0.575 0.576 0.577 0.578 **0.579**

What is 5.2 + 3.5?

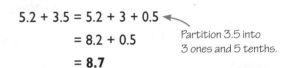

$5.2 + 3.5 = 5.2 + 3 + 0.5$

$= 8.2 + 0.5$

$= \mathbf{8.7}$

Partition 3.5 into
3 ones and 5 tenths.

Set A

Starting at 5, count forward:

1. 4 steps of 0.1
2. 5 steps of 0.01
3. 3 steps of 0.001

Starting at 3, count back:

4. 2 steps of 0.1
5. 1 step of 0.01
6. 6 steps of 0.001

Use the rules of these sequences
to find the next two terms:

7. Add 0.5:
   1.2   1.7   2.2   ☐ ☐
8. Subtract 0.2:
   4.8   4.6   4.4   ☐ ☐
9. Add 0.3:
   2.5   2.8   3.1   ☐ ☐
10. Subtract 0.4:
    8.8   8.4   8.0   ☐ ☐

Work out:

11. 5 + 0.8
12. 1 − 0.3
13. 0.4 + 0.6
14. 0.9 − 0.7
15. 3.5 + 0.4
16. 6.6 − 0.5
17. 8 − 1.2

Set B

How many steps of 0.001
are there between:

1. 0.543 and 0.548?
2. 0.387 and 0.381?
3. 0.847 and 0.854?
4. 0.67 and 0.68?
5. 0.1 and 0.2?
6. 7 and 7.5?

Count forward:

7. 4 steps of 0.2 from 0
8. 5 steps of 0.03 from 2.51
9. 3 steps of 0.005 from 5.420

Count back:

10. 3 steps of 0.3 from 2
11. 4 steps of 0.02 from 8.49
12. 5 steps of 0.004 from 0.5

Find the missing numbers:

13. 5 + ☐ = 5.9
14. 0.9 − ☐ = 0.1
15. ☐ − 0.3 = 3.6
16. 0.4 + ☐ = 4.2
17. ☐ + 0.8 = 6
18. ☐ − 0.5 = 7.8
19. 1 − ☐ = 0.55

Set C

Find the missing numbers
in these sequences:

1. 0.4   0.8   1.2   ☐ ☐
2. 5.0   4.5   4.0   ☐ ☐
3. 4.8   5.6   6.4   ☐ ☐
4. 3.2   2.8   2.4   ☐ ☐
5. 2.1   3.3   4.5   ☐ ☐

6. Find the missing decimals
   on this number line:

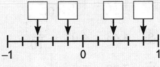

−1   0   1

Count back:

7. 2 steps of 0.002 from 0.632
8. 4 steps of 0.004 from 4.335
9. 5 steps of 0.005 from 0.501

Work out:

10. 5.8 + 1.8
11. 2.4 − 1.7
12. 3.4 + 2.6
13. 9.1 − 4.5
14. 1 − 0.14
15. 3.68 − 0.53
16. 6.94 + 1.2

I can count forward and backwards using decimals.

Writing Decimals as Fractions — 1

Decimals and fractions are two different ways to show the same number.
Have a look at these examples to see how you can easily change from a decimal to a fraction.

Examples

Write 0.7 as a fraction.

$$0.7 = 7 \text{ tenths} = \frac{7}{10}$$

A pool table is 2.83 m long.
Write this length as a mixed number.

$$2.83 = 2 + 0.83 = 2\frac{83}{100} \text{ m}$$

Set A

Write as a fraction:

1. 0.1
2. 0.3
3. 0.5
4. 0.9
5. 0.89
6. 0.77
7. 0.03

Find the missing numbers to complete these calculations:

8. $0.89 = 0.8 + \dfrac{\square}{100}$

9. $0.62 = \dfrac{\square}{10} + 0.02$

10. $0.21 = \dfrac{\square}{10} + \dfrac{1}{100}$

11. $0.47 = \dfrac{4}{10} + \dfrac{\square}{100}$

12. $0.69 = \dfrac{\square}{10} + \dfrac{\square}{100}$

Find the missing numbers to complete these mixed numbers:

13. $4.2 = 4\dfrac{\square}{10}$

14. $6.7 = \square\dfrac{7}{10}$

15. $9.3 = \square\dfrac{\square}{10}$

16. $1.89 = \square\dfrac{\square}{100}$

17. $3.13 = \square\dfrac{\square}{100}$

Set B

Write as a fraction:

1. 0.6
2. 0.2
3. 0.19
4. 0.41
5. 0.99
6. 0.07
7. 0.04

Write as mixed numbers:

8. 4.3
9. 5.7
10. 9.84
11. 15.15
12. 32.41
13. 3.05
14. 100.09

Find the missing numbers:

15. $3.89 = 3.8 + \dfrac{\square}{100}$

16. $2.43 = 2 + \dfrac{\square}{100}$

17. There are 0.23 g of salt in a glass of milk. Write this amount as a fraction.

18. Mike's thumb is 6.35 cm long. Write this as a mixed number.

Set C

Write as mixed numbers:

1. 8.1
2. 1.31
3. 8.83
4. 13.17
5. 38.47
6. 55.29
7. 209.03

Find the missing numbers to complete these calculations:

8. $1.17 = 1 + \dfrac{\square}{100}$

9. $4.43 = 4.03 + \dfrac{\square}{10}$

10. $7.89 = 7.5 + \dfrac{\square}{100}$

11. $10.75 = 10 + \dfrac{3}{10} + \dfrac{\square}{100}$

12. $15.29 = 15 + \dfrac{\square}{10} + \dfrac{19}{100}$

This table shows the weights of some items in Alia's pencil case.

Crayon	Ruler	Pen
5.74 g	23.45 g	54.08 g

13. Write the weight of each item as a mixed number.

14. Gabe's rope is 8.56 m long. He uses 8.1 m to make a swing. Write the amount he has left as a fraction.

I can write decimals as fractions.

Writing Decimals as Fractions — 2

More writing decimals as fractions coming right up — these ones are a little bit tougher.

Examples

Write 3.411 as a mixed number.

$$3.411 = 3 + 0.411 = 3\frac{411}{1000}$$

Find the missing number in $1.747 = 1.7 + \dfrac{\square}{1000}$

$$1.747 - 1.7 = 0.047 = \frac{47}{1000}$$

Set A

Write these as fractions:

1. 0.26
2. 0.69
3. 0.04
4. 0.912
5. 0.683
6. 0.709
7. 0.051

Find the missing numbers to complete these mixed numbers:

8. $3.21 = 3\dfrac{\square}{100}$
9. $8.41 = \square\,\dfrac{41}{100}$
10. $9.39 = \square\,\dfrac{\square}{100}$
11. $1.424 = 1\dfrac{\square}{1000}$
12. $5.103 = \square\,\dfrac{\square}{1000}$

13. Find the missing numbers on this number line. Give your answers as fractions.

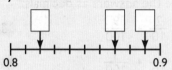

14. The mass of a piece of gold is 0.877 g. Write this mass as a fraction.

Set B

Write these as fractions:

1. 0.53
2. 0.390
3. 0.341
4. 0.874
5. 0.903
6. 0.007
7. 0.091

Write as mixed numbers:

8. 5.51
9. 8.08
10. 1.743
11. 3.246
12. 17.147
13. 28.914
14. 45.008

Find the missing numbers to complete these calculations:

15. $1.89 = 1.8 + \dfrac{\square}{100}$
16. $2.893 = 2 + \dfrac{\square}{1000}$
17. $1.008 = 1 + \dfrac{\square}{1000}$
18. $5.627 = 5.62 + \dfrac{\square}{1000}$
19. $1.213 = 1.013 + \dfrac{\square}{10}$

Set C

Write as mixed numbers:

1. 1.07
2. 9.471
3. 5.609
4. 9.003
5. 15.209
6. 25.031
7. 10.047

Find the missing numbers to complete these calculations:

8. $8.814 = 8 + \dfrac{\square}{1000}$
9. $2.547 = 2.5 + \dfrac{\square}{1000}$
10. $5.176 = 5.006 + \dfrac{\square}{100}$
11. $6.059 = 6 + \dfrac{3}{100} + \dfrac{\square}{1000}$
12. $3.307 = 3 + \dfrac{2}{10} + \dfrac{\square}{1000}$

Dan and Lina have a 200 m race. Lina finished 0.87 seconds after Dan. Write this time as a fraction with:

13. a denominator of 100
14. a denominator of 1000

Dan finished in 25.873 seconds.

15. Write this as a mixed number.

16. A lump of coal weighs 9.042 g. Write this as a mixed number.

I am confident writing decimals as fractions.

Write as a decimal:

1. $\dfrac{43}{100}$
2. $\dfrac{7}{100}$
3. $\dfrac{184}{1000}$
4. $\dfrac{475}{1000}$
5. $\dfrac{89}{1000}$
6. $\dfrac{7}{1000}$
7. $1\dfrac{88}{100}$
8. $2\dfrac{743}{1000}$
9. $7\dfrac{54}{1000}$
10. $23\dfrac{4}{1000}$

Write the answers as decimals:

11. $\dfrac{2}{10} + \dfrac{9}{100}$
12. $\dfrac{1}{10} + \dfrac{3}{100}$
13. $\dfrac{2}{10} + \dfrac{5}{100} + \dfrac{8}{1000}$
14. $\dfrac{7}{10} + \dfrac{6}{100} + \dfrac{7}{1000}$
15. $\dfrac{6}{100} + \dfrac{3}{1000}$
16. $\dfrac{8}{10} + \dfrac{2}{1000}$
17. $\dfrac{4}{10} + \dfrac{47}{1000}$
18. $\dfrac{2}{10} + \dfrac{19}{100}$
19. $\dfrac{5}{100} + \dfrac{32}{1000}$
20. $\dfrac{7}{10} + \dfrac{211}{1000}$

21. count forward 6 steps of 0.01 from 0
22. count forward 5 steps of 0.001 from 1
23. count back 8 steps of 0.001 from 9
24. count forward 2 steps of 0.02 from 0.241
25. count forward 5 steps of 0.003 from 2.542
26. count back 7 steps of 0.004 from 5.487

Find the missing numbers in these sequences:

27. 0.3   0.6   0.9   ☐ ☐
28. 3.5   3.0   2.5   ☐ ☐
29. 2.8   3.5   4.2   ☐ ☐
30. 7.2   6.0   4.8   ☐ ☐

Work out:

31. 6 + 0.3
32. 4 − 0.6
33. 0.2 + 0.5
34. 8.5 − 0.3
35. 9 − 1.8
36. 3.8 + 1.4
37. 9.2 − 4.5
38. 4.24 + 3.5

Write as a fraction:

39. 0.4
40. 0.7
41. 0.8
42. 0.17
43. 0.71
44. 0.97
45. 0.01
46. 0.09

Write as mixed numbers:

47. 2.3
48. 6.7
49. 1.13
50. 12.11
51. 28.01
52. 47.03

Find the missing numbers to complete these calculations:

53. $0.57 = 0.5 + \dfrac{\boxed{}}{100}$
54. $0.73 = \dfrac{\boxed{}}{10} + 0.03$
55. $0.49 = \dfrac{\boxed{}}{10} + \dfrac{9}{100}$
56. $7.29 = 7 + \dfrac{\boxed{}}{100}$
57. $3.65 = 3 + \dfrac{4}{10} + \dfrac{\boxed{}}{100}$

Write as a fraction:

58. 0.453
59. 0.789
60. 0.805
61. 0.230
62. 0.009
63. 0.054

Write as mixed numbers:

64. 1.323
65. 2.717
66. 8.401
67. 14.849
68. 21.007
69. 54.011

Find the missing numbers to complete these calculations:

70. $1.572 = 1 + \dfrac{\boxed{}}{1000}$
71. $8.735 = 8.73 + \dfrac{\boxed{}}{1000}$
72. $5.291 = 5.091 + \dfrac{\boxed{}}{10}$
73. $2.409 = 2.209 + \dfrac{\boxed{}}{10}$
74. $9.654 = 9 + \dfrac{6}{10} + \dfrac{\boxed{}}{1000}$

Fractions and decimals can be tricky, so if you got through those questions you're doing great!

Rounding Decimals — 1

You can use the rounding skills you already have to help you round decimals to the nearest whole number. Just look at the tenths digit — if it's less than 5 then round down, otherwise round up.

Examples

Round 32.43 to the nearest whole number.

32.43 is between 32 and 33.

The tenths digit is 4, so round down to **32**.

Charlotte's suitcase weighed 15.56 kg. What is this weight to the nearest kg?

15.56 is between 15 and 16.

The tenths digit is 5, so round up to **16 kg**.

Set A

Round these decimals to the nearest whole number:

1. 2.4
2. 5.7
3. 0.57
4. 1.38
5. 3.79
6. 6.52

7. Round each of these decimals to the nearest whole number.

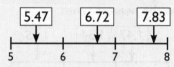

8. Which numbers in the box below round to 1 to the nearest whole number?

| 0.62 | 0.30 | 1.53 | 1.93 | 0.91 |

The lengths of some pieces of string are shown below. Round each length to the nearest cm:

9. 0.8 cm
10. 3.4 cm
11. 5.90 cm
12. 4.45 cm
13. 1.67 cm
14. 6.50 cm

Set B

Round these decimals to the nearest whole number:

1. 3.45
2. 9.74
3. 11.07
4. 23.51
5. 54.15
6. 89.88

Find the decimal in each box that rounds to a different whole number than the others:

7. | 8.75 | 9.45 | 8.49 |
8. | 12.57 | 12.97 | 13.56 |
9. | 54.15 | 55.21 | 55.49 |
10. | 87.12 | 87.49 | 87.52 |

Joe records the distance he cycles each day in this table:

Mon	Tues	Wed
8.47 km	17.29 km	29.85 km

To the nearest km, how far did he cycle on:

11. Monday?
12. Tuesday?
13. Wednesday?

Set C

Round these decimals to the nearest whole number:

1. 8.55
2. 16.83
3. 32.41
4. 108.54
5. 672.44
6. 499.87

The prices of some smartphones are shown below. Round each price to the nearest £.

7. Phone A: £96.29
8. Phone B: £160.85
9. Phone C: £299.49
10. Phone D: £305.50
11. Phone E: £489.99

Round each number to the nearest whole number to estimate the answers to these calculations:

12. 7.65 + 9.21
13. 14.74 − 6.55
14. 105.78 − 4.34
15. 321.57 + 599.57
16. 7.53 × 8.1

I can round decimals to the nearest whole number.

Rounding Decimals — 2

You need to be able to round decimals to the nearest tenth too — this time you look at the hundredths digit. If it's less than 5 then round down, if it's 5 or more then round up.

Examples

Round 65.42 to the nearest tenth.

> 65.42 is between 65.4 and 65.5
>
> The hundredths digit is 2,
> so round down to **65.4**

Tyson ran a 100 m race in 14.57 seconds. What was his time to one decimal place?

> 14.57 is between 14.5 and 14.6
>
> The hundredths digit is 7,
> so round up to **14.6 seconds**.

Rounding to one decimal place is the same as rounding to the nearest tenth.

Set A

Round these decimals to one decimal place:

1. 0.42
2. 0.54
3. 0.68
4. 0.15
5. 1.62
6. 3.39

7. Round each of these decimals to the nearest tenth.

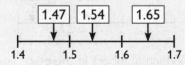

True or False?

8. 3.19 is 3.2 to the nearest tenth
9. 1.35 is 1.3 to the nearest tenth

Round these prices to the nearest 10p:

10. £0.87
11. £1.46
12. £1.82
13. £2.55
14. £3.33
15. £5.94

Set B

Round these decimals to one decimal place:

1. 0.22
2. 4.67
3. 8.44
4. 14.35
5. 36.18
6. 87.61

The weights of some garden furniture are shown below. Round each weight to one decimal place.

7. Chair: 9.48 kg
8. Hammock: 17.08 kg
9. Sun lounger: 22.65 kg
10. Table: 41.43 kg
11. Parasol: 63.84 kg

Here are times from a race:

Lane 1	28.58 seconds
Lane 2	29.94 seconds
Lane 3	29.03 seconds

To the nearest tenth of a second, what time was recorded in:

12. Lane 1?
13. Lane 2?
14. Lane 3?

Set C

Round these decimals to one decimal place:

1. 7.68
2. 47.85
3. 84.02
4. 73.05
5. 62.98
6. 89.95

Find the decimal in each box that rounds to a different number to the nearest tenth:

7. 0.75   0.65   0.72
8. 9.98   10.04   9.93
9. 19.26   19.21   19.33
10. 49.97   50.14   50.05

Estimate the answers to these calculations by rounding each number to one decimal place:

11. 3.55 + 2.29
12. 9.83 − 4.28
13. 15.75 + 2.98
14. 22.45 + 10.15
15. 32.51 − 20.04

I can round decimals to the nearest tenth.

Ordering Decimals

Now it's time to get some practice ordering decimals with up to three decimal places. As always, just compare the digits from left to right.

Example

Put these decimals in order, starting with the smallest.

8.457   8.688   8.524   8.599   ← All the numbers have 8 ones.

8.457   8.688   8.524   8.599   ← Look at the tenths: 4 is the smallest and 6 is the largest.
So 8.457 is the smallest and 8.688 is the largest.

8.524   8.599   ← Look at the hundredths: 2 is smaller than 9.
So 8.524 is smaller than 8.599

So the correct order is: **8.457   8.524   8.599   8.688**

Set A

Which decimal is bigger:

1. 1.85 or 1.93?
2. 2.53 or 2.55?
3. 3.87 or 3.78?
4. 5.48 or 5.45?
5. 7.842 or 7.538?
6. 4.561 or 7.558?

7. Look at this number line.

```
├────────┼────────┤
1.42     1.43     1.44
```

Which of the numbers in this box will lie on the number line above?

1.442	1.431	1.412
1.454	1.425	1.439

Put these decimals in order, starting with the smallest:

8. | 0.47 | 0.59 | 0.49 |
9. | 9.82 | 8.85 | 9.88 |
10. | 4.262 | 4.357 | 4.255 |
11. | 7.994 | 7.948 | 7.950 |

Set B

Which symbol (< or >) should go in each box?

1. 0.25 ☐ 0.28
2. 8.44 ☐ 8.45
3. 7.395 ☐ 7.299
4. 9.147 ☐ 9.138
5. 5.402 ☐ 5.408
6. 6.112 ☐ 6.15

What is the largest number with two decimal places:

7. between 13.1 and 13.4?
8. between 29.3 and 29.8?

What is the smallest number with three decimal places:

9. between 13.12 and 13.13?
10. between 8.8 and 8.9?

Put these decimals in order, starting with the largest:

11. | 0.337 | 0.373 | 0.733 |
12. | 4.872 | 4.8 | 4.806 |
13. | 9.88 | 9.879 | 9.893 |
14. | 2.051 | 2.05 |
    | 2.008 | 2.115 |

Set C

Which decimal is the biggest?

1. 7.63, 7.68 or 7.65?
2. 1.89, 1.84 or 1.8?
3. 1.315, 1.457 or 1.448?
4. 7.405, 7.54 or 7.450?
5. 3.48, 3.477 or 3.472?
6. 5.844, 5.8 or 5.85?

Put these decimals in order, starting with the smallest:

7. | 0.89 | 0.885 | 0.902 |
8. | 2.5 | 2.508 | 2.485 | 2.55 |
9. | 9.472 | 9.47 | 9.55 | 9.04 |
10. | 5.811 | 5.808 | 5.8 | 5.81 |

A gymnast got these scores in four different gymnastics events.

Rings	9.699
Floor	9.68
Bar	9.685
Vault	9.689

In which event did they get:

11. a score between 9.69 and 9.7?
12. their lowest score?
13. their second highest score?

I can compare and order decimals.

Solving Problems with Decimals

Now let's see how you use all those decimal skills to solve problems. The examples below
will guide you through a few of the different question types that you might see.

Examples

The table on the right shows the heights and weights of some horses in a stable.

Who is the heaviest horse in the stable?

385.45 kg is the largest weight so **Venus** is the heaviest horse.

Name	Height (m)	Weight (kg)
Bullet	1.457	332.56
Muddle	1.846	380.89
Beauty	1.153	270.43
Patch	1.549	295.02
Shelly	1.62	340.65
Venus	1.68	385.45

Write Beauty's height as a mixed number.

$1.153 \text{ m} = 1 + 0.153 = \mathbf{1\frac{153}{1000}} \textbf{ m}$

What is Bullet's weight to the nearest whole kg?

Bullet's weight is 332.56 kg, which is between 332 kg and 333 kg.
The tenths digit is 5, so round up to **333 kg**.

What is Shelly's height to one decimal place?

Shelly's height is 1.62 m, which is between 1.6 m and 1.7 m.
The hundredths digit is 2, so round down to **1.6 m**.

Set A

Freda has a bowl with 0.3 kg of cake mix in it.
She also has some 0.5 kg packs of cake mix.
How much cake mix will be in the bowl if she:

1   adds one pack to the bowl?

2   adds three packs to the bowl?

The volume of water in three jugs is shown below.

Jug A	Jug B	Jug C
0.54 litres	0.57 litres	0.5 litres

3   Put the jugs in order, starting with the jug
that has the greatest volume of water.

4   Write the volume of water in jug B as a fraction.

5   0.3 litres of water are poured out of jug C.
How much water is in that jug now?

The temperature in the garden was 4 °C.
It was 0.8 °C warmer in the shed.
How warm was it in the shed?

6   Give your answer as a decimal.

7   Give your answer as a mixed number.

Lukas drives 8.56 km to the airport.
How far is this rounded to:

8   the nearest km?

9   one decimal place?

Jules measures the widths of her furniture.
Her drawers are 0.65 m wide
and her chair is $\frac{673}{1000}$ m wide.

10   Which is wider, her drawers or her chair?

11   What is the width of her drawers
to the nearest metre?

12   Edwin has £3.40 and Dennis has £4.20.
How much do they have in total to the
nearest pound?

13   Stan uses $\frac{4}{100}$ of a ribbon to wrap a
present and $\frac{3}{1000}$ to decorate a card.
How much of the ribbon has he used?
Give your answer as a decimal.

Felix has a grey rock and a brown rock in his garden. The grey rock has a mass of 3.1 kg and the brown rock is 0.3 kg heavier.

1. What is the mass of the brown rock?

2. What is the total mass of the two rocks?

3. A digital thermometer records the temperature of a pan of water as 47.54 °C. What is this temperature to one decimal place?

The exact lengths of coloured drawing pins are shown in the table below.

Colour	Length
Red	1.887 mm
Blue	1.893 mm
Green	1.885 mm
Yellow	1.89 mm

4. Which drawing pin is the longest?

5. What is the difference in lengths between the yellow and blue drawing pins?

Sam has 4.3 ml of eye drops left. Each drop is 0.2 ml. How much will be left if she uses:

6. 2 drops?

7. 6 drops?

8. The four judges in a dancing competition gave Rebecca these scores:

6.124	6.1	6.142	6.13

Put the scores in order, starting with her lowest score.

Celia finished a race in 8.51 seconds. Priya finished $\frac{7}{1000}$ of a second after Celia.

9. What was Priya's time?

10. What was Celia's time to the nearest second?

11. A restaurant has $3\frac{4}{1000}$ litres of olive oil and 3.04 litres of sunflower oil. The chef says, "we have the same amount of each oil." Is he correct? Explain your answer.

The results of a diving competition are shown in the table below.

Diver	Maddy	Tom	Steph
Points	232.75	233.85	233.2

1. Which diver got the most points?

2. The points are rounded to the nearest whole number. Which two divers have the same points when rounded?

3. A printer takes 6.7 seconds to print the first page and 1.2 seconds to print each page after that. How many seconds does it take to print the first four pages?

1.55 litres of orange juice, $1\frac{475}{1000}$ litres of pineapple juice and 1.45 litres of lemonade are mixed together to make some punch.

4. How many litres of orange juice are used, to the nearest one decimal place?

5. How much more pineapple juice than lemonade is in the punch? Give your answer as a decimal.

6. Simon cycled 7.45 km on Monday and 4.39 km on Tuesday. Round each distance to the nearest tenth of a km and estimate the total distance he cycled.

A lumberjack recorded the thickness of three tree branches in this table.

Branch A	Branch B	Branch C
8.714 cm	8.72 cm	8.719 cm

7. Put the branches in order, starting with the thinnest branch.

What is the difference in thickness between:

8. branch A and branch C?

9. branch B and branch A?

The mass of a battery is 28 grams to the nearest whole gram. What is the heaviest the battery could be:

10. to one decimal place?

11. to two decimal places?

I can solve problems with decimals up to three decimal places.

Fractions, Decimals and Percentages — Review 4

Round these decimals to the nearest whole number:

1 0.6

2 3.5

3 0.38

4 1.73

5 5.49

6 9.57

7 12.34

8 21.09

9 59.62

10 99.51

11 124.43

12 489.67

The weights of some bags of fruit are shown below. Round each weight to the nearest kg.

13 0.9 kg

14 2.5 kg

15 0.87 kg

16 1.27 kg

17 2.86 kg

18 5.50 kg

Estimate the answers to these calculations by rounding each number to the nearest whole number:

19 0.8 + 1.9

20 4.2 − 3.1

21 14.47 − 6.76

22 97.57 + 8.09

23 6.15 × 9.87

Round these decimals to one decimal place:

24 0.37

25 0.51

26 0.89

27 0.06

28 1.54

29 3.23

30 9.77

31 12.65

32 26.84

33 55.03

34 87.95

35 49.99

Find the decimal in each box that rounds to a different number to the nearest tenth:

36 0.87   0.95   0.93

37 5.68   5.66   5.64

38 15.09   15.15   15.13

39 30.05   29.99   30.01

Which symbol (< or >) should go in each box?

40 0.45 ☐ 0.49

41 2.89 ☐ 2.98

42 0.574 ☐ 0.575

43 3.513 ☐ 3.521

44 9.547 ☐ 9.54

45 4.855 ☐ 4.86

46 6.005 ☐ 6.011

47 7.301 ☐ 7.31

Put these decimals in order, starting with the smallest:

48 0.24   0.34   0.29

49 2.54   2.59   2.5

50 3.849   3.847   3.834   3.836

51 4.225   4.252   4.22   4.25

52 9.05   9.009   9.1   9.062

The weights of four parcels are shown in this table:

Parcel A	Parcel B	Parcel C	Parcel D
1.075 kg	1.12 kg	1.054 kg	1.09 kg

53 Which parcel is the lightest?

54 Which parcels weigh more than 1.06 kg?

Zeb has 5.5 litres of apple juice in a jug.
He also has some glasses that can hold 0.3 litres each.
How much apple juice is left in the jug if he fills:

55 one glass?

56 three glasses?

57 ten glasses?

Jan's garden is 9.87 m long.
Kerry's garden is $\frac{9}{1000}$ m longer than Jan's.

58 How long is Kerry's garden? Give your answer as a decimal.

59 What is the length of Jan's garden to the nearest metre?

60 Padma has £14.78 in her pocket and £34.76 in her purse. Round each number to the nearest pound to estimate how much money she has in total.

Decimals are no piece of cake but if you got through that lot you've cracked it!

Percentages

Per cent (or %) just means 'out of 100'. So the total amount of something is 100%.

Examples

What percentage of the grid below is shaded?

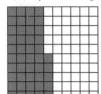

45 out of 100 squares are shaded.

So $\frac{45}{100}$ = **45%** is shaded.

Paula has completed 70% of a race. What percentage of the race has she got left?

100% − 70% = **30%**

The whole race is 100%.

Set A

The grid below is divided into 100 squares. Write the percentage of the grid that each of these shapes takes up:

1. A
2. B
3. C
4. D
5. E

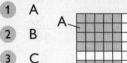

On a grid of 100 squares, how many squares are shaded if:

6. 30% is shaded?
7. 55% is shaded?
8. 80% is shaded?
9. Alex is painting a wall. He painted 15% yesterday and 30% today. What percentage of the wall is painted?

10. Patricia has eaten 35% of a packet of biscuits. What percentage of the packet of biscuits is left?

There are 100 cars parked along a road. 55 of them are red. What percentage of them are:

11. red?
12. not red?

Set B

The grid below is divided into 100 squares. Write the percentage of the grid that each of these shapes takes up:

1. A
2. B
3. C
4. D
5. E

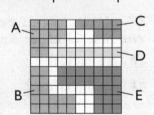

6. Eddie uses 52% of a tube of glue. What percentage of the tube of glue is left?

There are 100 children in Year 5. 43 of them are boys. What percentage of them are:

7. boys?
8. girls?

Paper clips come in boxes of 100. In one box, 25 are green, 48 are blue and 27 are yellow. What percentage of them are:

9. green?
10. yellow or blue?
11. Another box contains 61 pink paper clips. What percentage are not pink?

Set C

What percentages of these grids are shaded?

1.
2.
3.
4.

Nardev has mixed 100 g of ingredients together:

flour 31 g	butter 30 g
eggs 12 g	sugar 27 g

What percentage of the mixture is made up from:

5. flour
6. butter and eggs
7. sugar, flour and eggs

8. Una completed 32% of a video game in June and 43% in July. How much does she have left?

9. A shop sold 100 pens. Half the pens were blue, 18 pens were black and the rest were red. What percentage of the pens sold were red?

I understand and can use percentages.

Fractions, Decimals and Percentages — 1

To write percentages as fractions, just put the percentage as the numerator and 100 as the denominator.
To write percentages as decimals, all you have to do is divide by 100.

Examples

Write 9% as a decimal.

$$9\% = 9 \div 100 = \mathbf{0.09}$$

Yusuf got 60% of the marks on his science test.
What fraction of the marks did he get?

$$60\% = \frac{60}{100} \text{ or } \frac{6}{10} \text{ or } \frac{3}{5}$$

Set A

Write these percentages as fractions with a denominator of 100.

1   10%
2   30%
3   50%
4   15%
5   75%
6   95%

Write these percentages as decimals:

7   10%
8   25%
9   45%
10   70%
11   90%
12   82%

13   Match each percentage to an equivalent amount.

100%	$\frac{80}{100}$
40%	0.35
35%	1
20%	$\frac{20}{100}$
80%	0.4

Set B

Find the missing numbers to write these percentages as fractions:

1   $17\% = \dfrac{\square}{100}$

2   $61\% = \dfrac{\square}{100}$

3   $94\% = \dfrac{\square}{100} = \dfrac{\square}{50}$

4   $70\% = \dfrac{\square}{100} = \dfrac{\square}{10}$

5   $20\% = \dfrac{\square}{100} = \dfrac{\square}{5}$

Are the following statements true or false?

6   $10\% = 0.1$

7   $90\% = \dfrac{9}{100}$

8   $45\% = 0.54$

9   $70\% = 0.07$

10   $25\% = \dfrac{1}{4}$

11   $8\% = 0.8$

12   Find the equivalent fractions and decimals in this table:

Percentage	35%	48%	78%
Fraction			
Decimal			

39% of Lola's jumpers are knitted. What fraction of her jumpers:

13   are knitted?

14   are not knitted?

Set C

Find the missing numbers to write these percentages as fractions:

1   $37\% = \dfrac{\square}{100}$

2   $90\% = \dfrac{\square}{10}$

3   $38\% = \dfrac{\square}{50}$

4   $60\% = \dfrac{\square}{5}$

5   $80\% = \dfrac{\square}{5}$

Are the following statements true or false?

6   $4\% = 0.04$

7   $97\% = \dfrac{97}{100}$

8   $23\% = 2.3$

9   $58\% = \dfrac{27}{50}$

10   $84\% = 0.84$

11   $15\% = \dfrac{3}{20}$

12   Nev's hamster has eaten 34% of its food. Nev says, "My hamster has eaten $\frac{17}{50}$ of its food." Is he correct? Explain your answer.

13   Nadya has 1 m of string. She uses 43% to tie up a parcel and 0.4 m to hang a picture frame. How many metres of string does she have left?

I can convert from percentages to fractions and decimals.

Fractions, Decimals and Percentages — 2

To write fractions as percentages, make sure the fraction has 100 on the bottom —
the number on top is the percentage. To write decimals as percentages, just multiply by 100.

Examples

Write 0.63 as a percentage.

$0.63 \times 100 = \mathbf{63\%}$

Holly has eaten $\frac{7}{10}$ of a carrot.
What percentage of the carrot has she eaten?

Find an equivalent fraction
with 100 as the denominator. $\frac{7}{10} \rightarrow \frac{70}{100} = \mathbf{70\%}$

Set A

Write these decimals
as percentages:

1. 0.25
2. 0.45
3. 0.75
4. 0.95
5. 0.50
6. 0.80

Are the following
statements true or false?

7. $\frac{15}{100} = 5\%$
8. $\frac{35}{100} = 35\%$
9. $\frac{40}{100} = 40\%$
10. $\frac{6}{10} = 65\%$
11. $\frac{9}{10} = 9\%$

Ida had a 1 kg block of cheese.
She used $\frac{7}{100}$ to make some scones.

12. What percentage of the block
did she use for scones?

She used 0.15 kg of the 1 kg block
to make some cheese sauce.

13. What percentage of the
block did she use to make
the cheese sauce?

Set B

Write these decimals
as percentages:

1. 0.12
2. 0.29
3. 0.34
4. 0.55
5. 0.01
6. 0.9

Write these fractions
as percentages:

7. $\frac{27}{100}$
8. $\frac{56}{100}$
9. $\frac{4}{10}$
10. $\frac{1}{2}$
11. $\frac{1}{4}$

The visitors to a zoo voted
for their favourite animal.

$\frac{1}{5}$ of the visitors voted for the rhino.

12. What percentage of the
visitors voted for the rhino?

Twice as many visitors voted
for the lion as the rhino.

13. What percentage of the
visitors voted for the lion?

Set C

Write these decimals
as percentages:

1. 0.65
2. 0.42
3. 0.03
4. 0.09
5. 0.6
6. 0.8

Which is the correct
percentage:

7. $\frac{16}{100} = 16\%$ or 6%?
8. $\frac{3}{10} = 3\%$ or 30%?
9. $\frac{1}{2} = 50\%$ or 20%?
10. $\frac{3}{4} = 75\%$ or 25%?
11. $\frac{4}{5} = 60\%$ or 80%?

12. $\frac{7}{20}$ of Lizzi's friends have
a brother or a sister.
What percentage is this?

Eli got some money for his birthday.
He spent $\frac{2}{5}$ of it and saved the rest.
What percentage of the money did he:

13. spend?
14. save?

I can convert from fractions and decimals to percentages.

Fraction, Decimal and Percentage Problems

These problems contain a mix of fractions, decimals and percentages — being able to quickly convert from one to another will help you a lot with these questions.

Examples

70% of the audience at a cinema are adults.

What fraction of the audience are children?

100% − 70% = 30% are children

$30\% = \dfrac{30}{100} = \dfrac{3}{10}$ are children.

Mrs Riley has a bag of sweets. Her daughter takes 20% of the sweets and her son takes $\dfrac{1}{4}$ of them.

What percentage of the sweets are left?

Her son takes $\dfrac{1}{4}$ = 25% of the sweets.

So she has 100% − 20% − 25% = **55% left**.

A lift is carrying 20 people. 30% of them are women.

How many women is the lift carrying?

$30\% = \dfrac{3}{10}$
$\dfrac{3}{10}$ of 20 = 20 ÷ 10 × 3

= 2 × 3 = **6 women**

There are 50 sheep in a field. 34 of them are black sheep.

What percentage of the sheep are black?

$\dfrac{34}{50}$ of the sheep are black.

$\dfrac{34}{50} = \dfrac{68}{100}$ = **68%** of the sheep are black.

Set A

Winston's garden is made up of 100 white paving stones. He replaces some of them with grass:

1. What percentage of his garden is now made up of grass?

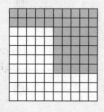

2. He wants to add a pond that will take up 25% of his garden. How many paving stones is this?

The ingredients to make 1 kg of fruit salad are shown on the right.

Apples	0.15 kg
Peaches	0.45 kg
Grapes	0.4 kg

What percentage of the fruit salad is made up of:

3. apples?

4. peaches?

5. grapes?

6. $\dfrac{60}{100}$ of the shoes in a shoe shop have laces. What percentage don't have laces?

Here are the percentages of each type of animal in the reptile house at a zoo:

- 50% lizards
- 27% snakes
- 18% tortoises
- 5% crocodiles

7. What fraction of the reptiles are snakes or tortoises?

8. What proportion of the reptiles are lizards or crocodiles? Write your answer as a decimal.

9. If there are 80 reptiles in total, how many are lizards?

Luca and Petra are playing a board game. The board is divided up into 10 squares and each person has their own coloured counters:

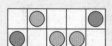

- Luca
- Petra

10. What percentage of the squares have Petra's counters on them?

11. Luca takes one of his counters off the board. What percentage of the squares don't have any counters on them?

The fraction of children in Year 5 with each hair colour are shown below:

- $\frac{5}{100}$ ginger
- $\frac{15}{100}$ blonde
- $\frac{60}{100}$ brown
- $\frac{20}{100}$ black

1. What percentage of the children have brown hair?

2. What percentage of the children have ginger or black hair?

3. $\frac{1}{4}$ of the children have short hair. What percentage of the children do not have short hair?

Terry buys a packet of 100 animal crackers.

4. Kim eats 35, Tom eats 20 and Terry eats the rest. What percentage of the animal crackers does Terry eat?

5. Terry also buys 10 cookies and gives 3 to Gio. What proportion of the cookies did he give to Gio? Give your answer as a decimal.

The pattern below is made up of plain, dotted and striped tiles. There are 50 tiles in total.

6. What percentage of the tiles are striped?

7. What percentage of the tiles are not plain?

Another pattern is 25% green, 10% blue, 5% black, and the rest is grey.

8. What proportion of this pattern is grey? Give your answer as a decimal.

Carrie's music shop displays CDs in boxes of 20.

9. She sells 10% of the CDs in one box. How many CDs is this?

10. She also sells 20% of another box. How many CDs has she sold in total?

11. Jo threw away $\frac{1}{10}$ of her toys and donated 35% of her toys to charity. What percentage of her toys does she have left?

1. A jug of lemonade is 39% full. What proportion of the jug is empty? Give your answer as a decimal.

Amelia has 35 plants in her greenhouse. The table shows the percentage of each plant.

2. How many of the plants are lettuces?

Lettuces	60%
Tomatoes	20%
Cucumbers	20%

3. In her garden she has 100 vegetable plants. 25% are cabbages and the rest are potatoes. How many potato plants are there?

Here are the ingredients to make a milkshake:

strawberries	milk
ice cream	raspberries

4. There is 15 ml of milk in 100 ml of milkshake. What percentage of the milkshake is not milk?

5. The milkshake is 74% fruit. If $\frac{6}{50}$ of the milkshake is raspberries, what fraction of the milkshake is strawberries?

6. At a football match, 37% of the fans are supporting the home side and $\frac{23}{100}$ are supporting the away side. The rest don't support either team. What percentage of the fans don't support either team?

A bathroom floor is made up of 20 tiles arranged in the pattern shown below.

What percentage of the tiles:

7. have a dot on them?

8. do not have a dot on them?

9. What proportion of the tiles have a cross on them? Give your answer as a decimal.

Lyndsey has 50 pairs of socks. 26 pairs are spotted, 9 pairs are striped and the rest are plain.

10. What percentage of the socks are plain?

11. Lyndsey loses 2 pairs of spotted socks and buys 2 pairs of striped socks. What percentage of her socks are now striped?

I can solve problems involving fractions, decimals and percentages.

What percentages of these grids are shaded?

  1

 2

  3

  4

  5

  6

A bricklayer is building a garden wall. He lays 32% of the bricks on Monday and 39% of the bricks on Tuesday.

7   What percentage of the bricks did he lay on Monday and Tuesday?

8   He finishes the wall on Wednesday. What percentage of the bricks did he lay on Wednesday?

Rory buys a box of 100 golf balls. 14 of the golf balls are orange, 19 are red and the rest are white.
What percentage of the golf balls are:

9   orange or red?

10 white?

11 not orange?

Find the missing numbers to write these percentages as fractions:

12 $19\% = \dfrac{\square}{100}$

13 $9\% = \dfrac{\square}{100}$

14 $10\% = \dfrac{\square}{100} = \dfrac{\square}{10}$

15 $30\% = \dfrac{\square}{100} = \dfrac{\square}{10}$

16 $40\% = \dfrac{\square}{100} = \dfrac{\square}{5}$

17 $14\% = \dfrac{\square}{100} = \dfrac{\square}{50}$

18 $12\% = \dfrac{\square}{100} = \dfrac{\square}{25}$

19 $55\% = \dfrac{\square}{100} = \dfrac{\square}{20}$

Write the percentages as decimals:

20 40%

21 60%

22 29%

23 72%

Clark has completed 57% of the puzzles in his puzzle book. What fraction of the puzzles has he:

24 completed?

25 not completed?

Write these decimals as percentages:

26 0.85

27 0.20

28 0.47

29 0.06

30 0.3

31 0.7

Write these fractions as percentages:

32 $\dfrac{15}{100}$

33 $\dfrac{78}{100}$

34 $\dfrac{6}{10}$

35 $\dfrac{9}{10}$

36 $\dfrac{65}{100}$

37 $\dfrac{8}{10}$

Cody counts the apples on the apple tree in his garden. He finds that there are 80 apples and 60% of them are ripe.

38 How many apples are ripe?

39 What fraction of the apples are not ripe?

There are 20 people watching a chess match.

40 7 of them are wearing glasses. What percentage of them are wearing glasses?

41 45% of the people are wearing trainers and $\dfrac{1}{5}$ are wearing sandals. What percentage of the people are not wearing trainers or sandals?

A 1 litre tropical drink is made up from water, mango juice and banana juice. The amounts of each liquid are shown in this table:

Water	0.25 litres
Mango Juice	0.6 litres
Banana Juice	0.15 litres

What percentage of the tropical drink is:

42 water?

43 water and banana juice?

44 not banana juice?

Well done for getting through that grisly lot — give yourself a pat on the back!

Fractions, Decimals and Percentages — Challenges

 1   A cafe gives each customer either $\frac{1}{5}$ of a carrot cake or $\frac{2}{9}$ of a cheesecake with their set lunch menu.

    a)   Copy and complete the table below to show the maximum amount of each cake the cafe would need for each number of customers. Give your answers as mixed numbers.

Number of customers	Carrot cakes	Cheesecakes
2	$\frac{2}{5}$	$\frac{4}{9}$
5		
7		
12		

    b)   One day, the cafe made 4 cheesecakes. 3 customers ordered cheesecake with their set lunch. How many cheesecakes do they have left? Give your answer as a mixed number.

    c)   Over a weekend, 90 customers ordered the set lunch menu.
$\frac{7}{10}$ ordered carrot cake and the rest ordered cheesecake.
Did the cafe serve more carrot cakes or cheesecakes that weekend?

 2   Farmer Jones is putting up a fence around his field. He has put five fence posts into the ground.
The proportion of each fence post that is sticking out of the ground is shown on the diagram below.

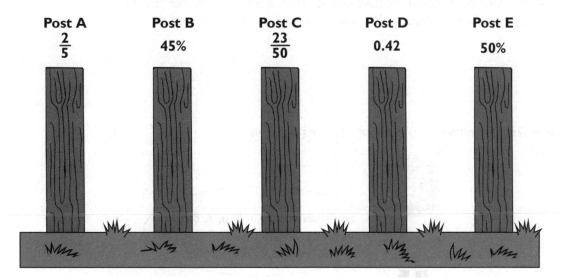

Post A $\frac{2}{5}$ **Post B** 45%   **Post C** $\frac{23}{50}$ **Post D** 0.42   **Post E** 50%

    a)   Which fence post is the longest?

    b)   Which fence post is the shortest?

    c)   Which fence post is the 2nd longest?

    d)   Make a diagram of your own fence posts and write the proportion that is sticking out of the ground. Give your diagram to a friend and see if they can find the longest and shortest fence posts.

3   Celeste has some musical note cards. They show the types of notes in her favourite song, and the fraction of a bar they take up. There are five types of card with different musical notes on them.

 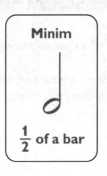   

Semibreve	Minim	Crotchet	Quaver	Semiquaver
1 bar	$\frac{1}{2}$ of a bar	$\frac{1}{4}$ of a bar	$\frac{1}{8}$ of a bar	$\frac{1}{16}$ of a bar

a)   Work out how many bars in the song each of these sets of cards would take up. Give any answers bigger than 1 as mixed numbers.

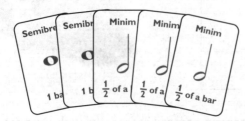   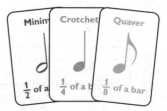

b)   Three bars of music from the song are shown below. Each bar should add up to 1. Which note needs to be added to each bar to complete it?

Bar 1   Bar 2   Bar 3

c)   Celeste picks out four notes from the song, totalling $\frac{5}{8}$ of a bar.

Which four notes could she have picked? There are two possible answers — can you find them both? You can use each note more than once.

4   Samir makes the following claim about rounding decimals.

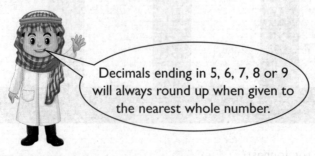

Decimals ending in 5, 6, 7, 8 or 9 will always round up when given to the nearest whole number.

a)   Find some examples to show that Samir is wrong.

b)   Rewrite Samir's statement so that it is correct.

c)   Write a similar statement about rounding decimals to the nearest one decimal place.

5   There are 60 children in Year 5 of Evermouth Primary School.
Mrs Watson asks all the children what their favourite colour is.
$\frac{3}{5}$ of the girls and 20% of the boys say purple. India and Tom have come to different results:

More girls than boys liked purple.

More boys than girls liked purple.

India   Tom

a)   There are 20 girls in Year 5. Who is correct, India or Tom?

b)   In Year 6, $\frac{1}{3}$ of the girls said purple was their favourite colour.
25% of the boys also chose purple. The same number of boys and girls chose purple.
There are 30 girls in Year 6. How many boys are there?

6   Some information about the colours of sweets inside this packet are shown below.

Fruity Chews

• $\frac{1}{3}$ of the sweets inside this pack are red.

• $\frac{1}{6}$ of the sweets inside this pack are green.

• $\frac{3}{8}$ of the sweets inside this pack are blue.

• The rest of the sweets are yellow.

a)   Gorka opens a packet and counts the sweets. He finds that there are 64 sweets in total.
Explain why the information on the packet must be wrong.

b)   What is the lowest amount of sweets that could be in the packet to make the information correct?

c)   What other amounts of sweets could be in the packet? Can you find a pattern?

Challenges complete — good job on giving them a go!

Metric Units — 1

Metric units include metres, grams and millilitres. Some units measure the same thing, e.g. centimetres and metres both measure distance. You need to be able to change between such units — this is called converting units.

Example

Convert 300 cm into m.

1 m = 100 cm
300 ÷ 100 = 3
So 300 cm = **3 m**

Convert 8300 g to kg.

1 kg = 1000 g
8300 ÷ 1000 = 8.3
So 8300 g = **8.3 kg**

Convert 2.35 litres into ml.

1 litre = 1000 ml
2.35 × 1000 = 2350
So 2.35 litres = **2350 ml**

Set A

Convert the following:

1. 5000 ml to litres
2. 4.6 kg to g
3. 6.7 m to cm
4. 320 mm to cm
5. 15 litres to ml
6. 9.8 km to m
7. 118 mm to cm

Find the missing values:

8. 25 litres = ☐ ml
9. 2300 m = ☐ km
10. 8.54 kg = ☐ g
11. 570 mm = ☐ cm
12. 1400 cm = ☐ m
13. 15 000 m = ☐ km
14. 405 mm = ☐ cm

True or false?

15. 43 m = 4300 cm
16. 6.5 km = 6500 cm
17. 2400 mm = 240 cm
18. 1100 cm = 1.1 m
19. 7700 g = 77 kg
20. 22 litres = 22 000 ml
21. 14 kg = 14 000 g

Set B

Convert the following:

1. 23 cm to m
2. 5.82 litres to ml
3. 12 000 g to kg
4. 6410 mm to cm
5. 3100 m to km
6. 5.72 cm to mm
7. 0.78 km to m

Find the missing values:

8. 8.96 kg = ☐ g
9. 23 400 m = ☐ km
10. 10 g = ☐ kg
11. 53 800 ml = ☐ litres
12. 1165 cm = ☐ m
13. 34.42 km = ☐ m
14. 240 m = ☐ km

Which is the largest measurement:

15. 3000 ml or 13 litres?
16. 4.1 kg or 4010 g?
17. 1.58 kg or 1550 g?
18. 1220 ml or 1.21 litres?
19. 21 km, 2100 m or 21 000 cm?
20. 3500 mm, 350 cm or 35 m?
21. 7.5 km, 75 000 m or 7500 cm?

Set C

Convert the following:

1. 3.41 kg to g
2. 8115 m to km
3. 41 900 cm to m
4. 16.7 cm to mm
5. 58 920 g to kg
6. 278 600 ml to litres
7. 523 mm to cm

Find the missing values and units:

8. 320 g = ☐ kg
9. 371 ☐ = 37.1 cm
10. 624.43 litres = ☐ ml
11. ☐ cm = 61.84 m
12. ☐ ml = 73.24 litres
13. 4750 ☐ = 4.75 km
14. 51 532 cm = ☐ m

Which is the largest measurement:

15. 0.7 litres, 70 ml or 750 ml?
16. 88 kg, 880 g or 8.8 kg?
17. 25 700 g, 2.6 kg or 26.6 kg?
18. 1000 mm, 1000 cm or 1 m?
19. 3.25 litres, 300 ml or 3300 ml?
20. 4461 mm, 446.1 cm or 44.61 m?
21. 5.5 km, 5555 m or 10 555 cm?

I can convert between different metric units.

Metric Units — 2

Remember that you need to convert all measurements to the same units if a question uses a mix of units.

Examples

A monkey weighs 8500 g.
What is its weight in kilograms?

1 kg = 1000 g
8500 ÷ 1000 = 8.5
So the monkey weighs **8.5 kg**.

Calculate 2.4 kg + 1300 g.
Give your answer in kg.

1 kg = 1000 g
1300 g = 1300 ÷ 1000 = 1.3 kg
2.4 kg + 1.3 kg = **3.7 kg**

Set A

1. Write the length shown below in centimetres.

2. Write the mass shown below in kilograms.

3. A rabbit weighs 1500 g. What is its weight in kg?

4. A mug contains 0.6 litres of tea. How much is this in ml?

5. A bungalow is 500 cm high. How high is this in m?

A flower is 120 mm tall.

6. How tall is it in cm?

7. How tall is it in m?

Look at the bottles below.

2.7 l   3100 ml

8. How much more does the orange bottle contain than the green one, in litres?

9. How much do the bottles contain in total, in litres?

Set B

1. A nail is 3.25 cm long. How long is this in mm?

2. A bath has 182 000 ml water inside. How much is this in litres?

3. A case weighs 17 290 g. How much is this in kg?

4. A road is 2710 m long. How long is this in km?

The chocolate cake weighs 0.6 kg. The vanilla cake weighs 200 g more.

5. How much does the vanilla cake weigh, in kilograms?

6. What is the total weight of the two cakes, in grams?

7. Harry has 450 ml of custard and uses 0.2 litres. How many ml of custard does he have left?

Find the missing values.

8. 5.5 kg + 3500 g = ☐ kg

9. 30 cm + 420 mm = ☐ cm

10. 550 mm − 35 cm = ☐ mm

11. 12 800 m − 4.2 km = ☐ km

12. 8.5 kg + 4150 g = ☐ g

13. 4250 ml + 9.75 litres = ☐ ml

14. 22.6 kg + 5400 g = ☐ kg

Set C

Look at the tables below.

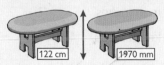

122 cm   1970 mm

1. What is the difference in height between the tables, in cm?

2. What would be the total height of a stack of 4 blue tables, in mm?

Look at the numbers below.

| 24 600 | 387 | 3.87 |
| 145 | 1450 | 24.6 |

Choose the correct number to fill each gap.

3. ☐ g = ☐ kg

4. ☐ cm = ☐ mm

5. ☐ cm = ☐ m

Find the missing values.

6. 0.05 kg + 16 700 g = ☐ kg

7. 28.9 litres − 6750 ml = ☐ ml

8. 18.25 km − 12 310 m = ☐ m

9. A candle is 94.5 mm when it is lit. It is 3.2 cm shorter after it has been blown out. How tall is it now, in cm?

I am confident converting between different metric units.

Imperial Units — 1

Imperial units are used less than metric units, but you've probably come across inches and feet before. It's still handy to know how to use them, so have a go at the questions below.

Example

You'll need these conversions for this page:
1 metre ≈ 3 feet   5 centimetres ≈ 2 inches

The '≈' sign means that the measurements are approximately equal.

A rabbit's ears are 15 cm long. Convert this length to inches.

5 cm ≈ 2 inches.
15 cm is 3 lots of 5 cm.
So 15 cm ≈ 3 × 2 inches = **6 inches**

Set A

Convert the following using approximations:

1. 2 metres to feet
2. 5 metres to feet
3. 9 metres to feet
4. 6 feet to metres
5. 12 feet to metres
6. 18 feet to metres

Find the missing values:

7. Convert 20 cm to inches.
   5 cm ≈ 2 inches
   20 cm is 4 lots of 5 cm.
   So 20 cm ≈ ☐ × 2 = ☐ inches

8. Convert 12 inches to cm.
   2 inches ≈ 5 cm
   12 inches is ☐ lots of 2 inches.
   So 12 inches ≈ ☐ × 5 = ☐ cm

Approximately:

9. how many inches is 10 cm?
10. how many inches is 25 cm?
11. how many cm is 10 inches?
12. how many cm is 16 inches?
13. House A is 8 m tall.
    House B is 27 feet tall.
    Which house is taller?

Set B

Convert the following using approximations:

1. 6 metres to feet
2. 13 metres to feet
3. 27 feet to metres
4. 33 feet to metres
5. 24 metres to feet
6. 45 feet to metres

Convert the following using approximations:

7. 30 centimetres to inches
8. 45 centimetres to inches
9. 80 centimetres to inches
10. 8 inches to centimetres
11. 14 inches to centimetres
12. 20 inches to centimetres

Which measurement is larger:

13. 20 m or 55 feet?
14. 44 inches or 100 cm?
15. 70 cm or 30 inches?
16. 100 inches or 300 cm?
17. A red rug is 55 cm wide.
    A blue rug is 28 inches wide.
    Which rug is wider?

Set C

Convert the following using approximations:

1. 25 metres to feet
2. 36 feet to metres
3. 40 cm to inches
4. 32 metres to feet
5. 66 feet to metres
6. 66 inches to cm

Which measurement is larger:

7. 93 feet or 32 m?
8. 100 cm or 36 inches?
9. 150 m or 400 feet?
10. 16 inches or 35 cm?
11. 210 m or 700 feet?
12. 80 inches or 240 cm?
13. 1212 feet or 360 m?

Approximate the following:

14. 0.5 m in inches
15. 0.4 km in feet
16. Fergus walked 1383 feet on Monday and 1.2 km on Tuesday.

    Approximate how much further Fergus walked on Tuesday than on Monday, in feet.

I understand and can use imperial units of length.

Imperial Units — 2

So you know your feet from your inches, but it's handy to know imperial units of mass and volume too. This page covers converting between metric units and pounds, ounces and pints.

Example

You'll need these conversions for this page:

1 kilogram ≈ 2 pounds
100 grams ≈ 4 ounces
1 litre ≈ 2 pints

A cauliflower has a mass of 500 g. Convert this mass to ounces.

100 g ≈ 4 ounces
500 g is 5 lots of 100 g.
So 500 g ≈ 5 × 4 ounces = **20 ounces**

Set A

Convert the following using approximations:

1. 5 kg to pounds
2. 15 kg to pounds
3. 24 pounds to kg
4. 8 litres to pints
5. 20 pints to litres
6. 32 pints to litres

Find the missing values:

7. Convert 200 g to ounces.
   100 g ≈ 4 ounces
   200 g is 2 lots of 100 g.
   So 200 g ≈ ☐ × 4 = ☐ ounces

8. Convert 12 ounces to g.
   4 ounces ≈ 100 g
   12 ounces is ☐ lots of 4 ounces.
   So 12 ounces ≈ ☐ × 100 = ☐ g

Approximately:

9. How many ounces is 400 g?
10. How many g is 24 ounces?

Jim has a small pond in his garden that has 90 litres of water inside.

11. How much is this in pints?

48 kg of rocks surround the pond.

12. How much is this in pounds?

Set B

Convert the following using approximations:

1. 35 kg to pounds
2. 44 litres to pints
3. 90 pounds to kg
4. 102 pints to litres
5. 85 litres to pints
6. 250 pounds to kg

Convert the following using approximations:

7. 600 grams to ounces
8. 800 grams to ounces
9. 28 ounces to grams
10. 900 grams to ounces
11. 40 ounces to grams
12. 56 ounces to grams

True or false?

13. 90 litres is less than 210 pints.
14. 200 kg is more than 450 pounds.
15. 1200 g is less than 50 ounces.

16. 126 litres of water fill a bath. How much is this in pints?

17. A recipe uses 350 g of sugar. How much is this in ounces?

Set C

Convert the following using approximations:

1. 55 kg to pounds
2. 700 g to ounces
3. 152 litres to pints
4. 410 pounds to kg
5. 84 ounces to grams
6. 120 ounces to grams

True or false?

7. 1600 g is more than 65 ounces
8. 510 pints is less than 240 litres
9. 230 kg is more than 450 pounds
10. 48 ounces is more than 1100 g
11. 125 pounds is more than 63 kg
12. 2000 g is less than 100 ounces
13. 118.5 litres is more than 205 pints

Approximate the following:

14. 2000 ml in pints
15. 1.5 kg in ounces
16. 9 pounds in grams

17. A cat weighs 180 ounces. A dog weighs 22 000 grams. Approximate how much _more_ the dog weighs, in ounces.

I understand and can use imperial units of mass and volume.

Measurement — Review 1

Convert the following:

(1) 7000 m to km

(2) 8 m to cm

(3) 3.5 km to m

(4) 9.37 kg to g

(5) 28.52 cm to mm

(6) 92 cm to m

(7) 7.42 litres to ml

(8) 610 mm to cm

(9) 986.24 m to cm

(10) 27 000 ml to litres

(11) 993 mm to cm

(12) 35 350 m to km

(13) 1950 g to kg

(14) 487 cm to m

Find the missing values and units:

(15) 31 kg = ⬚ g

(16) 3700 m = ⬚ km

(17) 781 ⬚ = 78.1 cm

Which measurement is largest:

(18) 1800 ml or 8.1 litres?

(19) 7 km, 8000 m or 9000 cm?

(20) 2.5 m, 25 cm or 250 mm?

Write the measurements shown below:

(21) in centimetres.

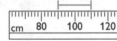

(23) in metres.

(22) in kilograms.

(24) in litres.

A little penguin is 290 mm tall.
An emperor penguin is 105 cm tall.

(25) Convert the little penguin's height into cm.

(26) Convert the emperor penguin's height into mm.

Find the missing values:

(27) 2400 m + 5.5 km = ⬚ km

(28) 12.3 cm + 324 mm = ⬚ mm

(29) 20.9 litres − 16 800 ml = ⬚ litres

Convert the following using approximations:

(30) 7 m to feet

(31) 9 feet to m

(32) 15 m to feet

(33) 30 feet to m

(34) 25 m to feet

(35) 99 feet to m

(36) 70 m to feet

(37) 20 cm to inches

(38) 4 inches to cm

(39) 50 cm to inches

(40) 16 inches to cm

(41) 60 cm to inches

(42) 80 inches to cm

(43) 125 cm to inches

(44) Gordon's new computer desk is 200 cm long. Approximately how long is his desk in inches?

Look at the lengths below.
Order them from shortest to longest.

(45) | 15 cm | 10 inches | 5 inches |

(46) | 5 km | 100 m | 50 feet |

(47) | 50 cm | 0.75 m | 12 inches |

Convert the following using approximations:

(48) 7 kg to pounds

(49) 12 litres to pints

(50) 64 pounds to kg

(51) 48 pints to litres

(52) 53 kg to pounds

(53) 120 pounds to kg

(54) 90 pints to litres

(55) 140 pounds to kg

(56) 50.5 kg to pounds

(57) 62.5 litres to pints

(58) 300 g to ounces

(59) 16 ounces to g

(60) 2100 g to ounces

(61) 48 ounces to g

(62) Jakob mixes 1 litre of ice cream and 4 litres of milk to make some milkshakes. Approximately how much milkshake does he have in pints?

Find the missing values:

(63) 22 litres + 13 pints ≈ ⬚ pints

(64) 30 kg + 24 pounds ≈ ⬚ pounds

(65) 700 g − 9 ounces ≈ ⬚ ounces

Phew, that was a lot of conversions — well done for getting through them!

Solving Problems with Length

You've got to grips with units, so now it's time to put your skills to the test.
For some of these length problems, you'll have to convert units to help you get the answer.

Example

A tree is 20 m tall.
It grows 150 cm each year.
How tall is the tree after five years?

150 cm × 5 = 750 cm = 7.5 m

The tree grows to 20 m + 7.5 m = **27.5 m**.

Set A

1. A paper clip is 2.7 cm long. A pencil case is ten times as long as the paper clip. How long is the pencil case? Give your answer in cm.

2. A worm travels 200 mm every minute. How many centimetres does the worm travel every minute?

Mo cuts a ribbon into two pieces. One piece is 70 cm long, the other is 1.2 m long.

3. How long was the ribbon to start with, in m?

Another ribbon is 6 m long. She cuts it into 3 pieces.

4. How long is each piece, in cm?

5. An athlete runs 1.5 km and swims 1800 m. How much further does she swim than run, in m?

6. A princess's hair is 110 cm long. A spell is cast and it grows four times as long. How long is the princess's hair now, in m?

Set B

1. A toy bus is 160 mm long. A toy car is a quarter the length of the toy bus. How long is the toy car, in mm?

2. A table is 750 mm long. It is extended by 24 cm. How long is the table now, in cm?

3. A bird takes off from the ground. It flies 720 m up then 0.5 km down. How high is the bird, in km?

4. Fred's blanket is 2.8 m long. It shrinks in the wash, and is now 18 cm shorter. How long is it now, in cm?

5. Tim has a plank which is 2 m long. He cuts off 0.5 m, then divides the rest of the plank into three equal pieces. How long is each piece, in cm?

6. A tower of cans is 0.6 m tall. There are 5 cans in the tower. How tall is each can? Give your answer in cm.

Set C

1. A frog hops 4 m. A toad hops 20% as far. In cm, how far does the toad hop?

2. Pam ran 4300 m. She dropped her keys after running 1.2 km. How far back does she have to run to get her keys, in m?

3. A bike race is four laps of a track. The race is 6 km long. How long is one lap, in m?

4. A string of sausages is 1160 mm long. A dog steals 34 cm of sausages. How long is the string that's left, in cm?

An eraser is 44 mm long.

5. How long would 5 erasers lined up be, in cm?

6. How many erasers fit on a line of 50 cm?

7. Pablo knits coloured squares with side length 20 cm. He sews them together to make a scarf that is 2.4 m long. How many squares does he make in total?

8. A plumber has 4.9 m of pipe. She cuts off 0.7 m, then divides the rest of the pipe into 4 equal pieces. How long is each piece of pipe, in cm?

I can solve problems involving length.

Solving Problems with Mass

Mass shouldn't cause you masses of problems — just read the questions carefully before answering.

Example

A deck of cards weighs 96 g.
A magician puts ten decks of cards in a bag.

What is the total mass of the cards in the bag?
Give your answer in kg.

96 g × 10 = 960 g
960 ÷ 1000 = 0.96 kg

The total mass of the cards in the bag is **0.96 kg**.

Set A

1. Kiera has 550 g of cheese. Joe has four times as much. How much cheese does Joe have, in grams?

2. Toby uses 125 g of butter, 300 g of oats and 175 g of sugar to make flapjack. What is the total mass of ingredients used, in kg?

3. Three pumpkins are weighed at a Halloween party.

Pumpkin A	2.8 kg
Pumpkin B	3.1 kg
Pumpkin C	3.4 kg

What is the difference between the heaviest and lightest pumpkin, in grams?

4. A bag of coins weighs 2 kg. The coins are evenly split into 4 smaller bags. What is the mass of each smaller bag, in grams?

5. Megan has 3 presents. They each weigh 250 g. What is the total mass of the presents, in kg?

Set B

1. A cow eats 12 kg of hay a day. It eats 25% of the hay in the morning. How many grams of hay does the cow eat in the morning?

2. Willow the rabbit weighs 2300 g. Toffee the rabbit weighs 2600 g. What is the total mass of the rabbits, in kg?

A box of 4 lettuces weighs 1.7 kg.
3. If the box weighs 300 g, what is the total mass of all of the lettuces, in grams?

4. How much does each lettuce weigh, in grams?

5. A basketball weighs 600 g. What is the mass of 4 basketballs, in kg?

6. An ostrich egg weighs 1.35 kg. What is the mass of two ostrich eggs, in grams?

7. Isla measures out 4.9 kg of pasta. She evenly divides it between 7 different dishes. How many grams of pasta is in each dish?

Set C

1. A TV weighs 14 kg. A laptop weighs one seventh as much as the TV. How much does the laptop weigh, in grams?

2. Two scooters have a combined weight of 5.5 kg. One weighs 500 g more than the other. What is the weight of each scooter, in grams?

3. "20 objects each with a mass of 0.2 kg weighs the same as 500 objects each with a mass of 10 g." Is this correct? Explain your answer.

4. A sloth weighs 8.82 kg. A koala weighs 4560 g more than the sloth. How much does the koala weigh, in kg?

5. Rudi can take 10 kg of luggage on a flight. His bag weighs 2.4 kg, and he puts an 800 g book in the bag. How many more kilograms can Rudi put in his bag?

6. Carl has a 250 g bag of sugar and a 0.65 kg bag of sugar. He shares all the sugar equally between 3 pots. How much is in each pot, in grams?

I can solve problems involving mass.

Solving Problems with Volume

Some problems about volume now — these questions are all about litres and millilitres.

Example

Eleanor has 1.3 litres of blue dye and 650 ml of red dye.

She mixes the two dyes together to make a purple dye. How much purple dye does she have, in litres?

Convert 650 ml to litres:
650 ml ÷ 1000 = 0.65 litres

Now add both litre values together:
1.3 + 0.65 = 1.95 litres

So Eleanor has **1.95 litres** of purple dye.

Set A

1) Aisling has 600 ml of cream. She puts a third of it in a trifle. How many ml of cream does she use?

2) A glass holds 0.3 litres. Ahmed pours 240 ml of water into the glass. How many more ml of water will fit in the glass?

3) Nicole buys two 0.2 litre bottles of glue for an art project. How much glue does she have, in ml?

Hayley records how much water her dog drinks.

Friday	280 ml
Saturday	0.4 litres
Sunday	320 ml

4) How much more does he drink on Saturday than on Friday, in ml?

5) What is the total over the three days, in litres?

6) One tin holds 0.5 litres of paint. Evan needs 2000 ml of paint in total. How many tins is this?

7) Gail buys three tins of peaches. She pours 150 ml of liquid out from each tin. How much liquid is this, in litres?

Set B

Some milkmaids collect milk one day:

Milkmaid	Milk Collected
Maggie	9 litres
Betty	7.4 litres
Dot	

1) Betty collected half as much as Dot. How much did Dot collect, in litres?

2) How much more milk did Maggie collect than Betty, in ml?

3) Karol shares 2.4 litres of water equally between 3 bowls to make jelly. How much water is in each bowl, in ml?

4) Erin has a 1.25 litre carton of apple juice. She drinks 275 ml.

How many ml of apple juice is left?

A witch's cauldron holds twelve times as much as a bottle. A bottle holds 1200 ml of potion.

5) How much potion can a cauldron hold, in litres?

A witch puts 4.8 litres of potion in bottles to sell.

6) How many bottles are needed in total?

Set C

1) Luna has 2 litres of soup. She eats 20% of it. How much soup is left over, in ml?

Johnny buys one 750 ml bottle of sauce and one 0.85 litre bottle of sauce.

2) What is the total amount, in ml?

3) He uses 290 ml of sauce from the second bottle. How much is left in that bottle, in litres?

4) A model village contains a 45 ml pond. The real pond has 2000 times as much water. How much water is in the real pond, in litres?

5) Alana pours three 0.83 litre bottles of cola into a jug. How much cola is there in total, in ml?

6) Ed has one 2 litre and two 1.5 litre bottles of water. He pours it all into cups so each has 250 ml of water. How many cups are there?

7) Mina buys 3.6 litres of paint. Mel buys one twelfth this amount. How much paint does Mel have, in ml?

I can solve problems involving volume.

Solving Problems with Money

Knowing how to figure out problems involving money is always useful — it's something that crops up a lot.

Example

Look at the advert for 'The Aquarium' on the right.

A group of eight children went to The Aquarium. How much did it cost them in total?

One child costs £1.15 = 115p

```
    1 1 5
  ×     8
    9 2 0
    1 4
```

920p = **£9.20**

The Aquarium
Open 9 am - 4 pm

Entry Prices
Adult: £3.70
Child: £1.15

Set A

1. Ursula has these six coins:

   | £1 50p 50p |
   | 10p 10p 5p |

   She buys a comic for £1.85. How much money does she have left?

2. Mishal buys 4 comics for £1.20 each. How much does she spend in total?

3. A pack of bow ties costs £1.40. There are 5 bow ties in a pack.

   What does one bow tie cost?

   A red hat costs £2.39 and a white hat costs £1.50.

4. What is the total cost of the two hats?

5. Iona has £3.05. How much more does she need to buy both hats?

6. Mason sells three CDs for £4.60 each. How much does he earn in total from selling the CDs?

7. Nathan earns £6.80 tidying his neighbour's garden. He gives £2.90 to his mum. How much does he keep?

Set B

Four tins of sweetcorn cost 92p. Five tins of beans cost £1.45.

1. How much does one tin of beans cost?

2. How much would 12 tins of sweetcorn cost?

3. A flying disc costs £11.49. Mika buys 4 discs.

   What is his total spend?

Look at the prices of rides at the fair:

Big wheel	£1.85
Dodgems	£1.25
Waltzers	?

4. Sam pays £4.05 to go on the big wheel and the waltzers. How much is a ride on the waltzers?

5. Jo goes on the big wheel twice and the dodgems three times. How much does she pay?

It costs £82.17 to hire a bouncy castle for 3 days.

6. What is the cost per day?

7. What would the cost be for 6 days?

8. 5 hats and 2 scarves cost £34. One scarf costs £4.50.

   What is the cost of one hat?

Set C

1. A cap costs £3.37. A T-shirt costs £4.61 more than a cap.

   Johan buys a cap and a T-shirt. What is the total cost?

2. Veronica buys a necklace for £9.50 and 2 identical rings. The total cost is £16.28. How much does 1 ring cost?

Marco buys 8 'Spooky Spiders' to stock in his shop. They each cost £10.43.

3. How much does he spend in total?

   He sells the 8 spiders for a total of £98.40.

4. How much does he sell each spider for?

5. Eve earns £8.25 an hour. How much will she earn in total if she works for 22 hours?

6. 4 rabbits cost the same amount as 7 guinea pigs. 1 rabbit costs £12.25. What is the cost of one guinea pig?

I can solve problems involving money.

Solving Problems with Time

Time can be a tricky thing, especially when you're converting from years to days or seconds to hours. Luckily, the next two pages will give you plenty of practice, so get stuck in.

Examples

Lucy went to see the dentist 3 times one year. Each visit lasted 10 minutes.

How many seconds did Lucy spend at the dentist that year?

Find the total number of minutes: 10 × 3 = 30 minutes.

60 seconds = 1 minute

So the total number of seconds is 30 × 60 = **1800**.

Flynn rode his bike every day for 128 days. How long is this in weeks and days?

There are 7 days in a week so divide by 7:

$$7\overline{)1\ ^12\ ^58}\quad \begin{array}{c}1\ 8\ r\ 2\end{array}$$

128 ÷ 7 = 18 remainder 2.
So 128 days is the same as **18 weeks and 2 days**.

Set A

Dennis took one and three-quarter minutes to run around a track.

1. How many seconds did it take him?

Francesca took 40 seconds longer than Dennis did to run around the track.

2. How long did it take her? Write your answer in minutes and seconds.

The table below shows how long three sports clubs open for each year:

Hockey	11 weeks
Basketball	14 weeks
Swimming	20 weeks
Volleyball	105 days

3. How many days does the hockey club open for?

4. How many more days is the basketball club open for than hockey?

5. How many days in a normal (not leap) year is the swimming club closed for?

6. How many weeks does the volleyball club open for?

7. A factory makes bars of soap non-stop for 6 days.

   How many hours is this?

8. It took Lena 2 minutes 30 seconds to do a wordsearch. It took Gary twice as long.

   How many minutes did it take Gary?

A website sells 7 books every second.

9. How many books does it sell in a minute?

The website also sells 4 TVs every hour.

10. How many TVs does it sell in a day?

11. Nikki started her morning run at the time on the clock. She finished her run at 7:40 am.

    Tim ran for three times as long as Nikki.

    How many hours did Tim run for?

12. Catriona went to stay with her uncle in New York for 69 days.

    How long is this in weeks and days?

Set B

Look at the table of circus classes below.

Class	Length of class
Juggling	80 minutes
Acrobatics	1 hour and 15 mins
Trapeze	135 minutes
Clowning	1 hour and 10 mins

1. Daisy goes to the juggling and clowning lessons. How many minutes is this in total?

2. The acrobatics class is made up of several activities. Each activity lasts 15 minutes. How many different activities are there?

3. Katya spends 210 minutes in classes. Which two classes does she go to?

The estimated time to finish a long distance boat race is 1 week and 2 days.

4. How many hours is this?

5. Nico starts this race in 98 days. How long is it until he starts, in weeks and days?

6. Daniel starts playing with his dog at the time on the right. They play for 180 seconds.

   What time do they finish playing?

7. It takes Mila a quarter of an hour to eat her breakfast every day. Over 8 days, how many hours does she spend eating breakfast?

8. It takes Nisha 8 minutes and 20 seconds to make a card. Hiran spends three times as long making a card.

   How many minutes did it take Hiran?

9. A snooker match lasted for 5 hours and 10 minutes. The players had two 20 minute breaks during the match. How many minutes were they playing snooker for?

10. Emilie went on a boat trip for 11 hours. She got off for 39 minutes to have lunch. How many minutes was she on the boat?

Set C

The table below shows the ages of three horses.

Frankie	5 years 4 months
Ginny	48 months
Stanley	84 months

1. How old is Ginny in years?

2. How much older is Frankie than Ginny? Write your answer in months.

3. How much older is Stanley than Ginny? Write your answer in years.

4. Pippa goes to a dance class for two hours. How many seconds is Pippa dancing for?

5. Charlie cycles 10 minutes to get to a shop. It takes him 9 minutes to cycle home. How many seconds was he cycling in total?

6. Caroline has an apple with her lunch for 298 days in a row. How long is this in weeks and days?

7. Vernon teaches a history lesson every week. It lasts three quarters of an hour. How many hours will Vernon have taught after 12 weeks?

8. Zara appeared on TV for 6 hours in June and 9 hours and 5 minutes in July. How many minutes was she on TV for in June and July in total?

A magician records how long she spends practising some tricks.

Card trick	3 days 12 hours
Escape act	120 hours
Disappearing act	240 hours
Fire-eating	1 day

9. How many more hours did she practise the escape act than the card trick?

10. How many days did she practise the disappearing act for?

11. How long did she spend practising fire-eating, in minutes?

I can solve problems involving time.

Measurement — Review 2

1. A flower grows 30 mm each week. How much does it grow in 5 weeks, in cm?

Matthew's hair is 4 cm long, Maya's hair is 0.3 m long and Alaia's hair is 0.18 m long.

2. How much longer is Maya's hair than Matthew's, in cm?

3. What is the total length of the three children's hair?

4. Angus cycles 3.3 km, then walks 415 m. How far does he travel in total, in km?

5. Sarah buys 400 g of apples, 250 g of oranges and 150 g of grapes at the market. What is the total mass of the fruit? Give your answer in kg.

6. Mike has 3 kg of paper. He splits it into 5 even piles. How much does each pile weigh, in g?

Jasmine weighs some of her books.

Dictionary	900 g
Textbook	0.35 kg
Atlas	650 g

7. How much more does the dictionary weigh than the textbook, in g?

8. How much do the books weigh in total, in kg?

9. How much would 4 atlases weigh in total, in kg?

10. Calum has four 350 ml bottles of vinegar. How much is this in litres?

11. Patrick makes 1.2 litres of gravy. He pours it into three equal jugs. How much gravy is in each jug, in ml?

Aimee buys 3 tins of paint. Each tin holds 2.3 litres.

12. How much paint does she have, in ml?

She uses 3840 ml of paint.

13. How much paint is left over, in litres?

14. A box of crisps costs £2.15. It contains 5 packets. How much is each packet of crisps?

15. Farah goes to a restaurant and has 3 courses. She spends £20.25. If the starter and dessert cost £4.25 each, how much was the main course?

16. A notepad costs £4.86. A set of colouring pencils costs £2.49 more than a notepad.

    What is the total cost of a notepad and a set of colouring pencils?

17. It took George 45 days to read a book. How long is this in weeks and days?

Look at the table below.

Cat	Age
Honey	8 and a half years
Roy	58 months

18. Write Roy's age in years and months.

19. What is the age difference between Honey and Roy, in months?

Howard leaves a wheel of cheese to ripen for 1 week and 3 days.

20. How many hours is this?

21. Dave leaves his cheese to ripen for five times as long as Howard's cheese. How long does Dave leave his cheese to ripen for, in weeks and days?

22. Jabari cooks some vegetables for 5 and a half minutes. He then adds some noodles and cooks it all for another 3 and a quarter minutes. How many seconds does he cook for in total?

23. Madeleine went swimming for an hour and a half. How many seconds was she swimming for?

24. Kelly draws for 5 and a half hours each week for three weeks. How many minutes does she spend drawing over the three weeks?

That was a lot of problems to get through — good going!

Perimeter

Perimeter is the distance around the outside of a shape. These pages are about shapes made up of squares and rectangles — you might need to do a bit of detective work to find missing lengths before working out the perimeter.

Examples

Calculate the perimeter of the shape below.

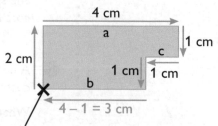

Find the missing length:
side b = side a − side c
= 4 cm − 1 cm = 3 cm

Pick a corner and go around the shape, adding the lengths of all the sides.

So the perimeter is:
2 + 4 + 1 + 1 + 1 + 3 = **12 cm**.

The rectangle below has a perimeter of 36 cm. Find the length of side c.

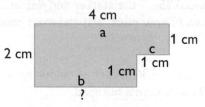

Perimeter = 36 cm

Opposite sides of a rectangle are equal, so the perimeter is:
c + 12 + c + 12 = 36
2c + 24 = 36
2c = 36 − 24 = 12
c = 12 ÷ 2
c = 6

So the length of side c = **6 cm**.

Set A

Find the perimeter of these shapes:

1
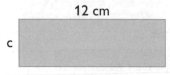

2
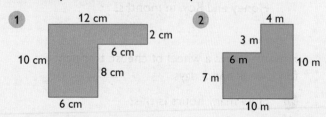

6 A square has a perimeter of 32 cm. What is the length of one side?

Use a ruler to measure the perimeter of the shapes below. Give your answers in cm.

3

4
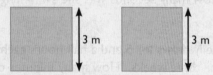

Look at the shapes below.

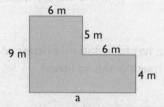

7 What is the length of side a?

8 What is the perimeter of the shape?

5 Two identical squares are shown below.

The squares are joined together to form a rectangle. What is the perimeter of the new shape?

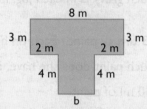

9 What is the length of side b?

10 What is the perimeter of the shape?

Set B

Measure the perimeter of the shapes below.
Give your answers in cm.

1
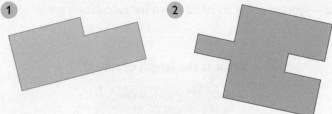

2
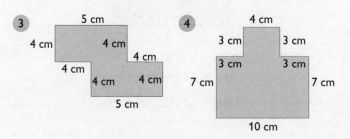

Work out the perimeter of these shapes:

3
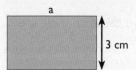
5 cm
4 cm   4 cm
4 cm
4 cm
4 cm   4 cm
5 cm

4
4 cm
3 cm   3 cm
3 cm   3 cm
7 cm   7 cm
10 cm

5 Look at the rectangle below.
It has a perimeter of 16 cm.

a
3 cm

What is the length of side a?

Look at shape X
on the right.

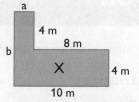
a
4 m
8 m
b
X   4 m
10 m

6 Work out the
lengths of sides
a and b.

7 What is the perimeter of shape X?

8 What is the perimeter of the shape below?

12 cm
3 cm
8 cm
12 cm
8 cm
3 cm

9 What is the perimeter of the shape below?

0.1 m
0.1 m
0.3 m
0.6 m   0.3 m
0.3 m
0.1 m
0.8 m

Set C

Work out the perimeter of the shapes below.

1
1 cm
4 cm
5 cm
5 cm
1 cm

2
1 m
1 m
3 m
3 m
1 m   1 m

3
25 cm
7 cm
12 cm   7 cm
5 cm
7 cm
5 cm

4
7 cm
2.5 cm
3 cm
5 cm
2.5 cm
5 cm

Work out the perimeter of the shapes below.
Give your answer in cm.

5
0.5 m
0.1 m
0.2 m
0.5 m
0.5 m
0.2 m

6
0.06 m
0.03 m   0.03 m
0.01 m   0.01 m
0.02 m   0.02 m

7 Measure the perimeter of this shape.
Give your answer in cm.

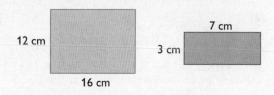

8 A rectangle has a perimeter of 19 cm.
The rectangle's length is 6 cm.
What is the width of the rectangle?

Two rectangles are shown below:

12 cm
16 cm
7 cm
3 cm

9 Sketch two shapes with different
perimeters that you could make by
joining the rectangles together.

10 What is the perimeter of each shape
you have made?

I can calculate the perimeter of shapes made up of rectangles.

Area — 1

You might want to brush up on your multiplication skills — you're going to need them for calculating areas.

Examples

Calculate the area of the rectangle below.

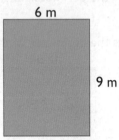

6 m

9 m

This rectangle's sides are 6 m and 9 m.
So the area = $9 \times 6 = $ **54 m²**. ←

The sides are measured in metres, so the area is in m² (metres squared).

What is the length of side a?

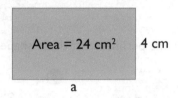

Area = 24 cm²   4 cm

a

Area = $a \times 4 = 24$
So $a = 24 \div 4 = 6$

Length of side a = **6 cm**

Calculate the area of the shape below.

2 cm

5 cm

3 cm

6 cm

Split the shape into two rectangles and calculate their areas.

2 cm

5 cm

$5 \times 2 = 10$ cm²

4 cm ←

3 cm

$4 \times 3 = 12$ cm²

You can work out the length of this side by subtracting the short side (2 cm) from the long side (6 cm).

Then add the two areas together to get the total area of the shape.

$10 + 12 = $ **22 cm²**

Set A

Work out the area of these shapes:

1 4 cm
10 cm

2 9 cm
7 cm

3 12 cm
5 cm

Work out the area of these squares:

4 3 cm

5 6 cm

6 8 cm

Work out the area of these shapes:

7 5 cm
5 cm

8 4 cm
4 cm
2 cm
2 cm

9 9 cm
3 cm
3 cm
7 cm

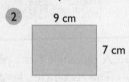

10 Copy the table below and fill in the missing values for squares of different lengths.

Length	Area
2 cm	4 cm²
4 cm	
	49 cm²

11 A square and rectangle are shown below. Which shape has the largest area?

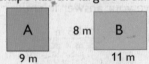

A   8 m   B

9 m   11 m

12 Look at the rectangle below. What is the length of side a?

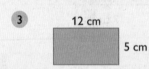

3 cm

Area = 6 cm²   a

Set B

Work out the area of these shapes:

1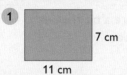
7 cm
11 cm

2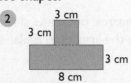
3 cm
3 cm
3 cm
8 cm

For each rectangle, identify the missing side:

3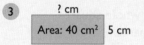
? cm
Area: 40 cm² 5 cm

5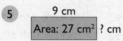
9 cm
Area: 27 cm² ? cm

4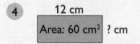
12 cm
Area: 60 cm² ? cm

6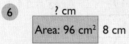
? cm
Area: 96 cm² 8 cm

Work out the area of the shapes below:

7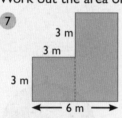
3 m
3 m
3 m
6 m

8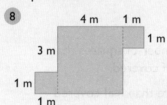
4 m 1 m
1 m
3 m
1 m
1 m

9 A smart phone screen has an area of 35 cm².

If the length of the screen is 7 cm, what is the width of the screen?

7 cm

10 Which of the shapes below has the smaller area?
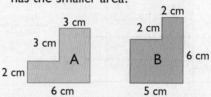
3 cm
3 cm
A
2 cm
6 cm

2 cm
2 cm
B
6 cm
5 cm

11 Harleen measures her laptop screen and a piece of paper. What is the difference between their areas?

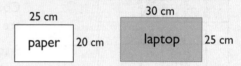
25 cm
paper 20 cm

30 cm
laptop 25 cm

Set C

Each rectangle below has an area of 48 cm². Work out the missing value:

1
?
6 cm

2
4 cm
?

3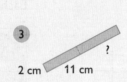
?
2 cm 11 cm

Work out the area of these shapes:

4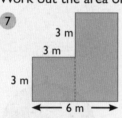
2 cm
4 cm
6 cm
3 cm
10 cm

5
20 cm
5 cm
3 cm 3 cm

6
1 m
11 m
8 m 3 m
3 m

7
2 m 2 m
4 m
12 m
4 m
2 m

Look at the shapes below.

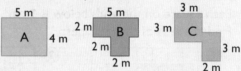
5 m
A
4 m

5 m
2 m
B
2 m
2 m

3 m
3 m
C
3 m
2 m

8 Order the shapes from smallest to largest area.

9 What is the difference in area between A and C?

10 This rectangle has an area of 72 cm².
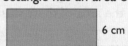
6 cm

What is the perimeter of the rectangle?

The diagram shows a purple rectangle with a square cut out of it.

Calculate the area:

11 of the square cut out.

12 of remaining purple part.

4 cm
8 cm
2 cm

I can calculate the area of shapes.

Area — 2

You've got the hang of working out the area of rectangles and squares, but some shapes are a bit trickier. Counting the squares on a grid is a way you can find or estimate the area of irregular shapes.

Examples

Find the area of the shape on the cm² grid below.

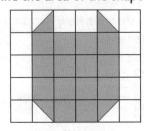

$\frac{1}{2}$

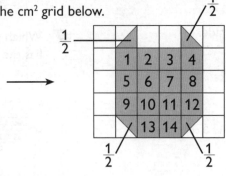

$\frac{1}{2}$

There are 14 whole squares and 4 half squares.

Area = $14 + \frac{1}{2} + \frac{1}{2} + \frac{1}{2} + \frac{1}{2}$ = **16 cm²**.

Estimate the area of the shape on the cm² grid below.

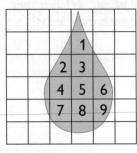

Count up the number of squares that are more than half covered.

9 squares are more than half covered by the raindrop, so you can estimate that its area is about **9 cm²**.

Set A

Each square on the grids below is 1 cm².
Find the area of these shapes:

1

2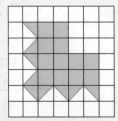

Each square on the grids below is 1 cm².
Estimate the area of these shapes:

3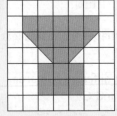

4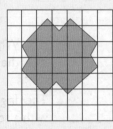

5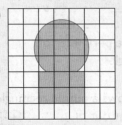

6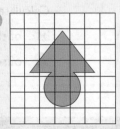

Each square on the grid below is 1 cm².

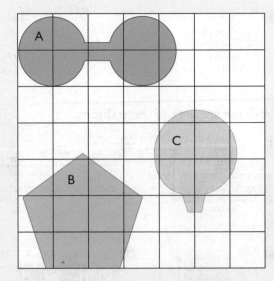

Which shape has an area of about:

7 4 cm²?

8 6 cm²?

9 Order the three shapes from smallest to largest area.

124   Section 5 — Measurement

Each square on the grids below is 1 cm².
Find the area of these shapes:

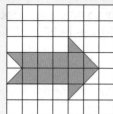

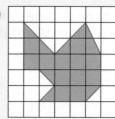

Each square on the grid below is 1 cm².

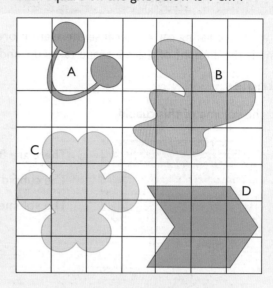

Each square on the grids below is 1 cm².
Estimate the area of these shapes:

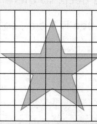

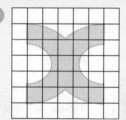

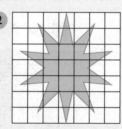

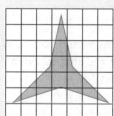

7   Order the shapes from largest to smallest estimated area.

8   What area did you estimate for the largest shape?

9   What area did you estimate for the smallest shape?

 Set C

Each square on the grids below is 1 cm².
Estimate the area of these shapes:

1

2

3

4

5   Naga cuts out 5 paper flowers to decorate her room.
The shape she uses is drawn on the 1 cm² grid on the right.

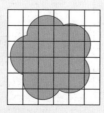

Estimate the total area of the cut out flowers.

Adele draws this shape on a 1 m² grid:

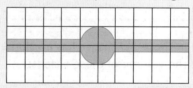

6   Estimate the area of this shape.

7   Is your estimate likely to be bigger or smaller than the actual area? Explain your answer.

Look at the spilled ink below.

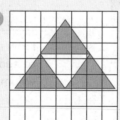

Each square has sides of 4 cm. Chloe says:
'The ink blob covers about 4 squares.
So, the area of the blob is about 4 × 4 = 16 cm².'

8   Is she correct? Explain your answer.

I can find and estimate the area of irregular shapes.

Volume and Capacity

Keep your calculating cap on because there are more questions on the way — it's time for volume and capacity. Volume is the amount of space a shape takes up, and capacity is the amount that something can hold.

Examples

Find the volume of this cuboid.

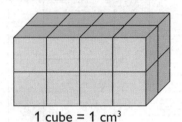

1 cube = 1 cm³

There are 8 cubes at the front of the cuboid.

The cuboid is 2 cubes deep, so there are 2 × 8 = 16 cubes in total.

The volume of each cube is 1 cm³, so the volume of the cuboid is **16 cm³**.

Find the capacity of the hole in this shape.

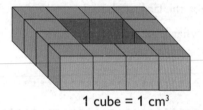

1 cube = 1 cm³

The hole in the middle of the shape is 4 cubes big, or 4 cm³.

This means that the capacity of the hole is **4 cm³**.

Set A

Each cube in these 3D shapes has a volume of 1 cm³.
Work out the volume of these shapes:

1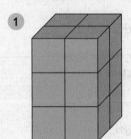

3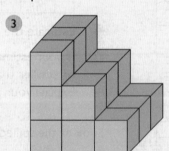

2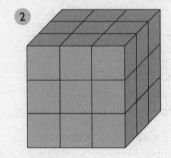

4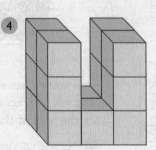

5 Look at the shape below.

1 cube = 1 cm³

How many cubes would you need to add to make the shape have a volume of 14 cm³?

6 What is the capacity of the hole in this shape?

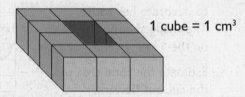

1 cube = 1 cm³

Each cube in these 3D shapes has a volume of 1 cm³.
Work out the volume of these shapes:

①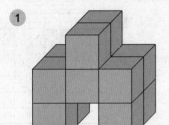

③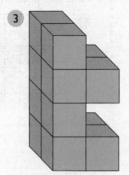

②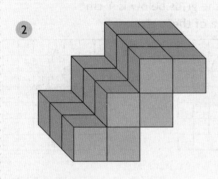

④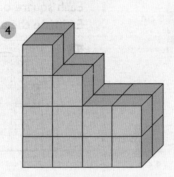

Bonnie builds this shape out of centimetre cubes.
Each layer is identical.

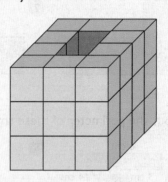

⑤ What is the capacity of the hole in the shape?

Bonnie builds another shape using identical layers to the shape above, but it is 7 cm tall.

⑥ Work out the capacity of the hole in the bigger shape.

Each cube in these 3D shapes has a volume of 1 cm³.
Work out the volume of these shapes:

①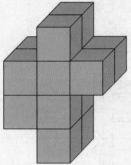

③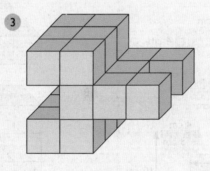

②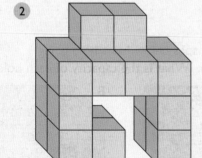

④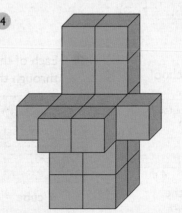

⑤ Sanjay builds this shape out of centimetre cubes.

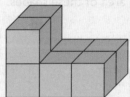

He makes an identical shape and joins the two shapes to make a bridge.

What is the bridge's volume?

⑥ The shape shown below is made of centimetre cubes.
Kim stacks up three of this shape.

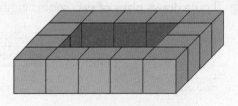

What is the capacity of the hole in Kim's stack?

I can find the volume of 3D shapes made from cubes.

  ✓ ✓   ✓

Measurement — Review 3

Use a ruler to measure the perimeter of the shapes below. Give your answers in cm.

①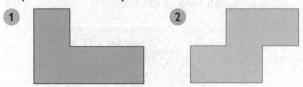

②

Work out the perimeter of these shapes:

③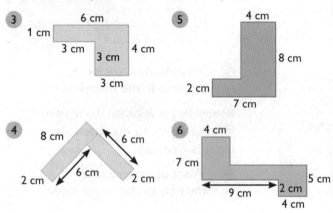

④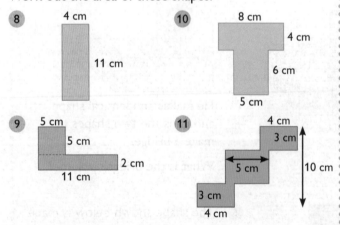

⑤

⑥

⑦ A rectangle has a perimeter of 60 cm. The width of the rectangle is 10 cm. What is its length?

Work out the area of these shapes:

⑧

⑩

⑨

⑪

⑫ Louie draws plans of two rooms in his school.

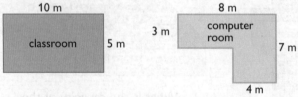

What is the difference in area between the classroom and the computer room, in m²?

Each square on the grids below is 1 cm². Find the area of these shapes:

⑬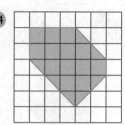

⑭

Each square on the grids below is 1 cm². Estimate the area of these shapes:

⑮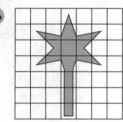

⑯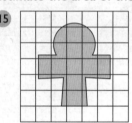

Each cube in these 3D shapes has a volume of 1 cm³. Work out the volume of these shapes:

⑰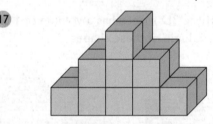

⑱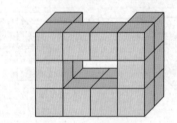

⑲ Each of the shapes below has a hole going through them. What is the capacity of each hole?

A

B

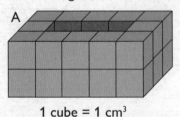

1 cube = 1 cm³

You've worked your way through another review, well done!

Measurement — Challenges

 1   Sasha and Jeremy are selling some things at a car boot sale.

 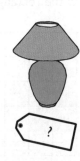  

£70.50   ?   ?   ?

Find the missing prices using the clues below.

- The lamp costs half the price of the chair.
- The teddy costs £23.95 less than the lamp.
- The globe costs twice as much as the teddy.

 2   Hassan is making a drink for his brother.
He needs the following ingredients for it.

600 g ketchup	250 g strawberry jam
5.5 l milk	3.5 kg custard

Conversions guide:
1 kilogram ≈ 2 pounds
100 grams ≈ 4 ounces
1 litre ≈ 2 pints

Choose the item which best matches the quantity Hassan needs.

a)

| 13 ounces | 24 ounces | 26 ounces |

b)

| 8 pints | 11 pints | 13 pints |

c)

| 7 ounces | 10 ounces | 12 ounces |

d)

| 7 pounds | 9 pounds | 15 pounds |

3   Look at the rectangle on the right.

2 cm

4 cm

a) Which shape shown on the grid below has the same area as the rectangle?

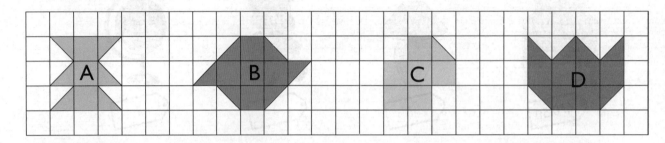

A   B   C   D

b) On a 1 cm² grid, draw a shape with the same area
    as the rectangle on the right which includes:

    (i)   2 half-covered squares.

    (ii) 4 half-covered squares.

    (iii) 6 half-covered squares.

3 cm

5 cm

4   Here are some weights.

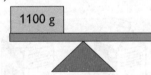   1.6 kg   1.8 kg   1200 g   900 g   0.7 kg   0.2 kg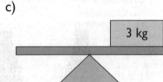

Choose the correct weights to balance each set of weighing scales below.
Two weights are needed for each set of scales. You can only use each weight once.

a)   b)   c)

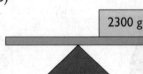

1100 g   2300 g   3 kg

5   Andy says, "Follow these clues to find the number I am thinking of."

•   Start with the number of whole weeks in 85 days.

•   Add on the number of years that's the same as 48 months.

•   Multiply by the number of minutes in 120 seconds.

a) What is Andy's number?

b) Write your own clues for finding a number, using different measures of time.
    Try them out with a friend — can they work out your number?

6   Some pupils have entered the models they've built in a competition.

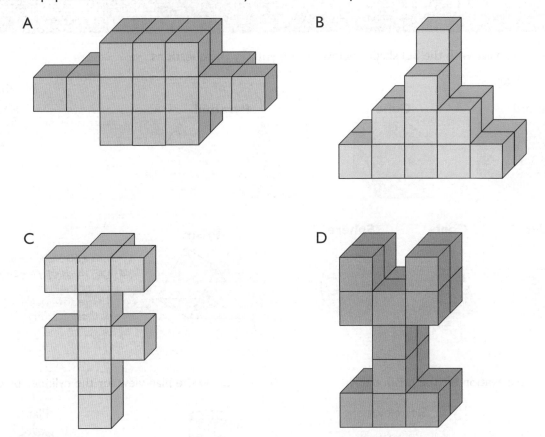

A

B

C

D

Use the information below to work out which model belongs to which pupil.

Tiana	Her model has a volume greater than 18 cm³.
Gregor	His model has a volume that is half the volume of Tiana's model.
Boris	His model has the greatest volume.
Mary	Her model has an odd number of blocks.

7   Lauren is trying to reach the mysterious gates. To do so, she has to cross
a path made up of various stones. But there are rules she must follow:

• She <u>cannot</u> stand on stones that have a perimeter of less than 35 cm.

• She can <u>only</u> stand on stones that have an area of more than 70 cm².

Choose which four stones she should stand on to get to the gates.

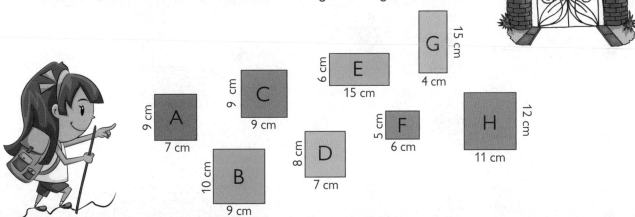

2D Views of 3D Shapes

Make sure you are familiar with the 3D shapes below before you try the questions.

Types of 3D shape

Cuboid **Cube** **Pyramid**

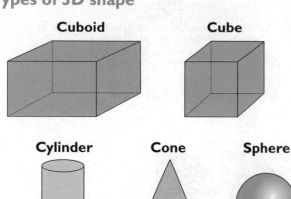

Triangle-based pyramids are also called tetrahedrons.

Cylinder **Cone** **Sphere**

Prism

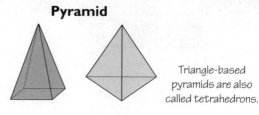

A prism is a 3D shape where both end faces are exactly the same.

So, cylinders and cuboids are also types of prism.

Examples

Draw the side elevation for the prism below.

Side elevation

→

This is the view from the <u>side</u> of the prism.

Draw the plan view for the cylinder below.

Plan

→

This is the view from <u>above</u> the cylinder.

Set A

Choose the correct plan view for each 3D shape below.

Sketch the elevation of each 3D shape, from the direction of the arrow.

    A   B

(1)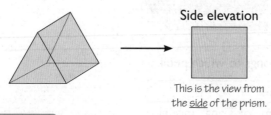

(6) 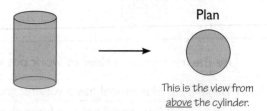 — Side

    A   B

(2)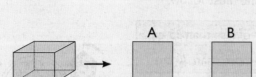

(7)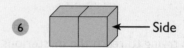

Front

    A   B

(3)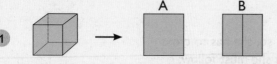

(8)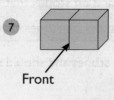

Front

    A   B

(4)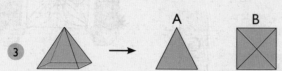

(9) 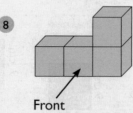 — Side

    A   B

(5)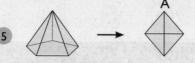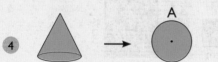

Sketch the plan view for each 3D shape below.

1 sphere

2 cuboid

3 cone (upside down)

4 hexagonal prism

5 tetrahedron

6 The table below includes the plan and front elevation of some 3D shapes.

Copy the table and complete the missing rows.

3D Shape	Plan	Front Elevation
Cube		Square
	Rectangle	Rectangle
Cylinder	Circle	

7 Cole makes three shapes out of building blocks.

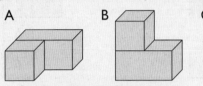

He draws the plan and front elevation of one of the shapes.

Plan: Front elevation:

Which shape did he choose?
Explain how you know.

Choose the name of a shape from the box that could have the plan view shown.

1 | cuboid   cylinder   pyramid |

2 | pyramid   cylinder   prism |

3 | cone   tetrahedron   prism |

4 | prism   cuboid   cylinder |

5 | pyramid   cylinder   prism |

6 Adele says: "A cube is the only 3D shape that has a front elevation of a square."

Describe a 3D shape to show that she isn't correct.

7 Look at the prism below.

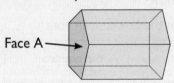

Face A

The prism is tipped over so that Face A touches the floor.

Describe the plan view of the tipped prism.

The shape below is made with 1 cm³ blocks.

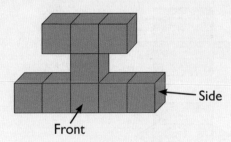

Side

Front

On a centimetre square grid, draw the:

8 front elevation of the shape.

9 side elevation of the shape.

10 plan of the shape.

I can use plans and elevations of 3D shapes.

Nets

A net is a pattern of flat shapes that can be folded up to make a 3D shape.
It can be tricky to work out how a net folds together in your head, so there's lots of practice coming up.

Example

Which of the three nets below would fold into a cube?

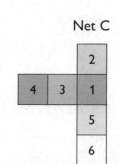

Net A

	2	
3	1	4
	5	
6	7	

No — cubes only have six faces.

Net B

	2	
3	1	4
	5	
	6	

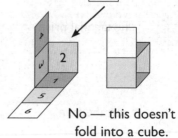

Yes — this makes a cube.

Net C

		2
4	3	1
		5
		6

No — this doesn't fold into a cube.

Set A

What 3D shape can be made from the nets below?

Use the names in the box to help you.

cuboid	tetrahedron
square-based pyramid	triangular prism

1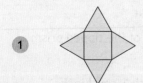

2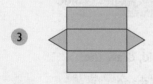

3

4

5 Identify the net below that can fold into a cube.

Net A   Net B

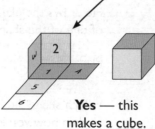

Net C   Net D

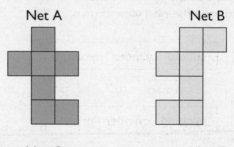

6 Harriet draws a net of the cuboid below.

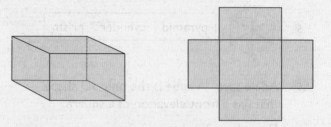

Has she drawn the net correctly?
Explain your answer.

Set B

1. Identify the nets below that can fold into a cuboid.

Net A

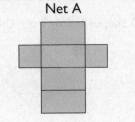

Net B

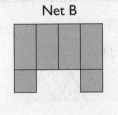

Net C

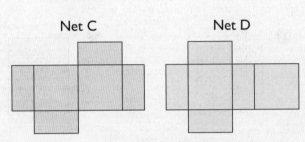

Net D

Sketch a net of the following 3D shapes:

2. tetrahedron

3. square-based pyramid

4. triangular prism

Copy the nets below on a centimetre square grid.

For each, shade in one more square to make a correct net of a cube.

5.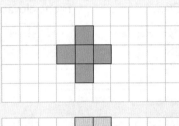

6.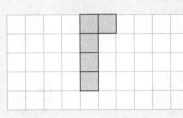

7.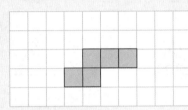

Set C

1. Identify the nets below that can fold into a cube.

Net A

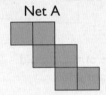

Net B

Net C

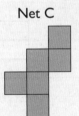

Net D

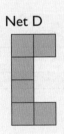

2. Look at the triangular prism below.

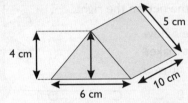

4 cm

5 cm

6 cm

10 cm

On a centimetre square grid, accurately draw a net of this prism.

Here are the plan views of some 3D shapes:

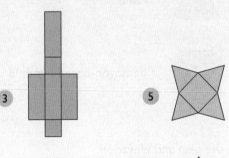

A   B   C

D   E   F

For each net below, write the letter of the plan view of the 3D shape the net could make.

3.

5.

4.

6.

I can identify nets of 3D shapes.

Geometry — Review 1

Give the name of the 3D shapes below from their plan and front elevation.

	Plan	Front elevation

1   (rectangle plan, rectangle front elevation)

2   (square with cross plan, triangle front)

3   (circle plan, circle front)

4   (triangle with lines plan, triangle front)

5   (circle plan, rectangle front)

6   (rectangle with line plan, triangle front)

Sketch the plan view for each shape below.

7   cuboid

8   cone

9   pentagon-based pyramid

Describe the plan and elevation of the following shapes:

10 cube

11 cone

12 pentagonal prism

Give the name of the 3D shapes below from their nets.

13

15

14

16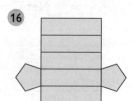

17 Which of the nets below fold into a cube?

Net A

Net B

Net C

Net D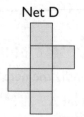

18 Copy and complete the net of the cuboid below on a centimetre square grid:

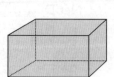

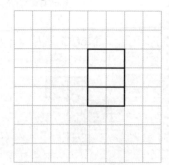

19 Ifrah draws the net on the right.

Which shape below does her net make? Explain your answer.

A   B   C   D

Your geometry skills are in tip top shape — good work!

Estimating Angles

You will have seen lots about angles before. Remember, they are just a measure of a turn.

Example

Circle the best estimate for each angle below.

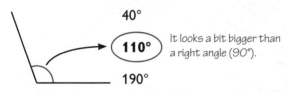

40°

110°   It looks a bit bigger than a right angle (90°).

190°

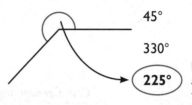

45°

330°

225°   It looks halfway between a half-turn (180°) and a three-quarter turn (270°).

Set A

Look at the three angles below.

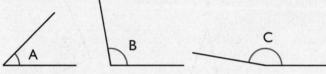

Choose the best estimate for each angle.

1. Angle A: 45° or 105°?
2. Angle B: 80° or 100°?
3. Angle C: 170° or 270°?

Sketch the following angles:

4. 80°
5. 120°
6. 190°

7. Look at the diagram on the right.

D

Estimate the size of angle D.

Set B

Look at the three angles below.

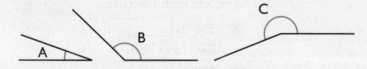

Which is the better estimate for each angle? Explain why.

1. Angle A: 20° or 70°?
2. Angle B: 95° or 135°?
3. Angle C: 200° or 260°?

Sketch the following angles:

4. 104°
5. 260°
6. 44°

7. Look at the diagram on the right.

Estimate the size of the blue angle, D.

D

Set C

Look at the shape below.

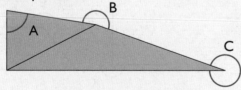

Which is the better estimate for each angle? Explain why.

1. Angle A: 80°, 95° or 100°?
2. Angle B: 190°, 260° or 330°?
3. Angle C: 240°, 300° or 340°?

Sketch the following angles:

4. 82°
5. 263°
6. 347°

7. Farrah says, "Angle D is 200°. Angle E looks about halfway between angle D and a three-quarter turn."

Estimate the size of angle E.

I can estimate angles.

Comparing Angles

A reflex angle is more than 180° (or 2 right angles). There are some coming up — make sure you can spot them.

Examples

Which of the angles below is a reflex angle?

 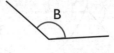 

C is a reflex angle because it is larger than 180°.

Order the angles below, from smallest to largest.

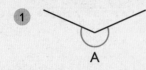 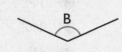

| This is a bit larger than two right angles (180°). | This is a bit smaller than two right angles (180°). | This is bigger than three right angles (270°). | This is about a right angle (90°). |

So the correct order is **Z, X, W, Y**.

Set A

Which angle in each pair is an obtuse angle?

1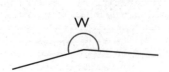

2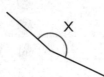

Order the angles in each group, from smallest to largest.

3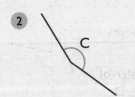

4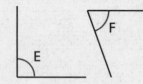

Use "smaller" or "larger" to complete each sentence.

5   300° is ☐ than a full turn.

6   190° is ☐ than half a turn.

7   100° is ☐ than a quarter turn.

8   330° is ☐ than a three-quarter turn.

Look at the three angles below.

 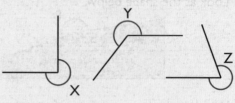

Which symbol (<, > or =) should go in each box?

9   X ☐ 270°

10   Y ☐ 180°

11   Z ☐ 360°

138   Section 6 — Geometry

1   Identify all the acute angles below.

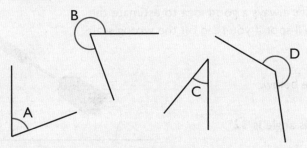

Three angles are labelled
on the picture below.

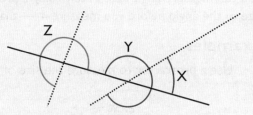

Order the angles in each group,
from smallest to largest.

2

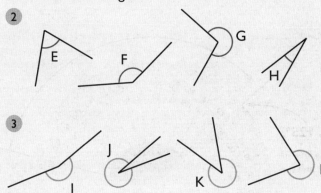

True or false?

4   angle X is the smallest angle.

5   angle Z is the largest angle.

Identify the smallest
reflex angle in each list:

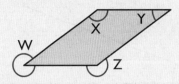

6 | 10° | 90° | 200° | 300° |

7 | 120° | 350° | 190° | 25° |

8 | 155° | 185° | 335° | 130° |

3

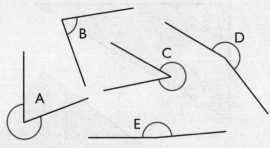

1   Identify all the reflex angles below.

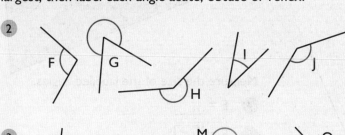

Look at the shape below.

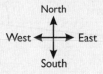

4   Order the angles,
from largest to smallest.

5   Which angle is between
180° and 270°?

Look at the compass below.

North

West ←——→ East

South

Order the angles in each group, from smallest to
largest, then label each angle acute, obtuse or reflex.

2

True or false? Explain your answers.

6   a turn clockwise from North
to South is a reflex angle.

7   300° is less than a clockwise turn
from West to South.

3

I can compare angles.

 ✓   ✓   ☺ ✓

Measuring Angles

You can measure angles accurately using a protractor. It's always a good idea to estimate the size of the angle before you measure it — that way you'll spot if you read off the wrong scale.

Examples

Use a protractor to measure the size of each angle below.

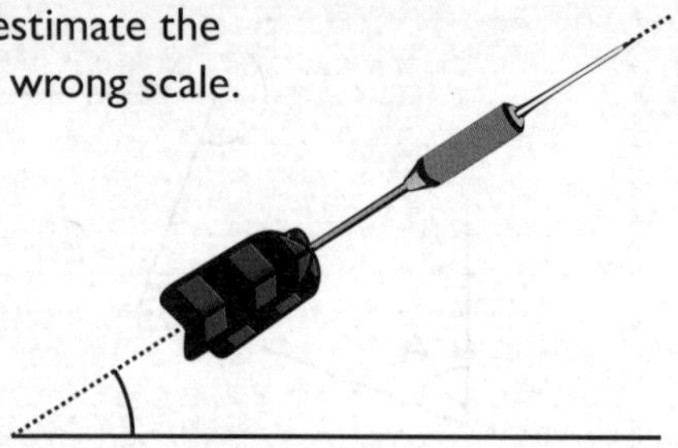

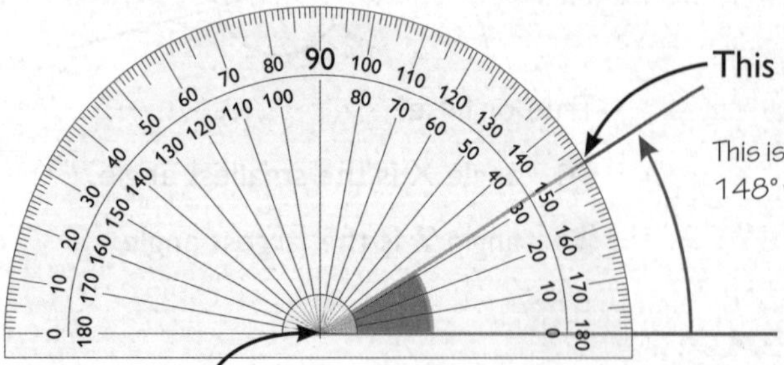

This angle is **32°**.

This is an acute angle — reading off 148° would give you the wrong answer.

Put the cross on the protractor over the vertex.

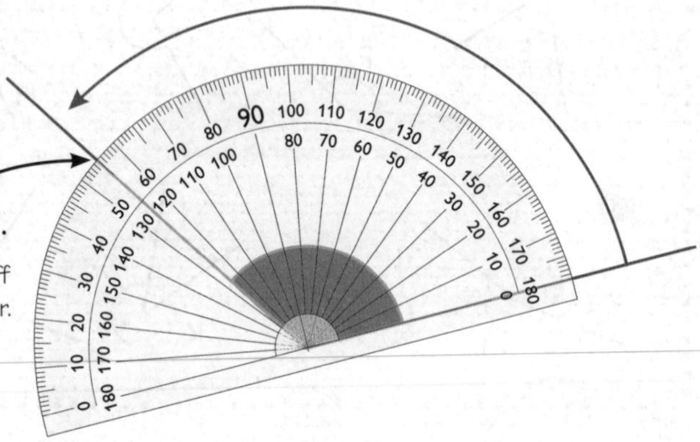

This angle is **125°**.

This is an obtuse angle — reading off 55° would give you the wrong answer.

Set A

Measure the size of each angle below.

1

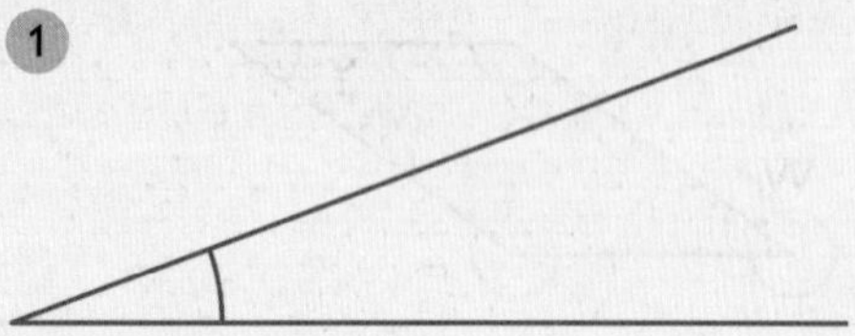

2

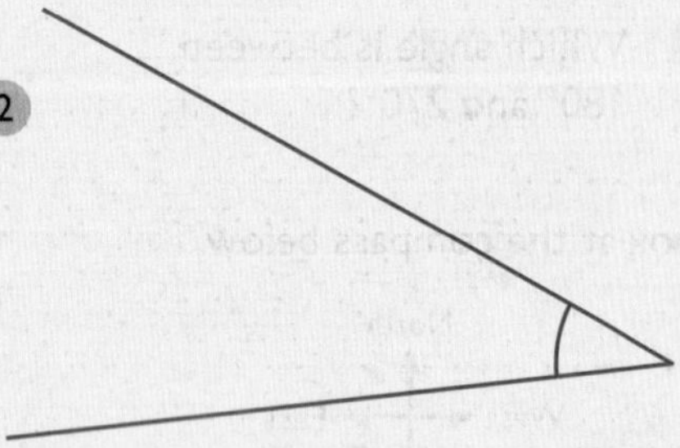

3

Look at the shapes below.

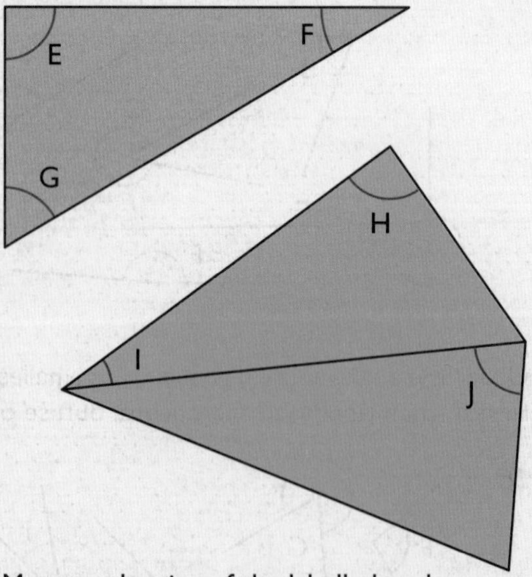

E

F

G

H

I

J

Measure the size of the labelled angles.

4 E = ☐ °

5 F = ☐ °

6 G = ☐ °

7 H = ☐ °

8 I = ☐ °

9 J = ☐ °

Look at the angles below.

Look at the triangles below.

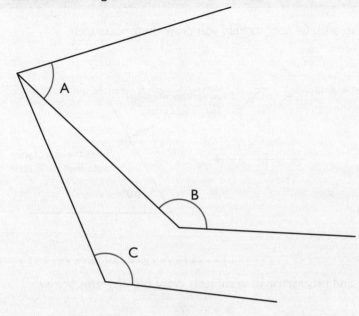

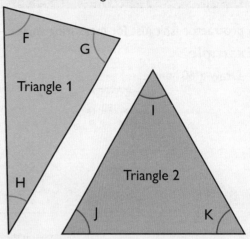

Measure the size of each angle.

4   Triangle 1:

F = ☐°, G = ☐°, H = ☐°

5   Triangle 2:

I = ☐°, J = ☐°, K = ☐°

6   What type of triangle is triangle 2? Explain your answer.

1   Measure the size of angle A.

2   Now measure the size of angles B and C.

3   How much bigger is angle B than angle C?

Look at the angles below.

Four angles are labelled in the diagram below.

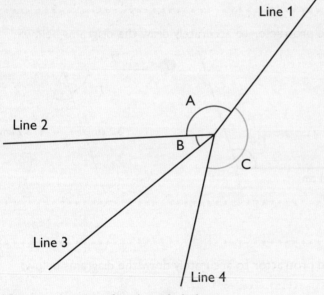

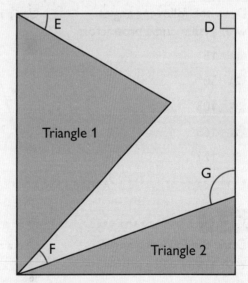

Measure the size of each angle below.

1   A = ☐°

2   B = ☐°

3   C = ☐°

Line 2 is removed.

4   What is the obtuse angle made by Line 1 and 3?

Measure the size of:

5   angle E.

6   the obtuse angle in the green shape.

7   the largest angle in triangle 1.

8   the smallest angle in triangle 2.

I can measure angles using a protractor.

Drawing Angles

A protractor isn't just for measuring angles — it is also a useful tool to help you draw them accurately.

Example

Draw a 60° angle.

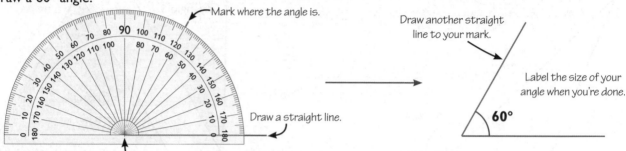

Mark where the angle is.

Draw a straight line.

Put the cross on the protractor over the end of the line.

Draw another straight line to your mark.

Label the size of your angle when you're done.

60°

Set A

Draw the following angles with a ruler and a protractor:

1. 20°
2. 45°
3. 95°
4. 115°
5. 140°

Use a ruler and protractor to accurately draw the diagrams below:

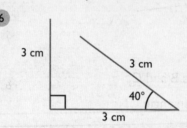

6

3 cm
3 cm
40°
3 cm

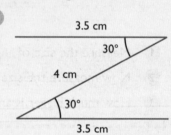

7

3.5 cm
30°
4 cm
30°
3.5 cm

Set B

Draw the following angles with a ruler and a protractor:

1. 15°
2. 58°
3. 103°
4. 165°
5. 177°

Use a ruler and protractor to accurately draw the diagrams below:

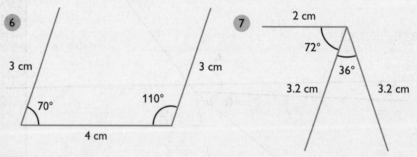

6

3 cm
3 cm
70°
110°
4 cm

7

2 cm
72°
36°
3.2 cm
3.2 cm

Set C

Draw the following angles with a ruler and a protractor:

1. 9°
2. 63°
3. 111°
4. 190°
5. 206°

Use a ruler and protractor to accurately draw the diagrams below:

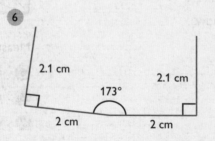

6

2.1 cm
2.1 cm
173°
2 cm
2 cm

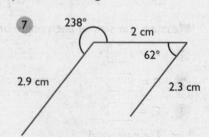

7

238°
2 cm
62°
2.9 cm
2.3 cm

I can draw angles using a protractor.

Geometry — Review 2

Choose the best estimate for each
angle below from the box on the right.

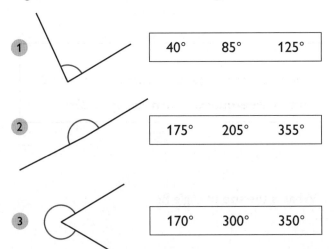

1 | 40°   85°   125°

2 | 175°   205°   355°

3 | 170°   300°   350°

4 | 20°   45°   60°

Identify the reflex angles in each group.

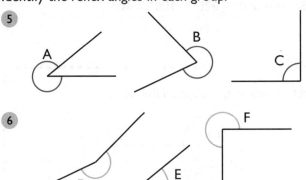

5

6

Order the angles in each group,
from smallest to largest.

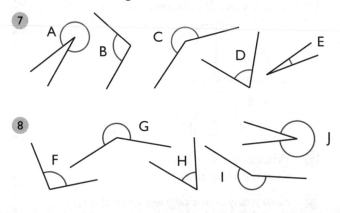

7

8

Measure the size of each angle below.

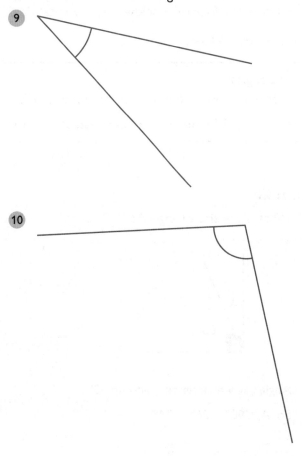

9

10

Draw the following angles with a ruler and protractor:

11   30°   14   102°

12   110°   15   168°

13   48°   16   250°

Use a ruler and protractor to
accurately draw the diagrams below:

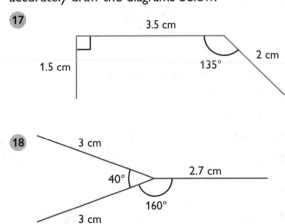

17

18

Estimating, ordering, measuring... your angle knowledge is impressive.

Angle Rules

There are some handy ways you can work out an angle without having to measure it.
Try and learn the four rules below before you tackle the questions.

Learn these rules

The angles:
- around a point (**a full turn**) add up to **360°**.
- on a straight line (**half a turn**) add up to **180°**.
- at a right angle (**quarter turn**) add up to **90°**.
- at a **three-quarter turn** add up to **270°**.

Examples

What is the size of angle A?

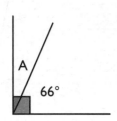

Angles at a quarter turn add up 90°.

So, A = 90° − 66° = **24°**

What is the size of angle B?

Angles around a point add up to 360°.

So, B = 360° − 220° − 100° = **40°**

Set A

Work out the size of each angle:

1. A = ☐ °
2. B = ☐ °

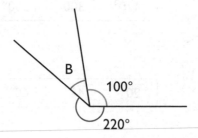

3. C = ☐ °
4. D = ☐ °

The dotted line in each diagram below is a straight line.

Work out the size of each angle:

5. E = ☐ °
6. F = ☐ °
7. G = ☐ °

 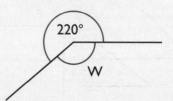 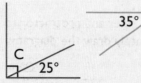 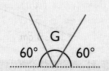

8. Look at the diagram below.

What is the size of angle W?

Look at the clock face below.

9. What is the size of angle X shown on the clock?

10. How many more degrees does the small hand have to turn to get to 12 o'clock?

Work out the size of each angle:

1. A = ☐ °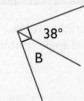

2. B = ☐ °

3. C = ☐ °

4. D = ☐ °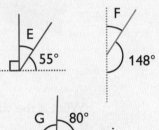

The dotted line in each diagram below is a straight line.

Work out the size of each angle:

5. E = ☐ °

6. F = ☐ °

7. G = ☐ °

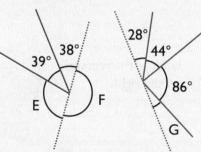

8. Look at the diagram below.

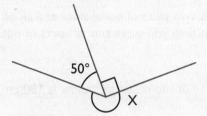

What is the size of angle X?

9. Ezara cuts a pizza into four equal slices.

She then cuts one slice into three equal slices.

What angle does each of the smaller slices make at the centre of the pizza?

Work out the size of each angle:

1. A = ☐ °

2. B = ☐ °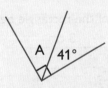

3. C = ☐ °

4. D = ☐ °

The dotted line in each diagram is a straight line.

Work out the size of each angle:

5. E = ☐ °

6. F = ☐ °

7. G = ☐ °

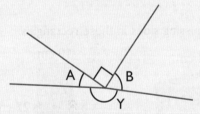

8. Look at the diagram below.

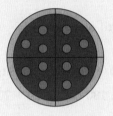

If A = 32° and B = 64°, what is the size of angle Y?

9. The angles in an equilateral triangle are equal and add up to 180°.

Shape A is an equilateral triangle. What is angle H?

10. Iona has three-quarters of a pie.

She cuts one slice measuring 36° and gives it to her sister.

How much pie is left? Give your answer in degrees.

I can find angles at a quarter, half, three-quarter and whole turn.

Rectangles

A rectangle has two pairs of equal sides and all of its angles are right angles.
These facts can help you work out all sorts of missing length and angle problems.

Examples

The perimeter of the rectangle below is 180 cm.

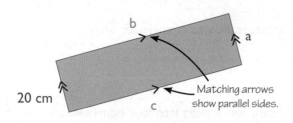

What is the length of side b?

a is 20 cm, because the side opposite it is 20 cm.

The perimeter is 180 cm, so 20 + 20 + b + c = 180 cm

b + c = 180 − 20 − 20 = 140 cm

b and c are opposite sides, so they have the same length.

b = 140 ÷ 2 = **70 cm** (and c = 70 cm)

Look at the rectangular flag below.

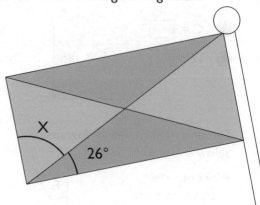

What is the size of angle X?

All of the angles in a rectangle are 90°.

So X = 90° − 26° = **64°**

Set A

Find the missing sides in these rectangles:

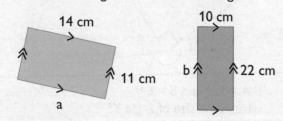

1. side a = ☐ cm

2. side b = ☐ cm

Find the missing angles in these rectangles:

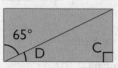

3. angle C = ☐ °

4. angle D = ☐ °

5. angle E = ☐ °

The perimeter of the rectangle below is 26 cm.

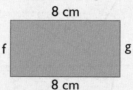

Copy and complete the sentences below to work out the missing sides of the rectangle.

6. f + g + 8 cm + 8 cm = ☐ cm

7. f + g = ☐ cm − 8 cm − 8 cm = ☐ cm

8. f and g are the same length,
   so f = ☐ cm and g = ☐ cm

Look at the rectangle on the right.

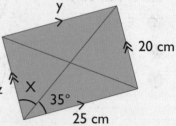

9. What is the size of angle X?

10. How much longer is side y than side z?

Set B

1 The rectangle below has a perimeter of 40 cm.

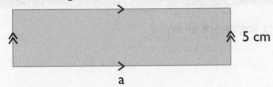

a

What is the length of side a?

Look at the two rectangles below.

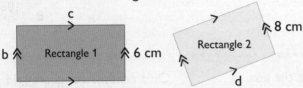

Use these facts to find the missing lengths:

- side c is twice the length of side b.
- the perimeters of rectangles 1 and 2 are the same.

2 side b = ☐ cm

3 side c = ☐ cm

4 side d = ☐ cm

Find the missing angles in this rectangle:

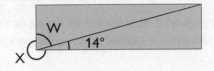

5 angle W = ☐°

6 angle X = ☐°

7 Lisa measures one of the angles in the shape below.

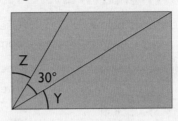

She says, "Angle Y plus angle Z equals sixty degrees."

Is she correct? Explain your answer.

Set C

1 The rectangle below has a perimeter of 38 cm.

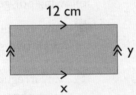

12 cm

y

x

How much longer is side x than side y?

Two shapes are joined to make a rectangle:

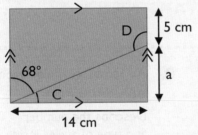

5 cm

a

14 cm

The perimeter of the rectangle is 50 cm.

2 What is the length of side a?

Angle D is 90° larger than angle C.

3 What is the size of angle C?

4 What is the size of angle D?

5 Amy labels the corners of a rectangle (A, B, C and D). She draws a diagonal line from corner A.
An angle of 12° is made at corner A. What is the size of the other angle?

The four triangle pieces of fabric below join together to make a rectangular banner.

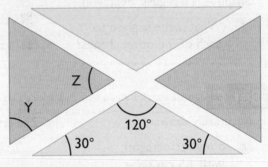

The top and bottom triangles are identical. The left and right triangles are identical.

Work out the missing angles. Explain your answers.

6 angle Y = ☐°

7 angle Z = ☐°

I can use facts about rectangles to find missing values.

Regular and Irregular Polygons

A polygon is regular if its sides are all the same length and its angles are all equal.
If that's not the case, it's called an irregular polygon.

Examples

What name is given to the shape below?

The shape has 7 sides.
The sides are not all the same length.

So this is an **irregular heptagon**.

Look at the regular pentagon on the right.

What is the size of angle A?   **108°**

What is the length of side B?   **5 cm**

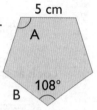

Set A

Look at the shapes below.

Shape A is a regular pentagon.

1   What name is given to
    each of the other shapes?

Use words from the box to
complete the sentences below:

| octagon seven angles |
| heptagon equal irregular |

2   A regular ⬚ has
    ⬚ sides and seven angles.

3   Its sides are ⬚ and
    its ⬚ are equal.

On a centimetre square grid,
copy and complete these shapes:

4   irregular
    pentagon

5   irregular
    hexagon

Set B

Look at the shapes below.

 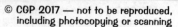 

Shape A is a regular heptagon.

1   What name is given to
    each of the other shapes?

This shape is a regular hexagon.

Side A is 5 cm. Angle y is 120°.

Explain how you also know:

2   the length of side B.

3   the size of angle z.

Accurately draw the
following polygons:

4   any irregular quadrilateral
    with two sides of 3 cm.

5   any irregular pentagon
    with three sides of 3.5 cm.

6   any irregular hexagon
    with four sides of 2.5 cm.

Set C

Accurately draw:

1   a regular octagon
    with 1.5 cm sides
    and 135° angles.

2   any irregular hexagon
    with three sides of 3 cm
    and 2 sides of 2.5 cm.

3   any 9-sided polygon with
    two sides of 2 cm and
    four sides of 1.5 cm.

Zac draws the shape below.

He says: "Each side is 2 cm,
so this is a regular quadrilateral."

4   Do you agree?
    Explain your answer.

5   What name is given to
    a regular quadrilateral?

6   An 'icosagon' is a polygon
    with twenty sides.

    Describe the number
    and type of angles inside
    a regular icosagon.

7   Angles in a 10-sided regular
    polygon add up to 1440°.

    What is the size of each
    angle in this shape?

I know the difference between regular and irregular polygons.

Geometry — Review 3

Work out the size of each angle:

1 A = ☐ °

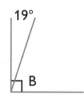

2 B = ☐ °

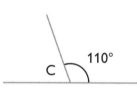

110°
C

3 C = ☐ °

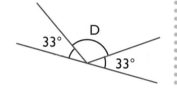

4 D = ☐ °

260°
E

5 E = ☐ °

F 160°

6 F = ☐ °

A circle is divided into three equal parts.
One equal part is shown below.

Without measuring,
what is the size of:

7 angle x?

8 angle y?

9 Look at the rectangle below.

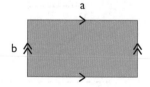

Copy and complete the table below
for different lengths of sides a and b.

Side a	Side b	Perimeter
3 cm		10 cm
	7 cm	36 cm
	15 cm	70 cm

Look at the rectangles below.

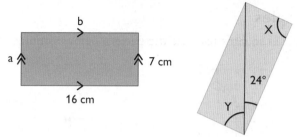

Are the following statements true or false?

10 Side a is 16 cm.

11 Side b is 16 cm.

12 The perimeter of the rectangle on the left is 44 cm.

13 Angle X is a right angle.

14 Angle Y is 76°.

15 Look at the shapes below.

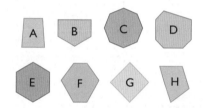

Shape A is an irregular quadrilateral.

What name is given to each of the other shapes?

16 The shape below is a regular nonagon.
One angle and one side have been labelled.

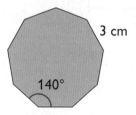

Describe what you know about the
other angles and sides of this shape.

On a centimetre square grid,
draw the following shapes:

17 a regular quadrilateral with sides of 2 cm.

18 an irregular hexagon with two sides of 2 cm.

19 an irregular octagon with four sides of 2 cm.

Angles rule and so do you — well done for tackling those questions!

Reflection

You'll have reflected shapes before in Year 4 — there's some more practice at it coming up.

Examples

Shade in squares to make the pattern below symmetrical in the mirror line.

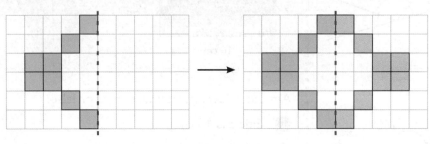

Copy out the diagram below and draw the reflection in both mirror lines.

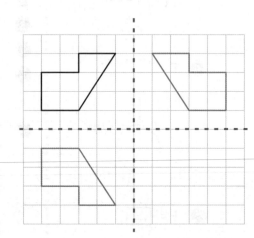

Set A

Copy out each diagram on squared paper and draw the reflection in the mirror line.

1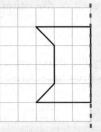

2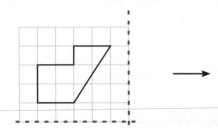

3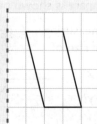

4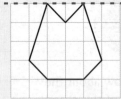

5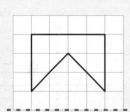

6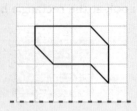

Copy out each diagram below and shade in squares to make each pattern symmetrical in the mirror line.

7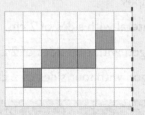

8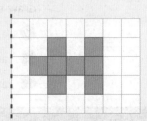

9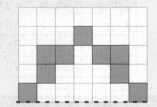

Copy out each diagram on squared paper and draw the reflection in both mirror lines.

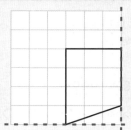 **1**

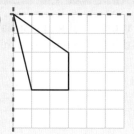 **2**

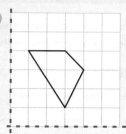 **3**

Copy the diagram on the right.

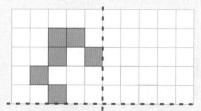

4 Reflect the shaded squares in the vertical mirror line.

5 Now reflect the whole pattern in the horizontal mirror line.

Look at the coordinate grid on the right.

Shape S is a reflection of Shape R in a vertical mirror line. The vertical mirror line goes through the point labelled P.

6 Copy out the grid and draw Shape R.

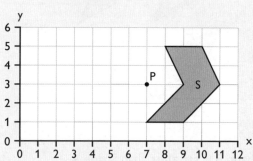

Copy out each diagram on squared paper and draw the reflection in both mirror lines.

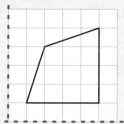 **1**

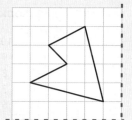 **2**

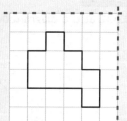 **3**

Copy out the grid on the right.

Shape A was reflected in a vertical mirror line to make Shape B. One side of Shape A is shown.

4 Draw the correct vertical mirror line.

5 Complete Shape A.

Shape C was reflected in a horizontal mirror line to make Shape D. One side of Shape C is shown.

6 Draw the correct horizontal mirror line.

7 Complete Shape C.

I can reflect shapes in vertical and horizontal lines.

Translation

Always check your answers when doing translations — if you translate a shape and it is bigger or smaller, or a rotation of the original shape, then you've made a mistake somewhere.

Examples

Look at the grid below.

Explain why Shape B and Shape C are not translations of Shape A.

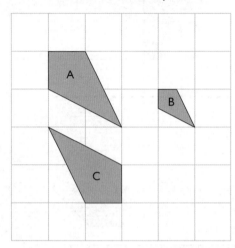

Shape B is **smaller** than Shape A.
Shape C is a **rotation** of Shape A.

So Shape B and Shape C are not translations of Shape A.

Look at the diagram below.

Describe the translation from P to Q.

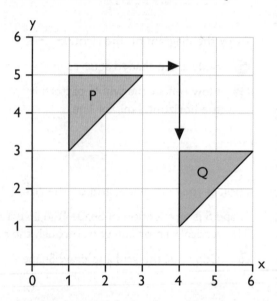

Shape P has been translated **3 squares right** and **2 squares down**.

Set A

Look at the diagram below.

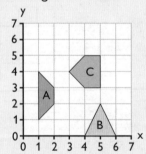

On a blank coordinate grid, draw the new position of each shape:

1. translate Shape A 3 squares right and 1 square down.

2. translate Shape B 2 squares left and 5 squares up.

3. translate Shape C 2 squares left and 1 square down.

4. The centre of a square is at coordinates (2, 5).

   The square is translated so that its centre is at (3, 6).

   Describe the translation.

Look at the diagram below.

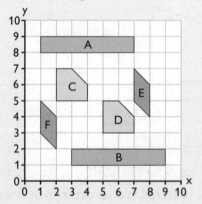

Describe the translation:

5. from A to B.

6. from C to D.

7. from E to F.

8. Look at the diagram on the right.

   Is Shape B a correct translation of Shape A?

   Explain your answer.

Set B

Look at the diagram below.

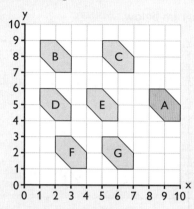

Shape A is translated to a new position on the grid.

Which letter shows the new position of Shape A if it was translated:

1. 3 squares left and 3 squares up.

2. 7 squares left and 3 squares up.

3. left and down by the same number of squares.

4. Look at the diagram on the right.

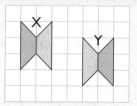

Is Shape Y a correct translation of Shape X?

Explain your answer.

5. Look at the diagram below.

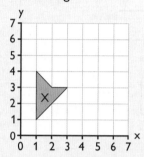

The diagram shows the new position of Shape X after it was translated 4 squares left and 2 squares down.

On a blank coordinate grid, draw the original position of Shape X.

Set C

Look at the diagram below.

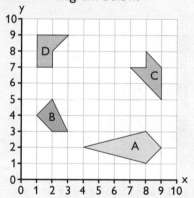

On a blank coordinate grid, draw the new position of each shape:

1. translate Shape A 1 square right and 6 squares up.

2. translate Shape B 7 squares right and 3 squares down.

3. translate Shape C 5 squares left and 2 squares down.

4. translate Shape D 3 squares right and 1 square up.

Look at the diagram below.

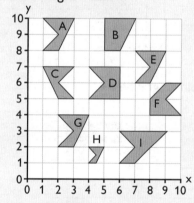

5. Which shapes are a translation of Shape A?

6. Describe all the translations of Shape A that you find.

A triangle has a vertex Z with coordinates (3, 1).

The triangle is translated 3 squares right and 8 squares up.

7. What are the new coordinates of vertex Z?

8. Describe a translation from the new coordinates to the original coordinates of vertex Z.

I can describe translations and translate shapes on a grid.

Geometry — Review 4

Copy out each diagram and draw
the reflection in both mirror lines.

1

2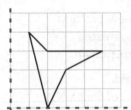

3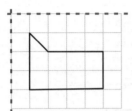

4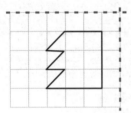

Look at the coordinate grid below.

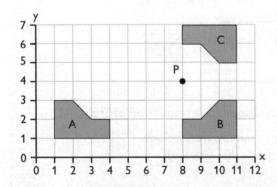

Describe the position of a mirror line that reflects:

5 Shape A onto Shape B.

6 Shape B onto Shape C.

A vertical mirror line goes
through the point labelled P.

7 On a copy of a coordinate grid, draw the
reflection of shape C in this mirror line.

Look at the diagram below.

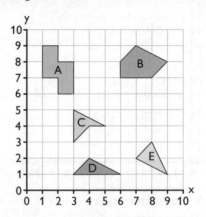

On a blank coordinate grid,
draw the new position of each shape:

8 translate shape A 1 square left and 2 squares down.

9 translate shape B 1 square right and 5 squares down.

10 translate shape C 3 squares right and 4 squares up.

11 translate shape D 2 squares left and 7 squares up.

12 translate shape E 6 squares left and 1 square down.

Look at the diagram below.

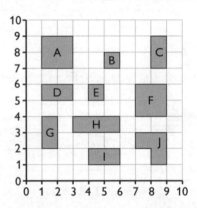

Complete the sentences:

13 Shape A is translated ☐ squares right
and ☐ squares down to make Shape F.

14 Shape I is translated ☐ squares left
and ☐ squares up to make Shape D.

15 Shape ☐ is translated 1 square left
and ☐ squares down to make Shape E.

16 Shape ☐ is translated ☐ squares ☐
and ☐ squares ☐ to make Shape G.

That's the end of another bunch of geometry questions. Superb work!

Geometry — Challenges

1 Look at Captain Pinkfeather's map below.

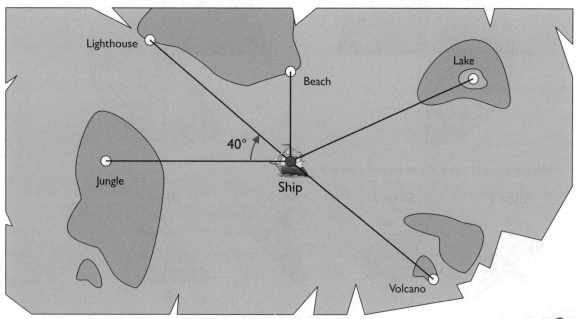

His ship is facing the jungle. He knows that if he turns the ship clockwise through an angle of 40° he would face the lighthouse.

Starting by facing the jungle, use a protractor to measure how many degrees clockwise his ship needs to turn through to face each location below.

a) the beach

b) the lake

c) the volcano

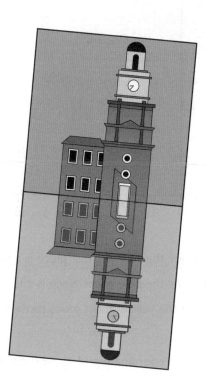

2 Look at the picture on the right.
A reflection of the building can be seen in the lake.

Phoebe thinks the picture isn't accurate because there is something wrong with the reflection.

Can you find anything wrong with the picture?
Discuss what you find with the person next to you.

3 Matthew has two cakes. He cuts two slices out of each.

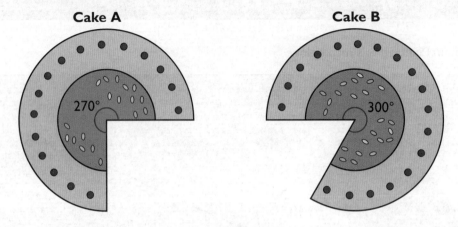

a) Which cake did the slices below come from?

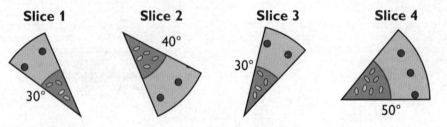

b) Matthew cuts one of the remaining cakes into 3 obtuse slices.

Did he cut cake A or cake B? Explain your answer.

 4 Mona is playing a game that uses yellow and blue ghost pieces on a coordinate grid.

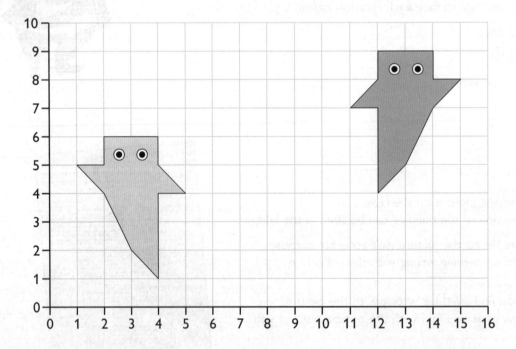

• A 'move' for the yellow ghost piece is a translation of 2 squares right and 1 square up.

• A 'move' for the blue ghost piece is a translation of 3 squares left and 1 square down.

Mona moves the yellow ghost piece three times and the blue ghost piece two times.

On a copy of a coordinate grid, draw the new positions of the two ghost pieces.

5 Rosie makes the shape on the right with three different sizes of rectangles. All of the rectangles are the same width.

She measures the width of the shape and finds it is 30 cm.
She then measures the perimeter of the shape and finds it is 156 cm.

Use the information above to find the length and width of rectangles A, B and C.

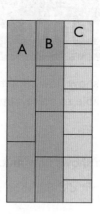

6 Dr. Angle looks through a microscope and sees the Poly-Germs below.

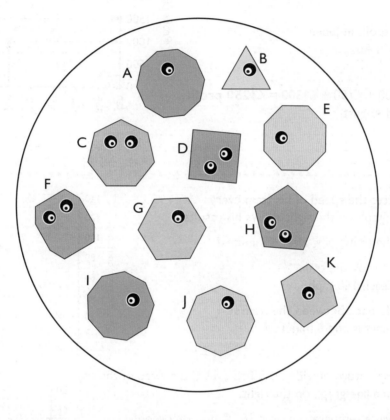

a) Work out which Poly-Germ is speaking:

    i) "I am a regular shape with two pairs of parallel sides."

    ii) "I have less than five sides and all of my angles are equal."

    iii) "I have two eyes and more than seven angles."

b) Sketch your own Poly-Germ. It must:

- be an irregular polygon.
- have up to 10 sides.
- have one or two eyes.

With a partner, describe your Poly-Germs to each other.
Once you're done, try and sketch their Poly-Germ from the description.

Fantastic — some of those challenges were very tricky!

Line Graphs — 1

Line graphs can show how something changes over time.
You need to be able to solve sum, difference and comparison problems using line graphs.

Example

This line graph shows how much profit a shop made in each month of a year.

How much profit did the shop make in total in June, July and August?

Read <u>up</u> from each month to the correct point, then read <u>across</u> to find the profit.

The shop made £1000 profit in June,
£750 in July and £1500 in August.

So the shop made £1000 + £750 + £1500 = **£3250 profit**
in total in June, July and August.

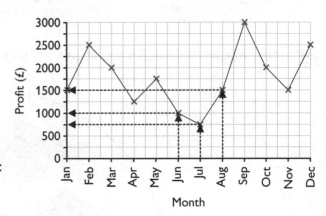

Set A

A train driver measures the speed of his train every
2 minutes. The line graph on the right shows his results.

1. How fast was the train going after 6 minutes?

2. True or false? It took the train
   12 minutes to reach 140 mph.

3. What is the difference between the train's
   speed after 4 minutes and 8 minutes?

Kyle records the temperature outside his office over the course of the day.
He shows the data in a line graph on the right.

4. At what time was a temperature over 16 °C first recorded?

5. What was the difference in temperature between 10 am and 3 pm?

6. True or false? It was warmer at 4 pm than at 10 am.

7. It was 8 °C warmer inside Kyle's office than outside at 5 pm.
   What was the temperature inside Kyle's office at 5pm?

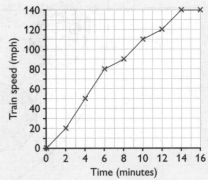

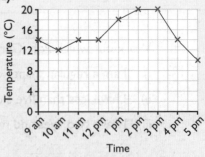

The line graph on the right shows how long it took
Molly and Tony to swim away from the shore.

What number is missing from each sentence?

8. Molly had swum ☐ m after 4 minutes.

9. It took Tony ☐ minutes to swim 600 m.

10. How far did Tony swim between 4 and 8 minutes?

11. What is the total distance that Molly and
    Tony had swum after 12 minutes?

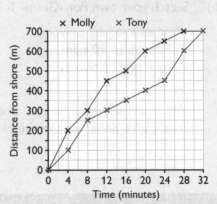

The line graph on the right shows the temperature
of a furnace between 6 pm and 6 am.

1 Was the furnace hotter at 11 pm or 6 am?

2 The maximum temperature of the furnace is 1400 °C.
How long did it take the temperature to fall to half this temperature?

Are the following statements true or false?

3 The temperature was the same at 5 am as it was at 1 am.

4 It took 5 hours for the temperature to drop from 800 °C to 200 °C.

5 The temperature of the furnace had dropped
by 1200 °C, from 6 pm to midnight.

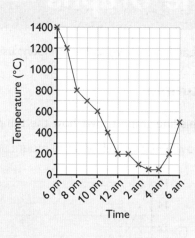

Two whales have radio tags that measure how deep they dive.
The line graph on the right shows how deep
each whale dived over 16 minutes.

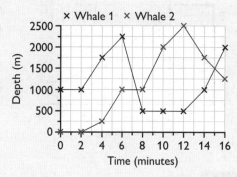

6 What is the difference between whale 1's
depth after 12 and 16 minutes?

7 How much deeper was whale 2 than
whale 1 after 14 minutes?

8 What was the total depth of the two whales at 6 minutes?

A gardener measured the height of
two sunflowers every three days.

The line graph on the right shows his results.

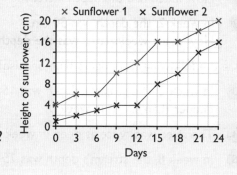

1 How tall was sunflower 1 on day 9?

2 True or false? Sunflower 2 grew
6 cm between day 15 and day 21.

3 Which sunflower grew the most between day 9 and day 24?

4 What is the total height of the sunflowers on day 18?

The line graph on the right shows the volume of water
in a water tank during the course of a week.

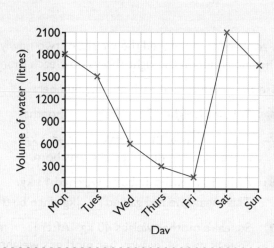

5 How much water was used between
Tuesday and Thursday?

6 On what day was the volume of water in the tank
exactly one third of the amount on Monday?

7 How much water was added to the tank
between Friday and Saturday?

8 What was the total volume of water
taken out of the tank during the week?

I can solve problems involving line graphs.

Line Graphs — 2

In Year 5, you have to be confident using line graphs to solve problems — the best way to do this is through practice.

Example

This line graph shows how the temperature of a mountain top changed after sunset.

How much colder was the mountain top after 5 hours than it was after 2 hours?

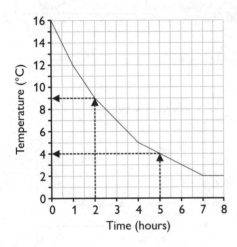

Read <u>up</u> from each time, and <u>across</u> to find the temperature.

After 2 hours, the temperature was 9 °C.
After 5 hours, the temperature was 4 °C.

So the mountain top was 9 – 4 = **5 °C colder** after 5 hours than it was after 2 hours.

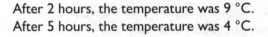

Set A

Eris records the depth of a stream each Saturday.
The line graph on the right shows how the depth changed over 8 weeks.

1. How much had the depth increased from week 0 to week 3?

2. In week 2, the depth was 30 cm.
   How many weeks later was the depth the same?

Are the following statements true or false?

3. In week 6, the stream's depth was 15 cm deeper than it was in week 0.

4. The river was twice as deep in week 4 than in week 1.

5. In week 8, the stream's depth was 25 cm shallower than it was in week 5.

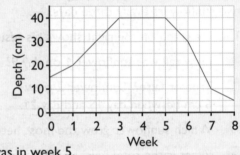

A zookeeper monitored the weight of two newly born monkeys, Bubbles and Squeak.
The line graph on the right shows how each monkey's weight changed.

Use the graph to find each missing number:

6. Bubbles weighed 2 kg after ☐ months.

7. After ☐ months Squeak weighed 2 kg more than she did when she was born.

8. After 18 months, Bubbles weighed 13 kg.
   This means he had gained ☐ kg since birth.

9. Squeak's mother weighs 40 kg. After ☐ months, Squeak was 34 kg away her mother's weight.

10. The total weight of the two monkeys after 8 months was ☐ kg.

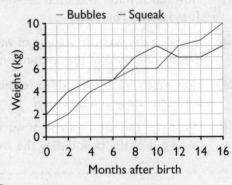

Joe did a skydive last month. The line graph shows how long it took him to fall to 1000 m after jumping from 4000 m.

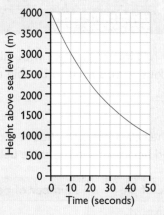

What numbers are missing from each sentence?

1) Joe fell ☐ m between 10 and 20 seconds.

2) It took Joe ☐ seconds to fall from 2250 m to 1500 m.

3) After 300 seconds, Joe reached the ground at 0 m. How long did it take him to fall the last 1000 m?

Mina planted two trees in her garden in 2007. The line graph on the right shows how the width of the trees changed over 9 years.

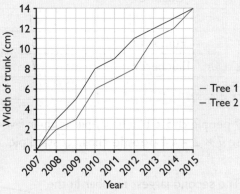

4) How much wider was tree 1's trunk in 2014 than 2012?

5) True or false? Tree 2's trunk was 8.5 cm wide in 2011.

6) How many years did it take before tree 1's trunk was 7 cm wide?

7) When was tree 2's width four times as wide as it was in 2008?

8) What was the total width of the tree trunks in 2012?

Coby and Fern each boiled a pan of water. The line graph shows how the temperature of the water changed over time.

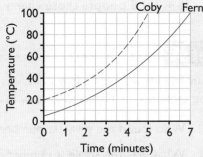

1) What temperature was Coby's water to start with?

2) How much cooler was Fern's pan of water after 3 minutes than Coby's?

3) By how many degrees did the temperature of Fern's water increase between 4 and a half and 7 minutes?

Arnie is flying a kite in his garden. The line graph below shows the height of the kite above the ground during the first 30 seconds of the flight.

4) How far did the kite fall between 5 and 10 seconds?

5) The height of the kite increased between 0 and 5 seconds. Find the two other time intervals when the height of the kite increased.

6) What was the total height gained by the kite during the three time intervals in Question 5?

Arnie writes down these statements about the flight.

- The height of the kite was above 20 m for 14 seconds in total.

- Once the kite was above 16 m, it didn't drop below 16 m again.

7) For each statement, work out if Arnie is correct and explain how you know.

I am confident solving problems involving line graphs.

Tables

You've already had lots of practice with tables. Tables are a good way of recording and representing data — you need to be able to read and write information in this format.

Example

Nina asked her classmates to choose their favourite type of pie from a list.
She recorded her results in the table below.

Type of pie	Number of people
Custard	
	11
Pumpkin	5
Blueberry	7

Complete the table using the following information:

- Twice as many people chose custard pie as blueberry pie.
- The second most popular type of pie was lime.
- Three more people chose cherry pie than pumpkin pie.

7 people chose blueberry pie as their favourite, so 7 × 2 = **14 people** chose custard pie.

The second largest number in the table is **11**, so that must be the number of people who chose lime pie.

5 people chose pumpkin pie, so 5 + 3 = **8 people** chose cherry pie.

Type of pie	Number of people
Custard	14
Lime	11
Pumpkin	5
Blueberry	7
Cherry	8

Set A

Four friends went on a frog hunt.
The table on the right shows how many frogs each person found:

	Number of frogs found
Henrietta	13
Rex	9
Mavis	24
Cayde	18

1. Who found the greatest number of frogs?

2. What was the smallest number of frogs found?

3. How many people found more than fifteen frogs?

Natalie is draining a water tank.
It takes 1 minute to drain 7 litres of water.

Time	Volume (litres)
1 minute	84
2 minutes	
3 minutes	70
4 minutes	

4. Copy and complete the table on the right.

5. Another tank contains 126 litres of water.
It takes 2 minutes to drain 9 litres. Draw a table to show how much water is left after 2, 4, 6 and 8 minutes.

Four friends take it in turns to roll a dice. They record the numbers they roll in the table on the right.

Giulia rolled the same total score as Leo.

Giulia	Leo	Ajay	Greta
3	4	6	1
6		5	
		6	3	5

	Giulia	Leo	Ajay	Greta
Total		11		10

6. Use this information to copy and complete the table.

7. Which number was rolled the most?

Three classes voted for their favourite pet:

	Hamster	Guinea pig	Rabbit	Goldfish
Class 5X	12	7	18	3
Class 5Y	6	15	10	9
Class 5Z	10	4	11	15

1. Which animal received the fewest votes in Class 5Y?

2. Which animal received the highest number of votes in total?

3. Jonni is in Class 5X. He voted for the third most popular animal. Which animal did he vote for?

4. How many more votes did 'rabbit' get in Class 5Z than 'goldfish' in Class 5X?

5. Tropical fruits are packed into crates before being delivered to a supermarket.

   Copy and complete the table using the information below:

Fruit	Number in each crate
Melon	38
	145
Mango	
	113

   • There are 145 lychees and 113 kiwi fruits in a crate.

   • There are 69 more mangoes than melons in a crate.

   • The number of pineapples in a crate is 40 less than the number of kiwi fruits.

The table below shows how many different sandwiches a shop sold on three days.

1. Copy and complete the table using the information below:

   • On Monday, the shop sold half as many cheese sandwiches as tuna sandwiches.

   • The shop sold 5 more egg sandwiches than cheese sandwiches on Wednesday.

	Monday	Wednesday	Friday
Chicken	6	25	
Egg	13		21
Tuna	28	9	23
Cheese		12	11

   • On Friday, the shop sold as many chicken sandwiches as egg and cheese sandwiches combined.

2. Which sandwich was the most popular over the three days?

3. How many sandwiches did the shop sell in total?

A website has a table of prices for two different tourist attractions.

4. Copy and complete the table using the information below:

   • Adult tickets at Ocean Encounters are half the price of its family ticket, and £4.25 less than an adult ticket at Jungle Perils.

   • Child tickets at Jungle Perils are a quarter of the family ticket price. Ocean Encounters charges £3.75 less.

	Ocean Encounters Aquarium	Jungle Perils Safari Park
Adult		
Child		
Family	£12.50	£28

5. Which is more expensive: 3 adult tickets at Jungle Perils or 2 family tickets and one adult ticket at Ocean Encounters?

I can read and write information in tables.

Timetables

Timetables do exactly what their name suggests — they show times in a table.
You have to learn how to read and write information in timetables.

Examples

Look at this extract from a train timetable:

Each column shows the times for one train. So this train leaves Treethorpes at 17:38.

Treethorpes	11:17	13:52	16:24	17:38
Oakville	11:35	14:10	16:42	17:56
Pineton	11:46	14:21	16:53	18:07
Willowford	12:07	14:42	17:14	18:28

All the trains take the same amount of time to travel between stations.

How long does it take to travel from Treethorpes to Pineton?

The train from the first column leaves at 11:17 and arrives at 11:46.

So it takes 13 + 16 = **29 minutes** to travel from Treethorpes to Pineton.

A train leaves Oakville at 21:40. When does it arrive at Willowford?

The train from the first column leaves at 11:35 and arrives at 12:07.

The journey takes 25 + 7 = 32 minutes. The train will arrive at Willowford 32 minutes after 21:40, so at **22:12**.

Set A

This is an extract from a tram timetable.

1. How long does it take the tram to travel between High Street and King's Way?

Miles lives on Nelson Road and works in Stuart Square.

2. He starts work at 9 am. On which days will the tram get him to work on time?

	Mon	Tues	Wed	Thurs
Nelson Road	08:15	09:10	08:40	09:05
Stuart Square	08:31	09:26	08:56	09:21
High Street	08:41	09:36	09:06	09:31
King's Way	08:58	09:53	09:23	09:48

Look at the ferry timetable on the right.

3. Stu is in Chalk Point at 11 am on Saturday. He wants to go to Pastel Cove. When is the next ferry he can catch?

4. Elena catches the first ferry from Burthaven on Sunday morning. She gets off at Pastel Cove. How long is her journey?

	Burthaven	Chalk Point	Pastel Cove
Saturday	08:30	09:40	10:35
	12:20	12:30	13:25
Sunday	10:10	11:20	13:15
	15:30	16:40	18:35

An extract from a bus timetable is shown on the right.

5. It takes 5 minutes to travel from Queen's Road to Ash Terrace. Use this information to complete the blank row in the timetable.

6. True or false? It takes 8 minutes to travel from Ash Terrace to Finley Park.

Queen's Road			
Ash Terrace	07:36	08:10	08:44
Finley Park	07:44	08:18	08:52

7. Sabine arrives at Ash Terrace at 08:15. How long will she wait for the next bus to Finley Park?

Look at this extract from a train timetable:

1 Copy and complete the timetable using the information below:

- It takes 25 minutes to travel between Milltown and Grainford.

- The journey from Grainford to Peakston is 10 minutes quicker than the journey from Milltown to Grainford.

Milltown	Grainford	Peakston
09:00		
10:20		
11:05		
12:00		

2 Walter arrives at Grainford at 12 noon. By how many minutes has he missed the previous train?

3 The 10:20 train is delayed by 45 minutes. At what time does it leave Milltown?

The timetable for a cable car is shown on the right.

4 Find the missing times in the timetable using the information below:

- The first cable car on Saturday leaves the mountain base 42 minutes before 10 am.

- On Sunday, the cable car arrives at the ski slopes 3 minutes before 11 am.

	Saturday	Sunday
Mountain base		10:32
Ice café	09:27	10:41
Ski slopes	09:43	

5 How long does it take to get from the mountain base to the ski slopes?

6 In winter, the cable car also opens on Fridays and journeys take the same amount of time. It leaves the mountain base 1 hour and 38 minutes before the cable car on Sunday. At what time will it arrive at the ice café?

Set C ··

The timetable on the right is part of a lake taxi schedule. All lake taxi journeys take the same amount of time.

Harbour	Beach	Promenade
18:15	18:29	18:46
19:10	19:24	19:41
20:05	20:19	20:36
21:00	21:14	21:31

1 How often do the taxis leave the harbour?

2 Wilma is at the harbour. She needs to be at the beach by 19:20. Which taxi should she get?

3 The last taxi of the evening arrives at the promenade at 23:21. What time does it leave the harbour?

4 Henry arrives at the beach at 6:30 pm. How many minutes will it take him to get to the promenade if he catches the next taxi?

Look at this extract from a bus timetable.

5 The bus takes 27 minutes to get to each stop. Copy and complete the timetable using this information.

6 How much later does the fourth bus arrive at Stop D than the fourth bus at Stop B?

Stop A	Stop B	Stop C	Stop D
05:32			
			07:06
	06:25		
	06:38		
		07:18	

It takes Lauren 15 minutes to walk to Stop A. What is the latest time she can leave the house if she needs to get to:

7 Stop B by 06:15?

8 Stop C by 07:00?

9 Stop D by 07:50?

I can read and write information in timetables.

Uri buys a painting and records its value every 4 years. He plots its value on the line graph below:

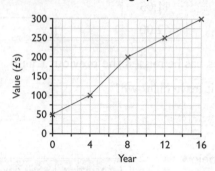

Find the missing numbers from the sentences below:

1. The value was £ ⬚ after 4 years.

2. After 12 years, the value was £ ⬚ more than its value at 0 years.

3. After 8 years, the value was £100 less than it was after ⬚ years.

Are the following statements true or false?

4. From 0 to 16 years, the value increased by £250.

5. The value increased by £100, from 0 to 4 years.

The line graph below shows how long it took a cyclist to finish a 120 km cycle race:

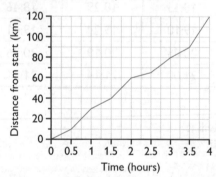

6. How far from the start was the cyclist after 1.5 hours?

7. How far from the finish was the cyclist after 3.5 hours?

8. True or false? It took the cyclist half an hour to travel from 30 km to 60 km.

9. When did the cyclist travel the furthest? Choose from the options below.

   A Between 0.5 and 1 hours.

   B Between 1.5 and 2.5 hours.

   C Between 3.5 and 4 hours.

The table below shows how many times Graeme had to repair four different things in his house.

	2014	2015	2016
Stereo	3		2
Games console	0	1	
TV	5		1
DVD player		3	0

10. Copy and complete the table using the information below:

    • Graeme didn't repair the stereo or the TV in 2015.

    • The games console needed twice as many repairs as the stereo did in 2016.

    • The number of repairs to the DVD player in 2015 was the same in 2014.

11. Graeme also had to repair his washing machine. He fixed it twice in 2014, twice in 2015 and three times in 2016. Add a row to your table to show this information.

12. Which item has been fixed the most?

13. What is the total number of repairs that Graeme has had to do?

Below is an extract from a train timetable. All trains take the same amount of time to get between stations.

Tineborough	13:08	13:39	14:10	14:41
Leadsford	13:31	14:02	14:33	15:04
Collingston	14:18	14:49	15:20	15:51
Mayforest	14:37	15:08	15:39	16:10

14. How long does it take to travel from Tineborough to Leadsford?

15. Hector arrives at Collingston at 15:25. How long does he have to wait for the next train to Mayforest?

16. Jasmine catches the train in Leadsford at 14:02. The train is delayed by 15 minutes in Collingston. At what time will it arrive in Mayforest?

17. Grayson lives in Leadsford and needs to be in Mayforest for 2:45 pm. Which train does he need to catch?

Phew! That was a mighty mountain of questions — nice work!

Statistics — Challenges

1 Some fishermen measured the change in the speed of a river during a rainstorm.

a) Find the missing values from the table using the line graph below.

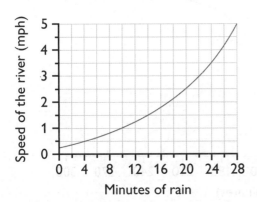

Minutes of rain	Speed (mph)
0	0.25
4	
8	0.8
12	
16	1.8
	2.5
	3.5
28	

b) Is the line graph or the table better for showing how the speed of the river changed during the rainstorm? Explain your answer.

2 A doctor is filling out her appointment diary for the week.

a) Copy and complete her blank diary using the sticky notes below:

	Monday	Wednesday	Thursday
09:00			
10:00			
13:00			
14:00			

Mr Limpson Wed 10.00

Mrs Beard Thurs 14.00

Mr Cester Mon 13.00

Miss Halton Mon 09.00

Miss Pageley Wed 09.00

Suzie & Warren Baxter Wed 14.00

Tyler Gattersly Thurs 09.00

Patients can book appointments in the remaining slots.

b) Mr Tinsley phones the doctor and gets an appointment on Thursday morning. At what time will his appointment be?

c) Miss Popperwell makes two appointments to see the doctor on different days. Write down all the possible appointment combinations she could have.

3 A boat travels between different towns on the edge of a lake. All boat journeys take the same amount of time.

Ripple Vale	Wavemouth	Little Eauton	Great Creek	Ripple Vale
09:42	10:00	10:25	10:46	11:05
11:20	11:38	12:03	12:24	12:43
14:08				
		16:39		

a) Find the missing times in the timetable.

b) Lorenzo gets on the boat at Ripple Vale at 14:08. He falls asleep halfway between Ripple Vale and Wavemouth, and wakes up 15 minutes before arriving back in Ripple Vale. How long was Lorenzo asleep for?

4   Sergio and Lowry climbed a mountain, using the same route.
    The line graph below shows how long it took each of them to reach the top.

a) When did Sergio overtake Lowry?

b) Sergio stopped for a 40 minute rest.
   After how many minutes did he stop for a rest? Explain how you know.

c) How much longer did it take Lowry to climb from 800 m to 1200 m than Sergio?

d) Another climber reached 1100 m in half the time that Lowry did. How long did it take him?

5   Constance works at a candle shop. She is counting the number of candles in the store room.

Each box has a picture to tell her what type of candle it is, and a number to tell her how many candles
are in the box. She also writes down how many of each box she finds in the store room.

LAVENDER	ROSE	COCONUT	STRAWBERRY

48	42	29	33
5 BOXES	3 BOXES	10 BOXES	5 BOXES

Use the information above to draw a table. Label your columns like this:

Type of candle	Total number of candles

Glossary and Index

2D	2D is short for <u>two-dimensional</u>. It means <u>flat</u>. p132-133
3D	3D is short for <u>three-dimensional</u>. A 3D shape is just the same as a <u>solid</u> shape. p126-127, p132-135
acute angle	An angle that measures <u>less than 90°</u>. It is <u>smaller</u> than a <u>right angle</u>. p137-141
area	The area of a shape is the <u>amount of surface</u> it covers. p122-125
capacity	The amount something can hold when it's <u>full</u>. Capacity is usually measured in <u>litres</u> or <u>millilitres</u>. p126-127
centimetre, cm	A unit for measuring <u>length</u> or <u>distance</u>. There are 100 cm in a metre. p108-110, p113
common factor	Factors which <u>two or more</u> numbers <u>share</u>. p44
coordinates	Tell you the <u>position</u> of a point from the <u>origin</u>. They're always written in the <u>same way</u>, for example, (3, 4). The first number gives the position on the <u>x-axis</u> and the second number gives the position on the <u>y-axis</u>. p152-153
cube number	The result of multiplying a number by itself <u>twice</u>. For example, $3 \times 3 \times 3 = 27$, so 27 is a cube number. p66
cubic centimetre, cm³	A unit for measuring <u>volume</u>. A cube with sides 1 cm long. p126-127
decimal places	The places in a number to the <u>right</u> of the <u>decimal point</u>. For example, the number 4.56 has 2 decimal places. p14, p88-97
decimal point	The <u>dot</u> you write in a <u>decimal number</u>. It comes between the <u>ones</u> and the <u>tenths</u>. p14, p88-97
degrees, °	The unit used to measure <u>angles</u>. For example, a right angle measures 90°. p137-148
denominator	The <u>bottom</u> number of a fraction. p14, p75-91
divide, ÷	Share equally or put into equal groups. For example, 6 ÷ 3 means 6 divided by 3 or 6 shared into 3 equal groups. p49, p52-53, p61-64
elevation	The <u>view</u> of an object from <u>one side</u>. p132-133
equivalent fractions	Fractions which are <u>written differently</u> but are <u>equal to</u> each other. For example, $\frac{3}{6}$ and $\frac{1}{2}$. p75-76
estimate	An estimate is a <u>sensible guess</u> at the answer. You can use <u>rounding</u> to help you estimate answers. p33-34, p124, p137
face	A <u>side</u> of a solid shape. Faces can be <u>flat</u>, as on cubes. They can also be <u>curved</u>, as on cylinders. p132-135
factor	A whole number that <u>divides exactly</u> into another whole number. For example, the factors of 6 are 1, 2, 3 and 6. p44, p46

Glossary and Index

gram, g	A unit for measuring <u>mass</u>. **1 kilogram = 1000 grams.** p108-109, p111, p114
heptagon	A flat shape with <u>seven straight sides</u>. p148
hexagon	A flat shape with <u>six straight sides</u>. p148
hour	A unit of <u>time</u>. An hour is 60 minutes. There are 24 hours in a day. p117-118
hundredth	The second digit to the right of the decimal point. One hundredth is written 0.01 or $\frac{1}{100}$. p88-97
imperial units	These are the old-fashioned units for measuring <u>distance</u>, <u>mass</u> and <u>capacity</u>. Imperial distance units include miles, yards, feet and inches. Imperial mass units include pounds and ounces. Imperial capacity units include pints. p110-111
improper fraction	A fraction with a numerator <u>bigger</u> than its denominator, for example, $\frac{9}{7}$. p79, p81-82
irregular polygon	In an irregular polygon, <u>not all sides</u> are of <u>equal length</u> and <u>not all of the angles are equal</u>. p148
kilogram, kg	A unit for measuring <u>mass</u>. **1 kilogram = 1000 grams.** p108-109, p111, p114
kilometre, km	A unit for measuring <u>length</u> or <u>distance</u>. **1 kilometre = 1000 metres.** p108-109, p113
length	A measure of <u>how long</u> or <u>how far</u> something is. Length is usually measured in millimetres, centimetres, metres or kilometres. p108-113
line graph	Line graphs can show how something <u>changes</u> over time. p158-161
line of symmetry	If you put a <u>mirror</u> on the line of symmetry, it looks like you can see the <u>whole shape</u>. It's the same thing as a <u>mirror line</u>. p150-151
litre, l	A unit for measuring <u>volume</u> or <u>capacity</u>. **1 litre = 1000 millilitres.** Orange juice often comes in 1 litre cartons. p108-109, p111, p115
mass	Mass is what most people mean when they say 'weight'. Mass is usually measured in <u>kilograms</u> or <u>grams</u>. p114
metre, m	A unit for measuring <u>length</u> or <u>distance</u>. **1 metre = 100 centimetres.** A door is about 2 m high. p108-110, p113
metric units	These are the modern units for measuring <u>distance</u>, <u>mass</u> and <u>capacity</u>. Metric distance units include mm, cm, m and km. Metric mass units include g and kg. Metric capacity units include ml and l. p108-109
millilitre, ml	A unit for measuring <u>volume</u> or <u>capacity</u>. There are 1000 millilitres in a litre. A teaspoon has a capacity of about 5 ml. p108-109, p111, p115
minute	A unit of <u>time</u>. There are 60 minutes in an hour, and 60 seconds in a minute. p117-118

Glossary and Index

mixed number	A mixed number has a whole-number part and a fraction part, for example, $3\frac{1}{2}$. p78, p81-86
month	A unit of time. There are 12 months in a year (January to December). p117-118
multiple	Multiples are the numbers in a times table. For example, the multiples of 4 are 4, 8, 12, 16... p43
multiply, ×	The proper maths word for 'times'. p48, p50-51, p55-59, p83-84
negative	Negative numbers are numbers below 0. For example, −1 or −10. p7-8
net	A 2D shape that will fold up to make a 3D shape. p134-135
numerator	The top number of a fraction. p14, p75-91
obtuse angle	An angle that measures more than 90° but less than 180°. It is between one and two right angles. p137-141
octagon	A flat shape with eight straight sides. p148
ordering	Putting in order. For example, to order 3, 1 and 2 from smallest to largest, start with the smallest, then the next smallest: 1, 2, 3. p9, p77, p95
parallel	Parallel lines are always the same distance apart. They will never meet or cross. p146-147
partition	Split a number up. You can partition numbers in many ways. For example, 173 = 100 + 70 + 3 or 173 = 150 + 20 + 3. p23, p25, p51, p53, p58, p89
pentagon	A flat shape with five straight sides. p148
perimeter	The distance around the outside of a 2D shape. p120-121, p146-147
place value	A digit's value in a number depends on its position in the number. Each position has a different place value. For example, the value of 2 in 827 is 2 tens. p2
plan	The view of an object from directly above. p132-133
polygon	Any flat shape with straight sides. p148
powers of 10	Numbers that are a 10 followed by just zeros: 10, 100, 1000, 10 000, 100 000 and 1 000 000 are powers of 10. p4-5
prime factor	A factor of a number that is also a prime number. For example, the prime factors of 20 are 5 and 2. p46
prime number	A number that has exactly two factors: 1 and itself. For example, 2, 3, 5, 7, etc. p45
proper fraction	A fraction that's less than 1. The numerator is smaller than the denominator. For example, $\frac{2}{5}$ or $\frac{3}{4}$. p75-91

Glossary and Index

protractor	You can use a protractor to measure angles. p140-142
quadrilateral	A flat shape with four straight sides. p148
rectangle	A quadrilateral with two pairs of equal sides and four right angles. p146-147
reflection	The image of a shape shown by a mirror across a mirror line. p150-151
reflex angle	Angles that are more than a $\frac{1}{2}$ turn (180°). p138-139
regular polygon	In a regular polygon, all the sides are equal lengths and all the angles are the same. p148
remainder	What's left over when you divide. For example, 7 ÷ 2 = 3 remainder 1. p62-64
right angle	A quarter turn, or 90°. p137-139, p146-147
Roman numerals	Letters that the Romans used to show numbers. For example, V = 5 and X = 10. p16-17
rounding	Finding a nearby number that's similar, but easier to use in calculations. For example, to round 27 to the nearest 10, you have to find the number that's nearest to 27 and a multiple of 10. 27 is between 20 and 30 but nearer to 30. p10, p33-34, p93-94
second	A unit of time. There are 60 seconds in a minute. p117-118
square centimetre, cm²	A unit for measuring area. A square with sides of length 1 cm. p122-125
square number	The result of multiplying a number by itself. For example, 2 × 2 = 4, 3 × 3 = 9. 4 and 9 are both square numbers. p66
tenth	The first digit after the decimal point. One tenth is written 0.1 or $\frac{1}{10}$. p88-97
thousandth	The third digit after the decimal point. One thousandth is written as 0.001 or $\frac{1}{1000}$. p14, p88-89, p91, p95-97
translation	When a shape moves from one place to another without rotating or flipping. p152-153
volume	The volume of a shape is the amount of space it takes up. p115, p126-127

M5PB21